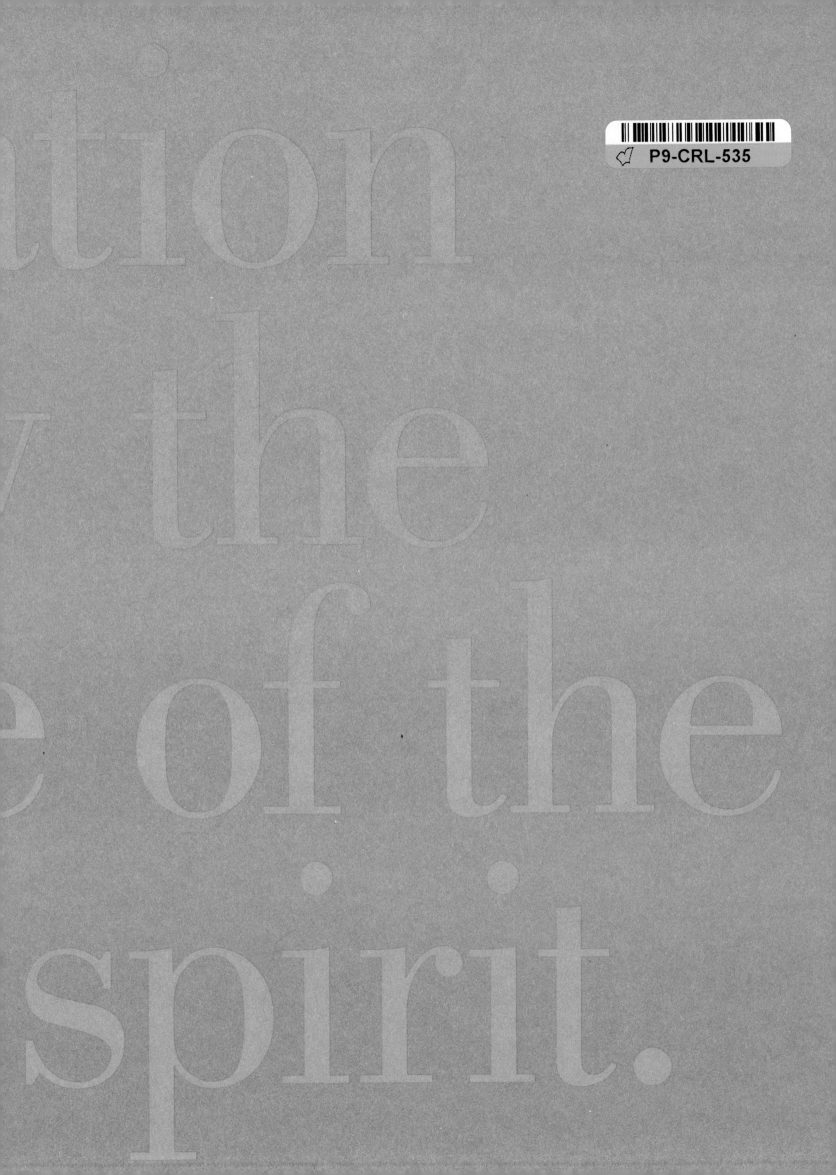

HAMMOND

EXPLORER

Atlas

OF THE WORLD

Contents

INTERPRETING MAPS

Designed to enhance your knowledge and enjoyment of the atlas, these pages explain map principles, scales, symbology and how to locate information quickly.

GEOGRAPHIC COMPARISONS

These eight pages contain flags and important facts about each independent country, plus dimensions of the earth's major mountains, longest rivers and largest lakes and islands.

MAPS OF THE WORLD

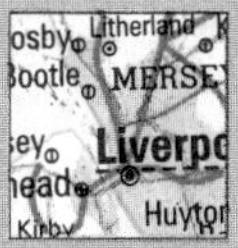

New maps, derived from a computer database, accurately present political detail while proprietary map projections show the most distortion-free views of the continents.

INDEX

A 6,000-entry A to Z index lists major places and geographic features in the atlas, complete with page numbers and easy-to-use alpha-numeric references.

ENTIRE CONTENTS
© COPYRIGHT 1996 BY
HAMMOND INCORPORATED
All rights reserved. No part of this book may be reproduced or utilized in any form or by any means, electronic or mechanical, including photocopying, recording or by any information storage and retrieval system, without permission in writing from the Publisher. Printed in The United States of America.

LIBRARY OF CONGRESS
CATALOGING-IN-
PUBLICATION DATA

Hammond Incorporated.
    Explorer atlas of the world.
    p. cm.
    At head of title: Hammond
    Includes index.
    ISBN 0-8437-1194-9
        (Hardcover)
    ISBN 0-8437-1186-8
        (Softcover)
    1. Atlases. I. Title.
G1021. H2457 1995 <G&M>
912--dc20   95-30419
                       CIP
                       MAP

Map Projections

Simply stated, the map-maker's challenge is to project the earth's curved surface onto a flat plane. To achieve this elusive goal, cartographers have developed map projections — equations which govern this conversion of geographic data.

This section explores some of the most widely used projections. It also introduces a new projection, the Hammond Optimal Conformal.

GENERAL PRINCIPLES AND TERMS

The earth rotates around its axis once a day. Its end points are the North and South poles; the line circling the earth midway between the poles is the equator. The arc from the equator to either pole is divided into 90 degrees of latitude. The equator represents 0° latitude. Circles of equal latitude, called parallels, are traditionally shown at every fifth or tenth degree.

The equator is divided into 360 degrees. Lines circling the globe from pole to pole through the degree points on the equator are called meridians, or great circles. All meridians are equal in length, but by international agreement the meridian passing through the Greenwich Observatory near London has been chosen as the prime meridian or 0° longitude. The distance in degrees from the prime meridian to any point east or west is its longitude.

While meridians are all equal in length, parallels become shorter as they approach the poles. Whereas one degree of latitude represents approximately 69 miles (112 km.) anywhere on the globe, a degree of longitude varies from 69 miles (112 km.) at the equator to zero at the poles. Each degree of latitude and longitude is divided into 60 minutes. One minute of latitude equals one nautical mile (1.15 land miles or 1.85 km.).

HOW TO FLATTEN A SPHERE: THE ART OF CONTROLLING DISTORTION

There is only one way to represent a sphere with absolute precision: on a globe. All attempts to project our planet's surface onto a plane unevenly stretch or tear the sphere as it flattens, inevitably distorting shapes, distances, area (sizes appear larger or smaller than actual size), angles or direction.

Since representing a sphere on a flat plane always creates distortion, only the parallels or the meridians (or some other set of lines) can maintain the same length as on a globe of corresponding scale. All other lines must be either too long or too short. Accordingly, the scale on a flat map cannot be true everywhere; there will always be different scales in different parts of a map. On world maps or very large areas, variations in scale may be extreme. Most maps seek to preserve either true area relationships (equal area projections) or true angles and shapes (conformal projections); some attempt to achieve overall balance.

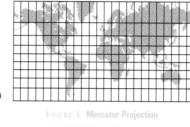

FIGURE 1 Mercator Projection

FIGURE 2 Robinson Projection

PROJECTIONS: SELECTED EXAMPLES

Mercator (Fig. 1): This projection is especially useful because all compass directions appear as straight lines, making it a valuable navigational tool. Moreover, every small region conforms to its shape on a globe — hence the name conformal. But because its meridians are evenly-spaced vertical lines which never converge (unlike the globe), the horizontal parallels must be drawn farther and farther apart at higher latitudes to maintain a correct relationship.

Only the equator is true to scale, and the size of areas in the higher latitudes is dramatically distorted.

Robinson (Fig. 2): To create the thematic maps in Global Relationships and the two-page world map in the Maps of the World section, the Robinson projection was used. It combines elements of both conformal and equal area projections to show the whole earth with relatively true shapes and reasonably equal areas.

Conic (Fig. 3): This projection has been used frequently for air navigation charts and to create most of the national and regional maps in this atlas. (See text in margin at left).

HAMMOND'S OPTIMAL CONFORMAL

As its name implies, this new conformal projection (Fig. 4) presents the optimal view of an area by reducing shifts in scale over an entire region to the minimum degree possible. While conformal maps generally preserve all small shapes, large shapes can become very distorted because of varying scales, causing considerable inaccuracy in distance measurements. The concept underlying the Optimal Conformal is that for any region on the globe, there is an ideal projection for which scale variation can be made as small as possible. Consequently, unlike other projections, the Optimal Conformal does not use one standard formula to construct a map. Each map is a unique projection — the optimal projection for that particular area.

After a cartographer defines the subject area, a sophisticated computer program evaluates the size and shape of the region, projecting the most distortion-free map possible. All of the continent maps in this atlas, except Antarctica, have been drawn using the Optimal projection.

The original idea of a conic projection is to cap the globe with a cone, and then project onto the cone from the planet's center the lines of latitude and longitude (the parallels and meridians). To produce a working map, the cone is simply cut open and laid flat. The conic projection used here is a modification of this idea. A cone can be made tangent to any standard parallel you choose. One popular version of a conic projection, the Lambert Conformal Conic, uses two standard parallels near the top and bottom of the map to further reduce errors of scale.

Like all conformal maps, the Optimal projection preserves angles exactly and minimizes distortion in shapes. This projection is more successful than any previous projection at spreading curvature across the entire map, producing the most distortion-free map possible.

Using This Atlas

How to Locate Information Quickly
Our Maps of the World section is organized by continent. If you're looking for a major region of the world, consult the Contents on page two.

Australia
Page/Location: 70
Area: 2,966,136 sq
7,682,300 s
Population: 17,2
Capital: Canh
Largest C

World Reference Guide
This concise guide lists the countries of the world alphabetically. If you're looking for the largest scale map of any country, you'll find a page and alpha-numeric reference at a glance, as well as information about each country, including its flag.

Merlimont, Fran
.9/F4 **Mersch**, Luxembou
68/A3 **Mers-les-Bains**, France
69/F4 **Mertert**, Luxembourg
69/F4 **Mertesdorf**, Germany
69/G6 **Mertzwiller**, France
68/B5 **Méru**, France
68/B2 **Merville**, France
69/F2 **Merzenich**, Germany
69/F5 **Merzig**, Germany
Messancy, Belo'
'F4 **Maxtat** Bal

Master Index
When you're looking for a specific place or physical feature, your quickest route is the Master Index. This 6,000-entry alphabetical index lists both the page number and alpha-numeric reference for major places and features in Maps of the World.

This new atlas is created from a unique digital database, and its computer-generated maps represent a new phase in map-making technology.

How Computer-Generated Maps Are Made

To build a digital database capable of generating this world atlas, the latitude and longitude of every significant town, river, coastline, natural and political border, transportation network and peak elevation was researched and digitized. Hundreds of millions of data points describing every important geographic feature are organized into thousands of different map feature codes.

There are no maps in this unique system. Rather, it consists entirely of coded points, lines and polygons. To create a map, cartographers simply determine what specific information they wish to show, based upon considerations of scale, size, density and importance of different features.

New technology developed by mathematical physicist Mitchell Feigenbaum uses fractal geometry to describe and re-configure coastlines, borders and mountain ranges to fit a variety of map scales and projections. Dr. Feigenbaum has also created a computerized type placement program which allows thousands of map labels to be placed accurately in minutes. After these steps have been completed, the computer then draws the final map.

Each section of this atlas has been designed to be both easy and enjoyable to use. Familiarizing yourself with its organization will help you to benefit fully from its use.

World Flags and Reference Guide

This colorful section portrays each nation of the world, its flag, important geographical data, such as size, population and capital, and its location in the Maps of the World section.

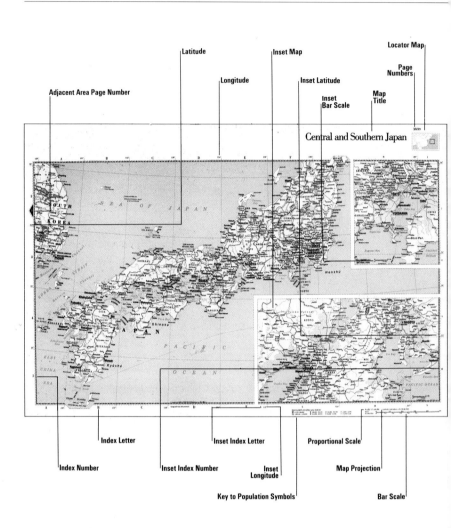

Symbols Used on Maps of the World

First Order (National) Boundary	City and Urban Area Limits	Rome — First Order (National) Capital
First Order Water Boundary	Demilitarized Zone	Belfast — Second Order (Internal) Capital
First Order Disputed Boundary	National Park/Preserve/Scenic Area	Hull — Third Order (Internal) Capital
Second Order (Internal) Boundary	National Forest/Forest Reserve	Neighborhood
Second Order Water Boundary	National Wilderness/Grassland	Pass
Second Order Disputed Boundary	National Recreation Area/Monument	Ruins
Third Order (Internal) Boundary	National Seashore/Lakeshore	Falls
Undefined Boundary	National Wildlife/Wilderness Area	Rapids
International Date Line	Native Reservation/Reserve	Dam
Shoreline, River	Military/Government Reservation	Point Elevation
Intermittent River	Lake, Reservoir	Park
Canal/Aqueduct	Intermittent Lake	Wildlife Area
Continental Divide	Dry Lake	Point of Interest
Highways/Roads	Salt Pan	Well
Railroads	Desert/Sand Area	International Airport
Ferries	Swamp	Other Airport
Tunnels (Road, Railroad)	Lava Flow	Air Base
Ancient Walls	Glacier	Naval Base

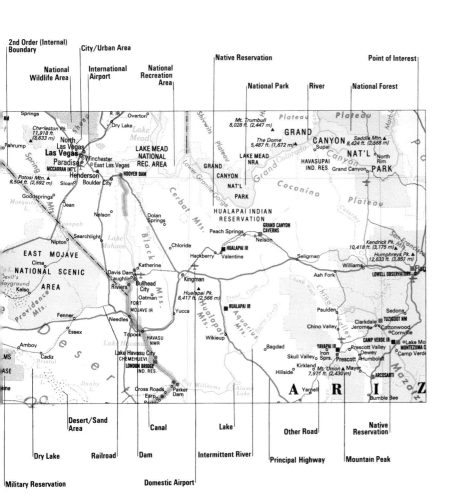

2nd Order (Internal) Boundary

National Wildlife Area

International Airport

National Recreation Area

City/Urban Area

Native Reservation

National Park

River

Point of Interest

National Forest

Desert/Sand Area

Canal

Lake

Other Road

Native Reservation

Dry Lake

Railroad

Dam

Intermittent River

Principal Highway

Mountain Peak

Military Reservation

Domestic Airport

PRINCIPAL MAP ABBREVIATIONS

ABOR. RSV.	ABORIGINAL RESERVE	IND. RES.	INDIAN RESERVATION	NWR	NATIONAL WILDLIFE RESERVE
ADMIN.	ADMINISTRATION	INT'L	INTERNATIONAL		
AFB	AIR FORCE BASE	IR	INDIAN RESERVATION	OBL.	OBLAST
AMM. DEP.	AMMUNITION DEPOT	ISTH.	ISTHMUS	OCC.	OCCUPIED
ARCH.	ARCHIPELAGO	JCT.	JUNCTION	OKR.	OKRUG
ARPT.	AIRPORT	L.	LAKE	PAR.	PARISH
AUT.	AUTONOMOUS	LAG.	LAGOON	PASSG.	PASSAGE
B.	BAY	LAKESH.	LAKESHORE	PEN.	PENINSULA
BFLD.	BATTLEFIELD	MEM.	MEMORIAL	PK.	PEAK
BK.	BROOK	MIL.	MILITARY	PLAT.	PLATEAU
BOR.	BOROUGH	MISS.	MISSILE	PN	PARK NATIONAL
BR.	BRANCH	MON.	MONUMENT	PREF.	PREFECTURE
C.	CAPE	MT.	MOUNT	PROM.	PROMONTORY
CAN.	CANAL	MTN.	MOUNTAIN	PROV.	PROVINCE
CAP.	CAPITAL	MTS.	MOUNTAINS	PRSV.	PRESERVE
C.G.	COAST GUARD	NAT.	NATURAL	PT.	POINT
CHAN.	CHANNEL	NAT'L	NATIONAL	R.	RIVER
CO.	COUNTY	NAV.	NAVAL	RA	RECREATION AREA
CR.	CREEK	NB	NATIONAL	RA.	RANGE
CTR.	CENTER		BATTLEFIELD	REC.	RECREATION(AL)
DEP.	DEPOT	NBP	NATIONAL	REF.	REFUGE
DEPR.	DEPRESSION		BATTLEFIELD PARK	REG.	REGION
DEPT.	DEPARTMENT	NBS	NATIONAL	REP.	REPUBLIC
DES.	DESERT		BATTLEFIELD SITE	RES.	RESERVOIR,
DIST.	DISTRICT	NHP	NATIONAL HISTORICAL		RESERVATION
DMZ	DEMILITARIZED ZONE		PARK	RVWY.	RIVERWAY
DPCY.	DEPENDENCY	NHPP	NATIONAL HISTORICAL	SA.	SIERRA
ENG.	ENGINEERING		PARK AND PRESERVE	SD.	SOUND
EST.	ESTUARY	NHS	NATIONAL HISTORIC	SEASH.	SEASHORE
FD.	FIORD, FJORD		SITE	SO.	SOUTHERN
FED.	FEDERAL	NL	NATIONAL LAKESHORE	SP	STATE PARK
FK.	FORK	NM	NATIONAL MONUMENT	SPR., SPRS.	SPRING, SPRINGS
FLD.	FIELD	NMEMP	NATIONAL MEMORIAL	ST.	STATE
FOR.	FOREST		PARK	STA.	STATION
FT.	FORT	NMILP	NATIONAL MILITARY	STM.	STREAM
G.	GULF		PARK	STR.	STRAIT
GOV.	GOVERNOR	NO.	NORTHERN	TERR.	TERRITORY
GOVT.	GOVERNMENT	NP	NATIONAL PARK	TUN.	TUNNEL
GD.	GRAND	NPP	NATIONAL PARK AND	TWP.	TOWNSHIP
GT.	GREAT		PRESERVE	VAL.	VALLEY
HAR.	HARBOR	NPRSV	NATIONAL PRESERVE	VILL.	VILLAGE
HD.	HEAD	NRA	NATIONAL	VOL.	VOLCANO
HIST.	HISTORIC(AL)		RECREATION AREA	WILD.	WILDLIFE,
HTS.	HEIGHTS	NRSV	NATIONAL RESERVE		WILDERNESS
I., IS.	ISLAND(S)	NS	NATIONAL SEASHORE	WTR.	WATER

WORLD STATISTICS

World Statistics lists the dimensions of the earth's principal mountains, islands, rivers and lakes, along with other useful geographic information.

MAPS OF THE WORLD

These detailed regional maps are arranged by continent, and introduced by a political map of that continent. The continent maps, which utilize Hammond's new Optimal Conformal projection, are distinguished by individual colors for each country to highlight political divisions.

On the regional maps, different colors and textures highlight distinctive features such as parks, forests, deserts and urban areas. These maps also provide considerable information concerning geographic features and political divisions.

MASTER INDEX

This is an A-Z listing of names found on the political maps. It also has its own abbreviation list which, along with other Index keys, appears on page 110.

MAP SCALES

A map's scale is the relationship of any length on the map to an identical length on the earth's surface. A scale of 1:3,000,000 means that one inch on the map represents 3,000,000 inches (47 miles, 76 km.) on the earth's surface. Thus, a 1:1,000,000 scale is larger than 1:3,000,000, just as 1/1 is larger than 1/3.

The most densely populated areas are shown at a scale of 1:1,170,000, while selected metropolitan areas are covered at either 1:587,000 or 1:1,170,000. Other populous areas are presented at 1:3,500,000 and 1:7,000,000, allowing you to accurately compare areas and distances of similar regions. Remaining regions are scaled at 1:10,500,000. The continent maps, as well as the United States, Canada, Russia, Pacific and World have smaller scales.

World Flags and Reference Guide

Afghanistan
Page/Location: 53/H2
Area: 250,775 sq. mi.
　　　649,507 sq. km.
Population: 16,903,000
Capital: Kabul
Largest City: Kabul
Highest Point: Noshaq
Monetary Unit: afghani

Albania
Page/Location: 39/F2
Area: 11,100 sq. mi.
　　　28,749 sq. km.
Population: 3,374,000
Capital: Tiranë
Largest City: Tiranë
Highest Point: Korab
Monetary Unit: lek

Algeria
Page/Location: 76/F2
Area: 919,591 sq. mi.
　　　2,381,740 sq. km.
Population: 27,895,000
Capital: Algiers
Largest City: Algiers
Highest Point: Tahat
Monetary Unit: Algerian dinar

Andorra
Page/Location: 35/F1
Area: 188 sq. mi.
　　　487 sq. km.
Population: 64,000
Capital: Andorra la Vella
Largest City: Andorra la Vella
Highest Point: Coma Pedrosa
Monetary Unit: Fr. franc, Sp. peseta

Angola
Page/Location: 82/C3
Area: 481,351 sq. mi.
　　　1,246,700 sq. km.
Population: 9,804,000
Capital: Luanda
Largest City: Luanda
Highest Point: Morro de Môco
Monetary Unit: kwanza

Antigua and Barbuda
Page/Location: 104/F3
Area: 171 sq. mi.
　　　443 sq. km.
Population: 65,000
Capital: St. John's
Largest City: St. John's
Highest Point: Boggy Peak
Monetary Unit: East Caribbean dollar

Argentina
Page/Location: 109/C4
Area: 1,072,070 sq. mi.
　　　2,776,661 sq. km.
Population: 33,913,000
Capital: Buenos Aires
Largest City: Buenos Aires
Highest Point: Cerro Aconcagua
Monetary Unit: Argentine peso

Armenia
Page/Location: 45/H5
Area: 11,506 sq. mi.
　　　29,800 sq. km.
Population: 3,522,000
Capital: Yerevan
Largest City: Yerevan
Highest Point: Alagez
Monetary Unit: dram

Australia
Page/Location: 70
Area: 2,966,136 sq. mi.
　　　7,682,300 sq. km.
Population: 18,077,000
Capital: Canberra
Largest City: Sydney
Highest Point: Mt. Kosciusko
Monetary Unit: Australian dollar

Austria
Page/Location: 33/L3
Area: 32,375 sq. mi.
　　　83,851 sq. km.
Population: 7,955,000
Capital: Vienna
Largest City: Vienna
Highest Point: Grossglockner
Monetary Unit: schilling

Azerbaijan
Page/Location: 45/H4
Area: 33,436 sq. mi.
　　　86,600 sq. km.
Population: 7,684,000
Capital: Baku
Largest City: Baku
Highest Point: Bazardyuzyu
Monetary Unit: manat

Bahamas
Page/Location: 104/B2
Area: 5,382 sq. mi.
　　　13,939 sq. km.
Population: 273,000
Capital: Nassau
Largest City: Nassau
Highest Point: 207 ft. (63 m)
Monetary Unit: Bahamian dollar

Bahrain
Page/Location: 52/F3
Area: 240 sq. mi.
　　　622 sq. km.
Population: 586,000
Capital: Manama
Largest City: Manama
Highest Point: Jabal Dukhān
Monetary Unit: Bahraini dinar

Bangladesh
Page/Location: 60/E3
Area: 55,126 sq. mi.
　　　142,776 sq. km.
Population: 125,149,000
Capital: Dhākā
Largest City: Dhākā
Highest Point: Keokradong
Monetary Unit: taka

Barbados
Page/Location: 104/G4
Area: 166 sq. mi.
　　　430 sq. km.
Population: 256,000
Capital: Bridgetown
Largest City: Bridgetown
Highest Point: Mt. Hillaby
Monetary Unit: Barbadian dollar

Belarus
Page/Location: 18/F3
Area: 80,154 sq. mi.
　　　207,600 sq. km.
Population: 10,405,000
Capital: Minsk
Largest City: Minsk
Highest Point: Dzerzhinskaya
Monetary Unit: Belarusian ruble

Belgium
Page/Location: 30/C2
Area: 11,781 sq. mi.
　　　30,513 sq. km.
Population: 10,063,000
Capital: Brussels
Largest City: Brussels
Highest Point: Botrange
Monetary Unit: Belgian franc

Belize
Page/Location: 102/D2
Area: 8,867 sq. mi.
　　　22,966 sq. km.
Population: 209,000
Capital: Belmopan
Largest City: Belize City
Highest Point: Victoria Peak
Monetary Unit: Belize dollar

Benin
Page/Location: 79/F4
Area: 43,483 sq. mi.
　　　112,620 sq. km.
Population: 5,342,000
Capital: Porto-Novo
Largest City: Cotonou
Highest Point: Nassoukou
Monetary Unit: CFA franc

Bhutan
Page/Location: 62/E2
Area: 18,147 sq. mi.
　　　47,000 sq. km.
Population: 1,739,000
Capital: Thimphu
Largest City: Thimphu
Highest Point: Kula Kangri
Monetary Unit: ngultrum

Bolivia
Page/Location: 106/F7
Area: 424,163 sq. mi.
　　　1,098,582 sq. km.
Population: 7,719,000
Capital: La Paz; Sucre
Largest City: La Paz
Highest Point: Nevado Ancohuma
Monetary Unit: Bolivian peso

Bosnia and Herzegovina
Page/Location: 40/C3
Area: 19,940 sq. mi.
　　　51,645 sq. km.
Population: 4,651,000
Capital: Sarajevo
Largest City: Sarajevo
Highest Point: Maglič
Monetary Unit: —

Botswana
Page/Location: 82/D5
Area: 224,764 sq. mi.
　　　582,139 sq. km.
Population: 1,359,000
Capital: Gaborone
Largest City: Gaborone
Highest Point: Tsodilo Hills
Monetary Unit: pula

Brazil
Page/Location: 105/D3
Area: 3,284,426 sq. mi.
　　　8,506,663 sq. km.
Population: 158,739,000
Capital: Brasília
Largest City: São Paulo
Highest Point: Pico da Neblina
Monetary Unit: cruzeiro real

Brunei
Page/Location: 66/D2
Area: 2,226 sq. mi.
　　　5,765 sq. km.
Population: 285,000
Capital: Bandar Seri Begawan
Largest City: Bandar Seri Begawan
Highest Point: Bukit Pagon
Monetary Unit: Brunei dollar

Bulgaria
Page/Location: 41/G4
Area: 42,823 sq. mi.
　　　110,912 sq. km.
Population: 8,800,000
Capital: Sofia
Largest City: Sofia
Highest Point: Musala
Monetary Unit: lev

Burkina Faso
Page/Location: 79/E3
Area: 105,869 sq. mi.
　　　274,200 sq. km.
Population: 10,135,000
Capital: Ouagadougou
Largest City: Ouagadougou
Highest Point: 2,405 ft. (733 m)
Monetary Unit: CFA franc

Burma
Page/Location: 63/G3
Area: 261,789 sq. mi.
　　　678,034 sq. km.
Population: 44,277,000
Capital: Rangoon
Largest City: Rangoon
Highest Point: Hkakabo Razi
Monetary Unit: kyat

Burundi
Page/Location: 82/E1
Area: 10,747 sq. mi.
　　　27,835 sq. km.
Population: 6,125,000
Capital: Bujumbura
Largest City: Bujumbura
Highest Point: 8,760 ft. (2,670 m)
Monetary Unit: Burundi franc

Cambodia
Page/Location: 65/D3
Area: 69,898 sq. mi.
　　　181,036 sq. km.
Population: 10,265,000
Capital: Phnom Penh
Largest City: Phnom Penh
Highest Point: Phnum Aoral
Monetary Unit: riel

Cameroon
Page/Location: 76/H7
Area: 183,568 sq. mi.
475,441 sq. km.
Population: 13,132,000
Capital: Yaoundé
Largest City: Douala
Highest Point: Mt. Cameroon
Monetary Unit: CFA franc

Canada
Page/Location: 86
Area: 3,851,787 sq. mi.
9,976,139 sq. km.
Population: 28,114,000
Capital: Ottawa
Largest City: Toronto
Highest Point: Mt. Logan
Monetary Unit: Canadian dollar

Cape Verde
Page/Location: 74/K9
Area: 1,557 sq. mi.
4,033 sq. km.
Population: 423,000
Capital: Praia
Largest City: Praia
Highest Point: 9,282 ft. (2,829 m)
Monetary Unit: Cape Verde escudo

Central African Republic
Page/Location: 77/J6
Area: 242,000 sq. mi.
626,780 sq. km.
Population: 3,142,000
Capital: Bangui
Largest City: Bangui
Highest Point: Mt. Kayagangiri
Monetary Unit: CFA franc

Chad
Page/Location: 77/J4
Area: 495,752 sq. mi.
1,283,998 sq. km.
Population: 5,467,000
Capital: N'Djamena
Largest City: N'Djamena
Highest Point: Emi Koussi
Monetary Unit: CFA franc

Chile
Page/Location: 109/B3
Area: 292,257 sq. mi.
756,946 sq. km.
Population: 13,951,000
Capital: Santiago
Largest City: Santiago
Highest Point: Nevado Ojos del Salado
Monetary Unit: Chilean peso

China
Page/Location: 48/J6
Area: 3,691,000 sq. mi.
9,559,690 sq. km.
Population: 1,190,431,000
Capital: Beijing
Largest City: Shanghai
Highest Point: Mt. Everest
Monetary Unit: yuan

Colombia
Page/Location: 106/D3
Area: 439,513 sq. mi.
1,138,339 sq. km.
Population: 35,578,000
Capital: Bogotá
Largest City: Bogotá
Highest Point: Pico Cristóbal Colón
Monetary Unit: Colombian peso

Comoros
Page/Location: 74/G6
Area: 719 sq. mi.
1,862 sq. km.
Population: 530,000
Capital: Moroni
Largest City: Moroni
Highest Point: Karthala
Monetary Unit: Comorian franc

Congo
Page/Location: 74/D5
Area: 132,046 sq. mi.
342,000 sq. km.
Population: 2,447,000
Capital: Brazzaville
Largest City: Brazzaville
Highest Point: Lékéti Mts.
Monetary Unit: CFA franc

Costa Rica
Page/Location: 103/F4
Area: 19,575 sq. mi.
50,700 sq. km.
Population: 3,342,000
Capital: San José
Largest City: San José
Highest Point: Cerro Chirripó Grande
Monetary Unit: Costa Rican colón

Côte d'Ivoire
Page/Location: 78/D5
Area: 124,504 sq. mi.
322,465 sq. km.
Population: 14,296,000
Capital: Yamoussoukro
Largest City: Abidjan
Highest Point: Mt. Nimba
Monetary Unit: CFA franc

Croatia
Page/Location: 40/C3
Area: 22,050 sq. mi.
57,110 sq. km.
Population: 4,698,000
Capital: Zagreb
Largest City: Zagreb
Highest Point: Veliki Troglav
Monetary Unit: Kuna

Cuba
Page/Location: 103/F1
Area: 44,206 sq. mi.
114,494 sq. km.
Population: 11,064,000
Capital: Havana
Largest City: Havana
Highest Point: Pico Turquino
Monetary Unit: Cuban peso

Cyprus
Page/Location: 49/C2
Area: 3,473 sq. mi.
8,995 sq. km.
Population: 730,000
Capital: Nicosia
Largest City: Nicosia
Highest Point: Olympus
Monetary Unit: Cypriot pound

Czech Republic
Page/Location: 27/H4
Area: 30,449 sq. mi.
78,863 sq. km.
Population: 10,408,000
Capital: Prague
Largest City: Prague
Highest Point: Sněžka
Monetary Unit: Czech koruna

Denmark
Page/Location: 20/C5
Area: 16,629 sq. mi.
43,069 sq. km.
Population: 5,188,000
Capital: Copenhagen
Largest City: Copenhagen
Highest Point: Yding Skovhøj
Monetary Unit: Danish krone

Djibouti
Page/Location: 77/P5
Area: 8,880 sq. mi.
23,000 sq. km.
Population: 413,000
Capital: Djibouti
Largest City: Djibouti
Highest Point: Moussa Ali
Monetary Unit: Djibouti franc

Dominica
Page/Location: 104/F4
Area: 290 sq. mi.
751 sq. km.
Population: 88,000
Capital: Roseau
Largest City: Roseau
Highest Point: Morne Diablotin
Monetary Unit: Dominican dollar

Dominican Republic
Page/Location: 104/D3
Area: 18,704 sq. mi.
48,443 sq. km.
Population: 7,826,000
Capital: Santo Domingo
Largest City: Santo Domingo
Highest Point: Pico Duarte
Monetary Unit: Dominican peso

Ecuador
Page/Location: 106/C4
Area: 109,483 sq. mi.
283,561 sq. km.
Population: 10,677,000
Capital: Quito
Largest City: Guayaquil
Highest Point: Chimborazo
Monetary Unit: sucre

Egypt
Page/Location: 77/L2
Area: 386,659 sq. mi.
1,001,447 sq. km.
Population: 60,765,000
Capital: Cairo
Largest City: Cairo
Highest Point: Mt. Catherine
Monetary Unit: Egyptian pound

El Salvador
Page/Location: 102/D3
Area: 8,260 sq. mi.
21,393 sq. km.
Population: 5,753,000
Capital: San Salvador
Largest City: San Salvador
Highest Point: Santa Ana
Monetary Unit: Salvadoran colón

Equatorial Guinea
Page/Location: 76/G7
Area: 10,831 sq. mi.
28,052 sq. km.
Population: 410,000
Capital: Malabo
Largest City: Malabo
Highest Point: Pico de Santa Isabel
Monetary Unit: CFA franc

Eritrea
Page/Location: 52/C5
Area: 36,170 sq. mi.
93,679 sq. km.
Population: 3,783,000
Capital: Asmara
Largest City: Asmara
Highest Point: Soira
Monetary Unit: birr

Estonia
Page/Location: 42/E4
Area: 17,413 sq. mi.
45,100 sq. km.
Population: 1,617,000
Capital: Tallinn
Largest City: Tallinn
Highest Point: Munamägi
Monetary Unit: kroon

Ethiopia
Page/Location: 77/N6
Area: 435,606 sq. mi.
1,128,220 sq. km.
Population: 54,927,000
Capital: Addis Ababa
Largest City: Addis Ababa
Highest Point: Ras Dashen Terara
Monetary Unit: birr

Fiji
Page/Location: 68/G6
Area: 7,055 sq. mi.
18,272 sq. km.
Population: 764,000
Capital: Suva
Largest City: Suva
Highest Point: Tomaniivi
Monetary Unit: Fijian dollar

Finland
Page/Location: 20/H2
Area: 130,128 sq. mi.
337,032 sq. km.
Population: 5,069,000
Capital: Helsinki
Largest City: Helsinki
Highest Point: Kahperusvaara
Monetary Unit: markka

France
Page/Location: 32/D3
Area: 210,038 sq. mi.
543,998 sq. km.
Population: 57,840,000
Capital: Paris
Largest City: Paris
Highest Point: Mont Blanc
Monetary Unit: French franc

Gabon
Page/Location: 76/H7
Area: 103,346 sq. mi.
267,666 sq. km.
Population: 1,139,000
Capital: Libreville
Largest City: Libreville
Highest Point: Mt. Iboundji
Monetary Unit: CFA franc

Gambia
Page/Location: 78/B3
Area: 4,127 sq. mi.
10,689 sq. km.
Population: 959,000
Capital: Banjul
Largest City: Banjul
Highest Point: 98 ft. (30 m)
Monetary Unit: dalasi

Georgia
Page/Location: 45/G4
Area: 26,911 sq. mi.
69,700 sq. km.
Population: 5,681,000
Capital: Tbilisi
Largest City: Tbilisi
Highest Point: Kazbek
Monetary Unit: lari

Germany
Page/Location: 26/E3
Area: 137,753 sq. mi.
356,780 sq. km.
Population: 81,088,000
Capital: Berlin
Largest City: Berlin
Highest Point: Zugspitze
Monetary Unit: Deutsche mark

Ghana
Page/Location: 79/E4
Area: 92,099 sq. mi.
238,536 sq. km.
Population: 17,225,000
Capital: Accra
Largest City: Accra
Highest Point: Afadjoto
Monetary Unit: cedi

Greece
Page/Location: 39/G3
Area: 50,944 sq. mi.
131,945 sq. km.
Population: 10,565,000
Capital: Athens
Largest City: Athens
Highest Point: Mt. Olympus
Monetary Unit: drachma

World Flags and Reference Guide

Grenada
Page/Location: 104/F5
Area: 133 sq. mi.
344 sq. km.
Population: 94,000
Capital: St. George's
Largest City: St. George's
Highest Point: Mt. St. Catherine
Monetary Unit: East Caribbean dollar

Guatemala
Page/Location: 102/D3
Area: 42,042 sq. mi.
108,889 sq. km.
Population: 10,721,000
Capital: Guatemala
Largest City: Guatemala
Highest Point: Tajumulco
Monetary Unit: quetzal

Guinea
Page/Location: 78/C4
Area: 94,925 sq. mi.
245,856 sq. km.
Population: 6,392,000
Capital: Conakry
Largest City: Conakry
Highest Point: Mt. Nimba
Monetary Unit: Guinea franc

Guinea-Bissau
Page/Location: 78/B3
Area: 13,948 sq. mi.
36,125 sq. km.
Population: 1,098,000
Capital: Bissau
Largest City: Bissau
Highest Point: 689 ft. (210 m)
Monetary Unit: Guinea-Bissau peso

Guyana
Page/Location: 106/G2
Area: 83,000 sq. mi.
214,970 sq. km.
Population: 729,000
Capital: Georgetown
Largest City: Georgetown
Highest Point: Mt. Roraima
Monetary Unit: Guyana dollar

Haiti
Page/Location: 103/H2
Area: 10,694 sq. mi.
27,697 sq. km.
Population: 6,491,000
Capital: Port-au-Prince
Largest City: Port-au-Prince
Highest Point: Pic la Selle
Monetary Unit: gourde

Honduras
Page/Location: 102/E3
Area: 43,277 sq. mi.
112,087 sq. km.
Population: 5,315,000
Capital: Tegucigalpa
Largest City: Tegucigalpa
Highest Point: Cerro de las Minas
Monetary Unit: lempira

Hungary
Page/Location: 40/D2
Area: 35,919 sq. mi.
93,030 sq. km.
Population: 10,319,000
Capital: Budapest
Largest City: Budapest
Highest Point: Kékes
Monetary Unit: forint

Iceland
Page/Location: 20/N7
Area: 39,768 sq. mi.
103,000 sq. km.
Population: 264,000
Capital: Reykjavík
Largest City: Reykjavík
Highest Point: Hvannadalshnúkur
Monetary Unit: króna

India
Page/Location: 62/C3
Area: 1,269,339 sq. mi.
3,287,588 sq. km.
Population: 919,903,000
Capital: New Delhi
Largest City: Calcutta
Highest Point: Nanda Devi
Monetary Unit: Indian rupee

Indonesia
Page/Location: 67/E4
Area: 788,430 sq. mi.
2,042,034 sq. km.
Population: 200,410,000
Capital: Jakarta
Largest City: Jakarta
Highest Point: Puncak Jaya
Monetary Unit: rupiah

Iran
Page/Location: 51/H3
Area: 636,293 sq. mi.
1,648,000 sq. km.
Population: 65,615,000
Capital: Tehrän
Largest City: Tehrän
Highest Point: Qolleh-ye Damävand
Monetary Unit: Iranian rial

Iraq
Page/Location: 50/E3
Area: 172,476 sq. mi.
446,713 sq. km.
Population: 19,890,000
Capital: Baghdad
Largest City: Baghdad
Highest Point: Haji Ibrahim
Monetary Unit: Iraqi dinar

Ireland
Page/Location: 21/A4
Area: 27,136 sq. mi.
70,282 sq. km.
Population: 3,539,000
Capital: Dublin
Largest City: Dublin
Highest Point: Carrantuohill
Monetary Unit: Irish pound

Israel
Page/Location: 49/D3
Area: 7,847 sq. mi.
20,324 sq. km.
Population: 5,051,000
Capital: Jerusalem
Largest City: Tel Aviv-Yafo
Highest Point: Har Meron
Monetary Unit: shekel

Italy
Page/Location: 18/E4
Area: 116,303 sq. mi.
301,225 sq. km.
Population: 58,138,000
Capital: Rome
Largest City: Rome
Highest Point: Monte Rosa
Monetary Unit: Italian lira

Jamaica
Page/Location: 103/G2
Area: 4,411 sq. mi.
11,424 sq. km.
Population: 2,555,000
Capital: Kingston
Largest City: Kingston
Highest Point: Blue Mountain Pk.
Monetary Unit: Jamaican dollar

Japan
Page/Location: 55/M4
Area: 145,730 sq. mi.
377,441 sq. km.
Population: 125,107,000
Capital: Tokyo
Largest City: Tokyo
Highest Point: Fujiyama
Monetary Unit: yen

Jordan
Page/Location: 49/E4
Area: 35,000 sq. mi.
90,650 sq. km.
Population: 3,961,000
Capital: Ammän
Largest City: Ammän
Highest Point: Jabal Ramm
Monetary Unit: Jordanian dinar

Kazakhstan
Page/Location: 46/G5
Area: 1,048,300 sq. mi.
2,715,100 sq. km.
Population: 17,268,000
Capital: Aqmola
Largest City: Alma-Ata
Highest Point: Khan-Tengri
Monetary Unit: tenge

Kenya
Page/Location: 77/M7
Area: 224,960 sq. mi.
582,646 sq. km.
Population: 28,241,000
Capital: Nairobi
Largest City: Nairobi
Highest Point: Mt. Kenya
Monetary Unit: Kenya shilling

Kiribati
Page/Location: 69/H5
Area: 291 sq. mi.
754 sq. km.
Population: 78,000
Capital: Bairiki
Largest City: —
Highest Point: Banaba Island
Monetary Unit: Australian dollar

Korea, North
Page/Location: 58/D2
Area: 46,540 sq. mi.
120,539 sq. km.
Population: 23,067,000
Capital: P'yŏngyang
Largest City: P'yŏngyang
Highest Point: Paektu-san
Monetary Unit: North Korean won

Korea, South
Page/Location: 58/D4
Area: 38,175 sq. mi.
98,873 sq. km.
Population: 45,083,000
Capital: Seoul
Largest City: Seoul
Highest Point: Halla-san
Monetary Unit: South Korean won

Kuwait
Page/Location: 51/F4
Area: 6,532 sq. mi.
16,918 sq. km.
Population: 1,819,000
Capital: Al Kuwait
Largest City: Al Kuwait
Highest Point: 951 ft. (290 m)
Monetary Unit: Kuwaiti dinar

Kyrgyzstan
Page/Location: 46/H5
Area: 76,641 sq. mi.
198,500 sq. km.
Population: 4,698,000
Capital: Bishkek
Largest City: Bishkek
Highest Point: Pik Pobedy
Monetary Unit: som

Laos
Page/Location: 65/C2
Area: 91,428 sq. mi.
236,800 sq. km.
Population: 4,702,000
Capital: Vientiane
Largest City: Vientiane
Highest Point: Phou Bia
Monetary Unit: kip

Latvia
Page/Location: 42/E4
Area: 24,595 sq. mi.
63,700 sq. km.
Population: 2,749,000
Capital: Riga
Largest City: Riga
Highest Point: Gaizina Kalns
Monetary Unit: lats

Lebanon
Page/Location: 49/D3
Area: 4,015 sq. mi.
10,399 sq. km.
Population: 3,620,000
Capital: Beirut
Largest City: Beirut
Highest Point: Qurnat as Sawdä'
Monetary Unit: Lebanese pound

Lesotho
Page/Location: 80/E3
Area: 11,720 sq. mi.
30,355 sq. km.
Population: 1,944,000
Capital: Maseru
Largest City: Maseru
Highest Point: Thabana-Ntlenyana
Monetary Unit: loti

Liberia
Page/Location: 78/C4
Area: 43,000 sq. mi.
111,370 sq. km.
Population: 2,973,000
Capital: Monrovia
Largest City: Monrovia
Highest Point: Mt. Wuteve
Monetary Unit: Liberian dollar

Libya
Page/Location: 77/J2
Area: 679,358 sq. mi.
1,759,537 sq. km.
Population: 5,057,000
Capital: Tripoli
Largest City: Tripoli
Highest Point: Picco Bette
Monetary Unit: Libyan dinar

Liechtenstein
Page/Location: 37/F3
Area: 61 sq. mi.
158 sq. km.
Population: 30,000
Capital: Vaduz
Largest City: Vaduz
Highest Point: Grauspitz
Monetary Unit: Swiss franc

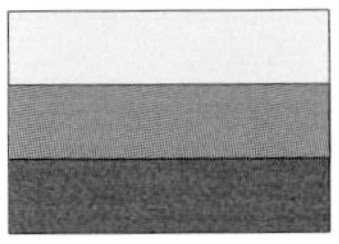

Lithuania
Page/Location: 42/D5
Area: 25,174 sq. mi.
65,200 sq. km.
Population: 3,848,000
Capital: Vilnius
Largest City: Vilnius
Highest Point: Nevaišių
Monetary Unit: litas

Luxembourg
Page/Location: 31/F4
Area: 999 sq. mi.
2,587 sq. km.
Population: 402,000
Capital: Luxembourg
Largest City: Luxembourg
Highest Point: Ardennes Plateau
Monetary Unit: Luxembourg franc

Macedonia
Page/Location: 39/G2
Area: 9,889 sq. mi.
25,612 sq. km.
Population: 2,214,000
Capital: Skopje
Largest City: Skopje
Highest Point: Korab
Monetary Unit: denar

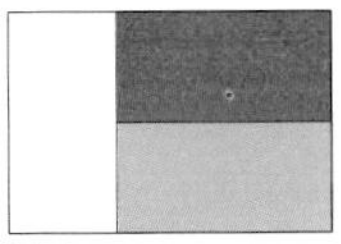

Madagascar
Page/Location: 81/H8
Area: 226,657 sq. mi.
587,041 sq. km.
Population: 13,428,000
Capital: Antananarivo
Largest City: Antananarivo
Highest Point: Maromokotro
Monetary Unit: Malagasy franc

Malawi
Page/Location: 82/F3
Area: 45,747 sq. mi.
118, 485 sq. km.
Population: 9,732,000
Capital: Lilongwe
Largest City: Blantyre
Highest Point: Mulanje Mts.
Monetary Unit: Malawi kwacha

Malaysia
Page/Location: 67/C2
Area: 128,308 sq. mi.
332,318 sq. km.
Population: 19,283,000
Capital: Kuala Lumpur
Largest City: Kuala Lumpur
Highest Point: Gunung Kinabalu
Monetary Unit: ringgit

Maldives
Page/Location: 48/G9
Area: 115 sq. mi.
298 sq. km.
Population: 252,000
Capital: Male
Largest City: Male
Highest Point: 20 ft. (6 m)
Monetary Unit: rufiyaa

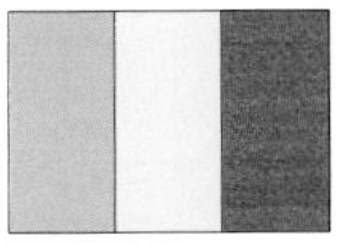

Mali
Page/Location: 76/E4
Area: 464,873 sq. mi.
1,204,021 sq. km.
Population: 9,113,000
Capital: Bamako
Largest City: Bamako
Highest Point: Hombori Tondo
Monetary Unit: CFA franc

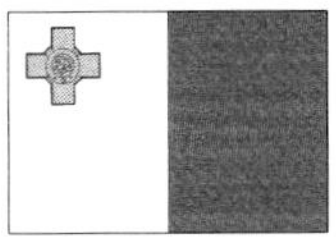

Malta
Page/Location: 38/D5
Area: 122 sq. mi.
316 sq. km.
Population: 367,000
Capital: Valletta
Largest City: Sliema
Highest Point: 830 ft. (253 m)
Monetary Unit: Maltese lira

Marshall Islands
Page/Location: 68/G3
Area: 70 sq. mi.
181 sq. km.
Population: 54,000
Capital: Majuro
Largest City: —
Highest Point: 20 ft. (6 m)
Monetary Unit: U.S. dollar

Mauritania
Page/Location: 76/C4
Area: 419,229 sq. mi.
1,085, 803 sq. km.
Population: 2,193,000
Capital: Nouakchott
Largest City: Nouakchott
Highest Point: Kediet Ijill
Monetary Unit: ouguiya

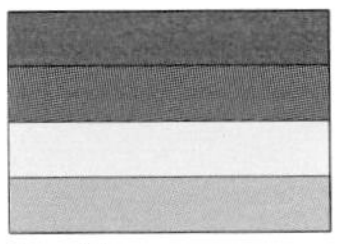

Mauritius
Page/Location: 81/S15
Area: 790 sq. mi.
2,046 sq. km.
Population: 1,117,000
Capital: Port Louis
Largest City: Port Louis
Highest Point: 2,713 ft. (827 m)
Monetary Unit: Mauritian rupee

Mexico
Page/Location: 84/G7
Area: 761,601 sq. mi.
1,972,546 sq. km.
Population: 92,202,000
Capital: Mexico City
Largest City: Mexico City
Highest Point: Citlaltépetl
Monetary Unit: Mexican peso

Micronesia
Page/Location: 68/D4
Area: 271 sq. mi.
702 sq. km.
Population: 120,347
Capital: Kolonia
Largest City: —
Highest Point: —
Monetary Unit: U.S. dollar

Moldova
Page/Location: 41/J2
Area: 13,012 sq. mi.
33,700 sq. km.
Population: 4,473,000
Capital: Chişinău
Largest City: Chişinău
Highest Point: 1,408 ft. (429 m)
Monetary Unit: leu

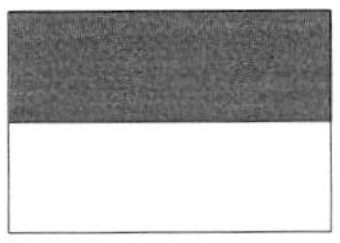

Monaco
Page/Location: 33/G5
Area: 368 acres
149 hectares
Population: 31,000
Capital: Monaco
Largest City: —
Highest Point: —
Monetary Unit: French franc

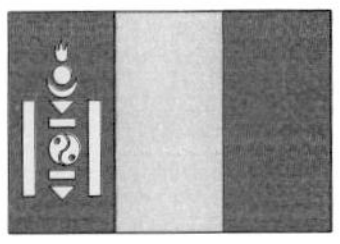

Mongolia
Page/Location: 54/D2
Area: 606,163 sq. mi.
1,569, 962 sq. km.
Population: 2,430,000
Capital: Ulaanbaatar
Largest City: Ulaanbaatar
Highest Point: Tavan Bogd Uul
Monetary Unit: tughrik

Morocco
Page/Location: 76/C1
Area: 172,414 sq. mi.
446,550 sq. km.
Population: 28,559,000
Capital: Rabat
Largest City: Casablanca
Highest Point: Jebel Toubkal
Monetary Unit: Moroccan dirham

Mozambique
Page/Location: 82/G4
Area: 303,769 sq. mi.
786,762 sq. km.
Population: 17,346,000
Capital: Maputo
Largest City: Maputo
Highest Point: Monte Binga
Monetary Unit: metical

Namibia
Page/Location: 82/C5
Area: 317,827 sq. mi.
823,172 sq. km.
Population: 1,596,000
Capital: Windhoek
Largest City: Windhoek
Highest Point: Brandberg
Monetary Unit: rand

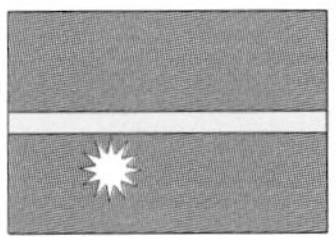

Nauru
Page/Location: 68/F5
Area: 7.7 sq. mi.
20 sq. km.
Population: 10,000
Capital: Yaren (district)
Largest City: —
Highest Point: 230 ft. (70 m)
Monetary Unit: Australian dollar

Nepal
Page/Location: 62/D2
Area: 54,663 sq. mi.
141,577 sq. km.
Population: 21,042,000
Capital: Kāthmāndu
Largest City: Kāthmāndu
Highest Point: Mt. Everest
Monetary Unit: Nepalese rupee

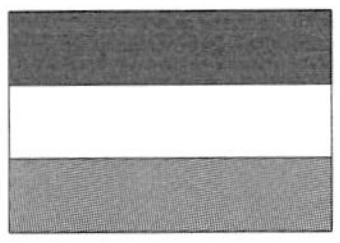

Netherlands
Page/Location: 28/B5
Area: 15,892 sq. mi.
41,160 sq. km.
Population: 15,368,000
Capital: The Hague; Amsterdam
Largest City: Amsterdam
Highest Point: Vaalserberg
Monetary Unit: Netherlands guilder

New Zealand
Page/Location: 71/Q10
Area: 103,736 sq. mi.
268,676 sq. km.
Population: 3,389,000
Capital: Wellington
Largest City: Auckland
Highest Point: Mt. Cook
Monetary Unit: New Zealand dollar

Nicaragua
Page/Location: 103/E3
Area: 45,698 sq. mi.
118,358 sq. km.
Population: 4,097,000
Capital: Managua
Largest City: Managua
Highest Point: Pico Mogotón
Monetary Unit: córdoba

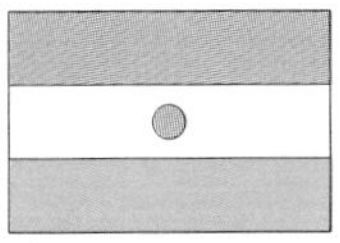

Niger
Page/Location: 76/G4
Area: 489,189 sq. mi.
1,267,000 sq. km.
Population: 8,972,000
Capital: Niamey
Largest City: Niamey
Highest Point: Bagzane
Monetary Unit: CFA franc

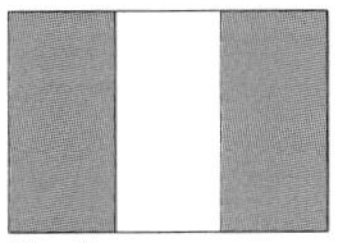

Nigeria
Page/Location: 76/G6
Area: 357,000 sq. mi.
924,630 sq. km.
Population: 98,091,000
Capital: Abuja
Largest City: Lagos
Highest Point: Dimlang
Monetary Unit: naira

Norway
Page/Location: 20/C3
Area: 125,053 sq. mi.
323,887 sq. km.
Population: 4,315,000
Capital: Oslo
Largest City: Oslo
Highest Point: Glittertjnden
Monetary Unit: Norwegian krone

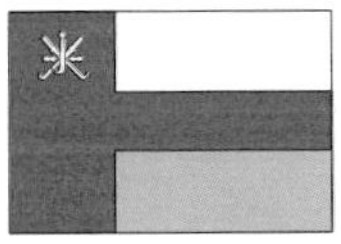

Oman
Page/Location: 53/G4
Area: 120,000 sq. mi.
310,800 sq. km.
Population: 1,701,000
Capital: Muscat
Largest City: Muscat
Highest Point: Jabal ash Shām
Monetary Unit: Omani rial

Pakistan
Page/Location: 53/H3
Area: 310,403 sq. mi.
803,944 sq. km.
Population: 128,856,000
Capital: Islāmābād
Largest City: Karāchi
Highest Point: K2 (Godwin Austen)
Monetary Unit: Pakistani rupee

Palau
Page/Location: 68/C4
Area: 177 sq. mi.
458 sq. km.
Population: 15,122
Capital: Koror
Largest City: Koror
Highest Point: 699 ft. (213m)
Monetary Unit: U.S. dollar

Panama
Page/Location: 103/F4
Area: 29,761 sq. mi.
77,082 sq. km.
Population: 2,630,000
Capital: Panamá
Largest City: Panamá
Highest Point: Barú
Monetary Unit: balboa

Papua New Guinea
Page/Location: 68/D5
Area: 183,540 sq. mi.
475,369 sq. km.
Population: 4,197,000
Capital: Port Moresby
Largest City: Port Moresby
Highest Point: Mt. Wilhelm
Monetary Unit: kina

World Flags and Reference Guide

Paraguay
Page/Location: 105/D5
Area: 157,047 sq. mi.
406,752 sq. km.
Population: 5,214,000
Capital: Asunción
Largest City: Asunción
Highest Point: Sierra de Amambay
Monetary Unit: guaraní

Peru
Page/Location: 106/C5
Area: 496,222 sq. mi.
1,285,215 sq. km.
Population: 23,651,000
Capital: Lima
Largest City: Lima
Highest Point: Nevado Huascarán
Monetary Unit: nuevo sol

Philippines
Page/Location: 48/M8
Area: 115,707 sq. mi.
299,681 sq. km.
Population: 69,809,000
Capital: Manila
Largest City: Manila
Highest Point: Mt. Apo
Monetary Unit: Philippine peso

Poland
Page/Location: 27/K2
Area: 120,725 sq. mi.
312,678 sq. km.
Population: 38,655,000
Capital: Warsaw
Largest City: Warsaw
Highest Point: Rysy
Monetary Unit: zloty

Portugal
Page/Location: 34/A3
Area: 35,549 sq. mi.
92,072 sq. km.
Population: 10,524,000
Capital: Lisbon
Largest City: Lisbon
Highest Point: Serra da Estrela
Monetary Unit: Portuguese escudo

Qatar
Page/Location: 52/F3
Area: 4,247 sq. mi.
11,000 sq. km.
Population: 513,000
Capital: Doha
Largest City: Doha
Highest Point: Dukhān Heights
Monetary Unit: Qatari riyal

Romania
Page/Location: 41/F3
Area: 91,699 sq. mi.
237,500 sq. km.
Population: 23,181,000
Capital: Bucharest
Largest City: Bucharest
Highest Point: Moldoveanul
Monetary Unit: leu

Russia
Page/Location: 46/H3
Area: 6,592,812 sq. mi.
17,075,400 sq. km.
Population: 149,609,000
Capital: Moscow
Largest City: Moscow
Highest Point: El'brus
Monetary Unit: Russian ruble

Rwanda
Page/Location: 82/E1
Area: 10,169 sq. mi.
26,337 sq. km.
Population: 8,374,000
Capital: Kigali
Largest City: Kigali
Highest Point: Karisimbi
Monetary Unit: Rwanda franc

Saint Kitts and Nevis
Page/Location: 104/F3
Area: 104 sq. mi.
269 sq. km.
Population: 41,000
Capital: Basseterre
Largest City: Basseterre
Highest Point: Mt. Misery
Monetary Unit: East Caribbean dollar

Saint Lucia
Page/Location: 104/F4
Area: 238 sq. mi.
616 sq. km.
Population: 145,000
Capital: Castries
Largest City: Castries
Highest Point: Mt. Gimie
Monetary Unit: East Caribbean dollar

Saint Vincent and the Grenadines
Page/Location: 104/F4
Area: 150 sq. mi.
388 sq. km.
Population: 115,000
Capital: Kingstown
Largest City: Kingstown
Highest Point: Soufrière
Monetary Unit: East Caribbean dollar

San Marino
Page/Location: 33/K5
Area: 23.4 sq. mi.
60.6 sq. km.
Population: 24,000
Capital: San Marino
Largest City: San Marino
Highest Point: Monte Titano
Monetary Unit: Italian lira

São Tomé and Príncipe
Page/Location: 76/G7
Area: 372 sq. mi.
963 sq. km.
Population: 137,000
Capital: São Tomé
Largest City: São Tomé
Highest Point: Pico de São Tomé
Monetary Unit: dobra

Saudi Arabia
Page/Location: 104/F3
Area: 829,995 sq. mi.
2,149,687 sq. km.
Population: 18,197,000
Capital: Riyadh
Largest City: Riyadh
Highest Point: Jabal Sawdā'
Monetary Unit: Saudi riyal

Senegal
Page/Location: 78/B3
Area: 75,954 sq. mi.
196,720 sq. km.
Population: 8,731,000
Capital: Dakar
Largest City: Dakar
Highest Point: Fouta Djallon
Monetary Unit: CFA franc

Seychelles
Page/Location: 74/H5
Area: 145 sq. mi.
375 sq. km.
Population: 72,000
Capital: Victoria
Largest City: Victoria
Highest Point: Morne Seychellois
Monetary Unit: Seychellois rupee

Sierra Leone
Page/Location: 78/B4
Area: 27,925 sq. mi.
72,325 sq. km.
Population: 4,630,000
Capital: Freetown
Largest City: Freetown
Highest Point: Loma Mansa
Monetary Unit: leone

Singapore
Page/Location: 66/B3
Area: 226 sq. mi.
585 sq. km.
Population: 2,859,000
Capital: Singapore
Largest City: Singapore
Highest Point: Bukit Timah
Monetary Unit: Singapore dollar

Slovakia
Page/Location: 27/K4
Area: 18,924 sq. mi.
49,013 sq. km.
Population: 5,404,000
Capital: Bratislava
Largest City: Bratislava
Highest Point: Gerlachovský Štít
Monetary Unit: Slovak koruna

Slovenia
Page/Location: 40/B3
Area: 7,898 sq. mi.
20,456 sq. km.
Population: 1,972,000
Capital: Ljubljana
Largest City: Ljubljana
Highest Point: Triglav
Monetary Unit: tolar

Solomon Islands
Page/Location: 68/E6
Area: 11,500 sq. mi.
29,785 sq. km.
Population: 386,000
Capital: Honiara
Largest City: Honiara
Highest Point: Mt. Makarakomburu
Monetary Unit: Solomon Islands dollar

Somalia
Page/Location: 77/Q6
Area: 246,000 sq. mi.
637,658 sq. km.
Population: 6,667,000
Capital: Mogadishu
Largest City: Mogadishu
Highest Point: Shimber Berris
Monetary Unit: Somali shilling

South Africa
Page/Location: 80/C3
Area: 455,318 sq. mi.
1,179,274 sq. km.
Population: 43,931,000
Capital: Cape Town; Pretoria
Largest City: Johannesburg
Highest Point: Injasuti
Monetary Unit: rand

Spain
Page/Location: 34/C2
Area: 194,881 sq. mi.
504,742 sq. km.
Population: 39,303,000
Capital: Madrid
Largest City: Madrid
Highest Point: Pico de Teide
Monetary Unit: peseta

Sri Lanka
Page/Location: 62/D6
Area: 25,332 sq. mi.
65,610 sq. km.
Population: 18,130,000
Capital: Colombo
Largest City: Colombo
Highest Point: Pidurutalagala
Monetary Unit: Sri Lanka rupee

Sudan
Page/Location: 77/L5
Area: 967,494 sq. mi.
2,505,809 sq. km.
Population: 29,420,000
Capital: Khartoum
Largest City: Omdurman
Highest Point: Jabal Marrah
Monetary Unit: Sudanese pound

Suriname
Page/Location: 107/G3
Area: 55,144 sq. mi.
142,823 sq. km.
Population: 423,000
Capital: Paramaribo
Largest City: Paramaribo
Highest Point: Juliana Top
Monetary Unit: Suriname guilder

Swaziland
Page/Location: 81/E2
Area: 6,705 sq. mi.
17,366 sq. km.
Population: 936,000
Capital: Mbabane
Largest City: Mbabane
Highest Point: Emlembe
Monetary Unit: lilangeni

Sweden
Page/Location: 20/E3
Area: 173,665 sq. mi.
449,792 sq. km.
Population: 8,778,000
Capital: Stockholm
Largest City: Stockholm
Highest Point: Kebnekaise
Monetary Unit: krona

Switzerland
Page/Location: 36/D4
Area: 15,943 sq. mi.
41,292 sq. km.
Population: 7,040,000
Capital: Bern
Largest City: Zürich
Highest Point: Dufourspitze
Monetary Unit: Swiss franc

Syria
Page/Location: 50/D3
Area: 71,498 sq. mi.
185,180 sq. km.
Population: 14,887,000
Capital: Damascus
Largest City: Damascus
Highest Point: Jabal ash Shaykh
Monetary Unit: Syrian pound

Taiwan
Page/Location: 61/J3
Area: 13,971 sq. mi.
36,185 sq. km.
Population: 21,299,000
Capital: Taipei
Largest City: Taipei
Highest Point: Yü Shan
Monetary Unit: new Taiwan dollar

Tajikistan
Page/Location: 46/H6
Area: 55,251 sq. mi.
143,100 sq. km.
Population: 5,995,000
Capital: Dushanbe
Largest City: Dushanbe
Highest Point: Communism Peak
Monetary Unit: Tajik ruble

Tanzania
Page/Location: 82/F2
Area: 363,708 sq. mi.
942,003 sq. km.
Population: 27,986,000
Capital: Dar es Salaam
Largest City: Dar es Salaam
Highest Point: Kilimanjaro
Monetary Unit: Tanzanian shilling

Thailand
Page/Location: 65/C3
Area: 198,455 sq. mi.
513,998 sq. km.
Population: 59,510,000
Capital: Bangkok
Largest City: Bangkok
Highest Point: Doi Inthanon
Monetary Unit: baht

Togo
Page/Location: 79/F4
Area: 21,622 sq. mi.
56,000 sq. km.
Population: 4,255,000
Capital: Lomé
Largest City: Lomé
Highest Point: Mt. Agou
Monetary Unit: CFA franc

Tonga
Page/Location: 69/H7
Area: 270 sq. mi.
699 sq. km.
Population: 105,000
Capital: Nuku'alofa
Largest City: Nuku'alofa
Highest Point: Kao Island
Monetary Unit: pa'anga

Trinidad and Tobago
Page/Location: 104/F5
Area: 1,980 sq. mi.
5,128 sq. km.
Population: 1,328,000
Capital: Port-of-Spain
Largest City: Port-of-Spain
Highest Point: El Cerro del Aripo
Monetary Unit: Trin. & Tobago dollar

Tunisia
Page/Location: 76/G1
Area: 63,378 sq. mi.
164,149 sq. km.
Population: 8,727,000
Capital: Tūnis
Largest City: Tūnis
Highest Point: Jabal ash Sha'nabī
Monetary Unit: Tunisian dinar

Turkey
Page/Location: 50/C2
Area: 300,946 sq. mi.
779,450 sq. km.
Population: 62,154,000
Capital: Ankara
Largest City: Istanbul
Highest Point: Mt. Ararat
Monetary Unit: Turkish lira

Turkmenistan
Page/Location: 46/F6
Area: 188,455 sq. mi.
488,100 sq. km.
Population: 3,995,000
Capital: Ashkhabad
Largest City: Ashkhabad
Highest Point: Rize
Monetary Unit: manat

Tuvalu
Page/Location: 68/G5
Area: 9.78 sq. mi.
25.33 sq. km.
Population: 10,000
Capital: Funafuti
Largest City: —
Highest Point: 16 ft. (5 m)
Monetary Unit: Australian dollar

Uganda
Page/Location: 77/M7
Area: 91,076 sq. mi.
235,887 sq. km.
Population: 19,859,000
Capital: Kampala
Largest City: Kampala
Highest Point: Margherita Peak
Monetary Unit: Ugandan shilling

Ukraine
Page/Location: 44/D2
Area: 233,089 sq. mi.
603,700 sq. km.
Population: 51,847,000
Capital: Kiev
Largest City: Kiev
Highest Point: Goverla
Monetary Unit: karbovanet

United Arab Emirates
Page/Location: 52/F4
Area: 32,278 sq. mi.
83,600 sq. km.
Population: 2,791,000
Capital: Abu Dhabi
Largest City: Dubayy
Highest Point: Hajar Mts.
Monetary Unit: Emirian dirham

United Kingdom
Page/Location: 21
Area: 94,399 sq. mi.
244,493 sq. km.
Population: 58,135,000
Capital: London
Largest City: London
Highest Point: Ben Nevis
Monetary Unit: pound sterling

United States
Page/Location: 88
Area: 3,540,542 sq. mi.
9,170,002 sq. km.
Population: 260,714,000
Capital: Washington
Largest City: New York
Highest Point: Mt. McKinley
Monetary Unit: U.S. dollar

Uruguay
Page/Location: 109/E3
Area: 72,172 sq. mi.
186,925 sq. km.
Population: 3,199,000
Capital: Montevideo
Largest City: Montevideo
Highest Point: Cerro Catedral
Monetary Unit: Uruguayan peso

Uzbekistan
Page/Location: 46/G5
Area: 173,591 sq. mi.
449,600 sq. km.
Population: 22,609,000
Capital: Tashkent
Largest City: Tashkent
Highest Point: Khodzha-Pir'yakh
Monetary Unit: som

Vanuatu
Page/Location: 68/F6
Area: 5,700 sq. mi.
14,763 sq. km.
Population: 170,000
Capital: Vila
Largest City: Vila
Highest Point: Tabwemasana
Monetary Unit: vatu

Vatican City
Page/Location: 38/C2
Area: 108.7 acres
44 hectares
Population: 821
Capital: —
Largest City: —
Highest Point: —
Monetary Unit: Italian lira

Venezuela
Page/Location: 106/E2
Area: 352,143 sq. mi.
912,050 sq. km.
Population: 20,562,000
Capital: Caracas
Largest City: Caracas
Highest Point: Pico Bolívar
Monetary Unit: bolívar

Vietnam
Page/Location: 65/D2
Area: 128,405 sq. mi.
332,569 sq. km.
Population: 73,104,000
Capital: Hanoi
Largest City: Ho Chi Minh City
Highest Point: Fan Si Pan
Monetary Unit: dong

Western Samoa
Page/Location: 69/H6
Area: 1,133 sq. mi.
2,934 sq. km.
Population: 204,000
Capital: Apia
Largest City: Apia
Highest Point: Mt. Silisili
Monetary Unit: tala

Yemen
Page/Location: 52/E5
Area: 188,321 sq. mi.
487,752 sq. km.
Population: 11,105,000
Capital: Sanaa
Largest City: Aden
Highest Point: Nabī Shu'ayb
Monetary Unit: Yemeni rial

Yugoslavia
Page/Location: 40/E3
Area: 38,989 sq. mi.
100,982 sq. km.
Population: 10,760,000
Capital: Belgrade
Largest City: Belgrade
Highest Point: Đaravica
Monetary Unit: Yugoslav new dinar

Zaire
Page/Location: 74/E5
Area: 905,063 sq. mi.
2,344,113 sq. km.
Population: 42,684,000
Capital: Kinshasa
Largest City: Kinshasa
Highest Point: Margherita Peak
Monetary Unit: zaire

Zambia
Page/Location: 82/E3
Area: 290,586 sq. mi.
752,618 sq. km.
Population: 9,188,000
Capital: Lusaka
Largest City: Lusaka
Highest Point: Sunzu
Monetary Unit: Zambian kwacha

Zimbabwe
Page/Location: 82/E4
Area: 150,803 sq. mi.
390,580 sq. km.
Population: 10,975,000
Capital: Harare
Largest City: Harare
Highest Point: Inyangani
Monetary Unit: Zimbabwe dollar

World Statistics

ELEMENTS OF THE SOLAR SYSTEM

	Mean Distance from Sun: in Miles	in Kilometers	Period of Revolution around Sun	Period of Rotation on Axis	Equatorial Diameter in Miles	in Kilometers	Surface Gravity (Earth = 1)	Mass (Earth = 1)	Mean Density (Water = 1)	Number of Satellites
Mercury	35,990,000	57,900,000	87.97 days	59 days	3,032	4,880	0.38	0.055	5.5	0
Venus	67,240,000	108,200,000	224.70 days	243 days†	7,523	12,106	0.90	0.815	5.25	0
Earth	93,000,000	149,700,000	365.26 days	23h 56m	7,926	12,755	1.00	1.00	5.5	1
Mars	141,730,000	228,100,000	687.00 days	24h 37m	4,220	6,790	0.38	0.107	4.0	2
Jupiter	483,880,000	778,700,000	11.86 years	9h 50m	88,750	142,800	2.87	317.9	1.3	16
Saturn	887,130,000	1,427,700,000	29.46 years	10h 39m	74,580	120,020	1.32	95.2	0.7	23
Uranus	1,783,700,000	2,870,500,000	84.01 years	17h 24m†	31,600	50,900	0.93	14.6	1.3	15
Neptune	2,795,500,000	4,498,800,000	164.79 years	17h 50m	30,200	48,600	1.23	17.2	1.8	8
Pluto	3,667,900,000	5,902,800,000	247.70 years	6.39 days(?)	1,500	2,400	0.03(?)	0.01(?)	0.7(?)	1

† Retrograde motion

DIMENSIONS OF THE EARTH

	Area in: Sq. Miles	Sq. Kilometers
Superficial area	196,939,000	510,073,000
Land surface	57,506,000	148,941,000
Water surface	139,433,000	361,132,000

	Distance in: Miles	Kilometers
Equatorial circumference	24,902	40,075
Polar circumference	24,860	40,007
Equatorial diameter	7,926.4	12,756.4
Polar diameter	7,899.8	12,713.6
Equatorial radius	3,963.2	6,378.2
Polar radius	3,949.9	6,356.8

Volume of the Earth	2.6×10^{11} cubic miles	10.84×10^{11} cubic kilometers
Mass or weight	6.6×10^{21} short tons	6.0×10^{21} metric tons
Maximum distance from Sun	94,600,000 miles	152,000,000 kilometers
Minimum distance from Sun	91,300,000 miles	147,000,000 kilometers

OCEANS AND MAJOR SEAS

	Area in: Sq. Miles	Sq. Kms.	Greatest Depth in: Feet	Meters
Pacific Ocean	64,186,000	166,241,700	36,198	11,033
Atlantic Ocean	31,862,000	82,522,600	28,374	8,648
Indian Ocean	28,350,000	73,426,500	25,344	7,725
Arctic Ocean	5,427,000	14,056,000	17,880	5,450
Caribbean Sea	970,000	2,512,300	24,720	7,535
Mediterranean Sea	969,000	2,509,700	16,896	5,150
South China Sea	895,000	2,318,000	15,000	4,600
Bering Sea	875,000	2,266,250	15,800	4,800
Gulf of Mexico	600,000	1,554,000	12,300	3,750
Sea of Okhotsk	590,000	1,528,100	11,070	3,370
East China Sea	482,000	1,248,400	9,500	2,900
Yellow Sea	480,000	1,243,200	350	107
Sea of Japan	389,000	1,007,500	12,280	3,740
Hudson Bay	317,500	822,300	846	258
North Sea	222,000	575,000	2,200	670
Black Sea	185,000	479,150	7,365	2,245
Red Sea	169,000	437,700	7,200	2,195
Baltic Sea	163,000	422,170	1,506	459

THE CONTINENTS

	Area in: Sq. Miles	Sq. Kms.	Percent of World's Land
Asia	17,128,500	44,362,815	29.5
Africa	11,707,000	30,321,130	20.2
North America	9,363,000	24,250,170	16.2
South America	6,875,000	17,806,250	11.8
Antarctica	5,500,000	14,245,000	9.5
Europe	4,057,000	10,507,630	7.0
Australia	2,966,136	7,682,300	5.1

MAJOR SHIP CANALS

	Length in: Miles	Kms.	Minimum Depth in: Feet	Meters
Volga-Baltic, Russia	225	362	–	–
Baltic-White Sea, Russia	140	225	16	5
Suez, Egypt	100.76	162	42	13
Albert, Belgium	80	129	16.5	5
Moscow-Volga, Russia	80	129	18	6
Volga-Don, Russia	62	100	–	–
Göta, Sweden	54	87	10	3
Kiel (Nord-Ostsee), Germany	53.2	86	38	12
Panama Canal, Panama	50.72	82	41.6	13
Houston Ship, U.S.A.	50	81	36	11

LARGEST ISLANDS

	Area in: Sq. Miles	Sq. Kms.
Greenland	840,000	2,175,600
New Guinea	305,000	789,950
Borneo	290,000	751,100
Madagascar	226,400	586,376
Baffin, Canada	195,928	507,454
Sumatra, Indonesia	164,000	424,760
Honshu, Japan	88,000	227,920
Great Britain	84,400	218,896
Victoria, Canada	83,896	217,290
Ellesmere, Canada	75,767	196,236
Celebes, Indonesia	72,986	189,034
South I., New Zealand	58,393	151,238
Java, Indonesia	48,842	126,501
North I., New Zealand	44,187	114,444
Newfoundland, Canada	42,031	108,860
Cuba	40,533	104,981
Luzon, Philippines	40,420	104,688
Iceland	39,768	103,000
Mindanao, Philippines	36,537	94,631
Ireland	31,743	82,214
Sakhalin, Russia	29,500	76,405
Hispaniola, Haiti & Dom. Rep.	29,399	76,143

	Area in: Sq. Miles	Sq. Kms.
Hokkaido, Japan	28,983	75,066
Banks, Canada	27,038	70,028
Ceylon, Sri Lanka	25,332	65,610
Tasmania, Australia	24,600	63,710
Svalbard, Norway	23,957	62,049
Devon, Canada	21,331	55,247
Novaya Zemlya (north isl.), Russia	18,600	48,200
Marajó, Brazil	17,991	46,597
Tierra del Fuego, Chile & Argentina	17,900	46,360
Alexander, Antarctica	16,700	43,250
Axel Heiberg, Canada	16,671	43,178
Melville, Canada	16,274	42,150
Southhampton, Canada	15,913	41,215
New Britain, Papua New Guinea	14,100	36,519
Taiwan, China	13,836	35,835
Kyushu, Japan	13,770	35,664
Hainan, China	13,127	33,999
Prince of Wales, Canada	12,872	33,338
Spitsbergen, Norway	12,355	31,999
Vancouver, Canada	12,079	31,285
Timor, Indonesia	11,527	29,855
Sicily, Italy	9,926	25,708

	Area in: Sq. Miles	Sq. Kms.
Somerset, Canada	9,570	24,786
Sardinia, Italy	9,301	24,090
Shikoku, Japan	6,860	17,767
New Caledonia, France	6,530	16,913
Nordaustlandet, Norway	6,409	16,599
Samar, Philippines	5,050	13,080
Negros, Philippines	4,906	12,707
Palawan, Philippines	4,550	11,785
Panay, Philippines	4,446	11,515
Jamaica	4,232	10,961
Hawaii, United States	4,038	10,458
Viti Levu, Fiji	4,010	10,386
Cape Breton, Canada	3,981	10,311
Mindoro, Philippines	3,759	9,736
Kodiak, Alaska, U.S.A.	3,670	9,505
Cyprus	3,572	9,251
Puerto Rico, U.S.A.	3,435	8,897
Corsica, France	3,352	8,682
New Ireland, Papua New Guinea	3,340	8,651
Crete, Greece	3,218	8,335
Anticosti, Canada	3,066	7,941
Wrangel, Russia	2,819	7,301

PRINCIPAL MOUNTAINS

	Height in : Feet	Meters		Height in : Feet	Meters		Height in : Feet	Meters
Everest, Nepal-China	29,028	8,848	Llullaillaco, Chile-Argentina	22,057	6,723	Blanc, France	15,771	4,807
K2 (Godwin Austen), Pakistan-China	28,250	8,611	Nevada Ancohuma, Bolivia	21,489	6,550	Klyuchevskaya Sopka, Russia	15,584	4,750
Makalu, Nepal-China	27,789	8,470	Chimborazo, Ecuador	20,561	6,267	Fairweather, Br. Col., Canada	15,300	4,663
Dhaulagiri, Nepal	26,810	8,172	McKinley, Alaska	20,320	6,194	Dufourspitze (Mte. Rosa), Italy-Switzerland	15,203	4,634
Nanga Parbat, Pakistan	26,660	8,126	Logan, Yukon, Canada	19,524	5,951	Ras Dashen, Ethiopia	15,157	4620
Annapurna, Nepal	26,504	8,078	Cotopaxi, Ecuador	19,347	5,897	Matterhorn, Switzerland	14,691	4,478
Rakaposhi, Pakistan	25,550	7,788	Kilimanjaro, Tanzania	19,340	5,895	Whitney, California, U.S.A.	14,494	4,418
Kongur Shan, China	25,325	7,719	El Misti, Peru	19,101	5,822	Elbert, Colorado, U.S.A.	14,433	4,399
Tirich Mir, Pakistan	25,230	7,690	Pico Cristóbal Colón, Colombia	18,947	5,775	Rainier, Washington, U.S.A.	14,410	4,392
Gongga Shan, China	24,790	7,556	Huila, Colombia	18,865	5,750	Shasta, California, U.S.A.	14,162	4,317
Communism Peak, Tajikistan	24,590	7,495	Citlaltépetl (Orizaba), Mexico	18,701	5,700	Pikes Peak, Colorado, U.S.A.	14,110	4,301
Pobedy Peak, Kyrgyzstan	24,406	7,439	Damavand, Iran	18,606	5,671	Finsteraarhorn, Switzerland	14,022	4,274
Chomo Lhari, Bhutan-China	23,997	7,314	El'brus, Russia	18,510	5,642	Mauna Kea, Hawaii, U.S.A.	13,796	4,205
Muztag, China	23,891	7,282	St. Elias, Alaska, U.S.A.-Yukon, Canada	18,008	5,489	Mauna Loa, Hawaii, U.S.A.	13,677	4,169
Cerro Aconcagua, Argentina	22,831	6,959	Dykh-tau, Russia	17,070	5,203	Jungfrau, Switzerland	13,642	4,158
Ojos del Salado, Chile-Argentina	22,572	6,880	Batian (Kenya), Kenya	17,058	5,199	Grossglockner, Austria	12,457	3,797
Bonete, Chile-Argentina	22,546	6,872	Ararat, Turkey	16,946	5,165	Fujiyama, Japan	12,389	3,776
Tupungato, Chile-Argentina	22,310	6,800	Vinson Massif, Antarctica	16,864	5,140	Cook, New Zealand	12,349	3,764
Pissis, Argentina	22,241	6,779	Margherita (Ruwenzori), Africa	16,795	5,119	Etna, Italy	10,902	3,323
Mercedario, Argentina	22,211	6,770	Kazbek, Georgia-Russia	16,558	5,047	Kosciusko, Australia	7,310	2,228
Huascarán, Peru	22,205	6,768	Puncak Jaya, Indonesia	16,503	5,030	Mitchell, North Carolina, U.S.A.	6,684	2,037

LONGEST RIVERS

	Length in : Miles	Kms.		Length in : Miles	Kms.		Length in : Miles	Kms.
Nile, Africa	4,145	6,671	Indus, Asia	1,800	2,897	Don, Russia	1,222	1,967
Amazon, S. America	3,915	6,300	Danube, Europe	1,775	2,857	Red, U.S.A.	1,222	1,966
Chang Jiang (Yangtze), China	3,900	6,276	Salween, Asia	1,770	2,849	Columbia, U.S.A.-Canada	1,214	1,953
Mississippi-Missouri-Red Rock, U.S.A.	3,741	6,019	Brahmaputra, Asia	1,700	2,736	Saskatchewan, Canada	1,205	1,939
Ob'-Irtysh-Black Irtysh, Russia-Kazakhstan	3,362	5,411	Euphrates, Asia	1,700	2,736	Peace-Finlay, Canada	1,195	1,923
Yenisey-Angara, Russia	3,100	4,989	Tocantins, Brazil	1,677	2,699	Tigris, Asia	1,181	1,901
Huang He (Yellow), China	2,877	4,630	Xi (Si), China	1,650	2,601	Darling, Australia	1,160	1,867
Amur-Shilka-Onon, Asia	2,744	4,416	Amudar'ya, Asia	1,616	2,601	Angara, Russia	1,135	1,827
Lena, Russia	2,734	4,400	Nelson-Saskatchewan, Canada	1,600	2,575	Sungari, Asia	1,130	1,819
Congo (Zaire), Africa	2,718	4,374	Orinoco, S. America	1,600	2,575	Pechora, Russia	1,124	1,809
Mackenzie-Peace-Finlay, Canada	2,635	4,241	Zambezi, Africa	1,600	2,575	Snake, U.S.A.	1,038	1,670
Mekong, Asia	2,610	4,200	Paraguay, S. America	1,584	2,549	Churchill, Canada	1,000	1,609
Missouri-Red Rock, U.S.A.	2,564	4,125	Kolyma, Russia	1,562	2,514	Pilcomayo, S. America	1,000	1,609
Niger, Africa	2,548	4,101	Ganges, Asia	1,550	2,494	Uruguay, S. America	994	1.600
Paraná-La Plata, S. America	2,450	3,943	Ural, Russia-Kazakhstan	1,509	2,428	Platte-N. Platte, U.S.A.	990	1,593
Mississippi, U.S.A.	2,348	3,778	Japurá, S. America	1,500	2,414	Ohio, U.S.A.	981	1,578
Murray-Darling, Australia	2,310	3,718	Arkansas, U.S.A.	1,450	2,334	Magdalena, Colombia	956	1,538
Volga, Russia	2,194	3,531	Colorado, U.S.A.-Mexico	1,450	2,334	Pecos, U.S.A.	926	1,490
Madeira, S. America	2,013	3,240	Negro, S. America	1,400	2,253	Oka, Russia	918	1,477
Purus, S. America	1,995	3,211	Dnieper, Russia-Belarus-Ukraine	1,368	2,202	Canadian, U.S.A.	906	1,458
Yukon, Alaska-Canada	1,979	3,185	Orange, Africa	1,350	2,173	Colorado, Texas, U.S.A.	894	1,439
St. Lawrence, Canada-U.S.A.	1,900	3,058	Irrawaddy, Burma	1,325	2,132	Dniester, Ukraine-Moldova	876	1,410
Rio Grande, Mexico-U.S.A.	1,885	3,034	Brazos, U.S.A.	1,309	2,107	Fraser, Canada	850	1,369
Syrdar'ya-Naryn, Asia	1,859	2,992	Ohio-Allegheny, U.S.A.	1,306	2,102	Rhine, Europe	820	1,319
São Francisco, Brazil	1,811	2,914	Kama, Russia	1,252	2,031	Northern Dvina, Russia	809	1,302

PRINCIPAL NATURAL LAKES

	Area in: Sq. Miles	Sq. Kms.	Max. Depth in: Feet	Meters		Area in: Sq. Miles	Sq. Kms.	Max. Depth in: Feet	Meters
Caspian Sea, Asia	143,243	370,999	3,264	995	Lake Eyre, Australia	3,500-0	9,000-0	–	–
Lake Superior, U.S.A.-Canada	31,820	82,414	1,329	405	Lake Titicaca, Peru-Bolivia	3,200	8,288	1,000	305
Lake Victoria, Africa	26,724	69,215	270	82	Lake Nicaragua, Nicaragua	3,100	8,029	230	70
Lake Huron, U.S.A.-Canada	23,010	59,596	748	228	Lake Athabasca, Canada	3,064	7,936	400	122
Lake Michigan, U.S.A.	22,400	58,016	923	281	Reindeer Lake, Canada	2,568	6,651	–	–
Aral Sea, Kazakhstan-Uzbekistan	15,830	41,000	213	65	Lake Turkana (Rudolf), Africa	2,463	6,379	240	73
Lake Tanganyika, Africa	12,650	32,764	4,700	1,433	Issyk-Kul', Kyrgyzstan	2,425	6,281	2,303	702
Lake Baykal, Russia	12,162	31,500	5,316	1,620	Lake Torrens, Australia	2,230	5,776	–	–
Great Bear Lake, Canada	12,096	31,328	1,356	413	Vänern, Sweden	2,156	5,584	328	100
Lake Nyasa (Malawi), Africa	11,555	29,928	2,320	707	Nettilling Lake, Canada	2,140	5,543	–	–
Great Slave Lake, Canada	11,031	28,570	2,015	614	Lake Winnipegosis, Canada	2,075	5,374	38	12
Lake Erie, U.S.A.-Canada	9,940	25,745	210	64	Lake Mobutu Sese Seko (Albert), Africa	2,075	5,374	160	49
Lake Winnipeg, Canada	9,417	24,390	60	18	Kariba Lake, Zambia-Zimbabwe	2,050	5,310	295	90
Lake Ontario, U.S.A.-Canada	7,540	19,529	775	244	Lake Nipigon, Canada	1,872	4,848	540	165
Lake Ladoga, Russia	7,104	18,399	738	225	Lake Mweru, Zaire-Zambia	1,800	4,662	60	18
Lake Balkhash, Kazakhstan	7,027	18,200	87	27	Lake Manitoba, Canada	1,799	4,659	12	4
Lake Maracaibo, Venezuela	5,120	13,261	100	31	Lake Taymyr, Russia	1,737	4,499	85	26
Lake Chad, Africa	4,000 –	10,360 –			Lake Khanka, China-Russia	1,700	4,403	33	10
	10,000	25,900	25	8	Lake Kioga, Uganda	1,700	4,403	25	8
Lake Onega, Russia	3,710	9,609	377	115	Lake of the Woods, U.S.A.-Canada	1,679	4,349	70	21J2

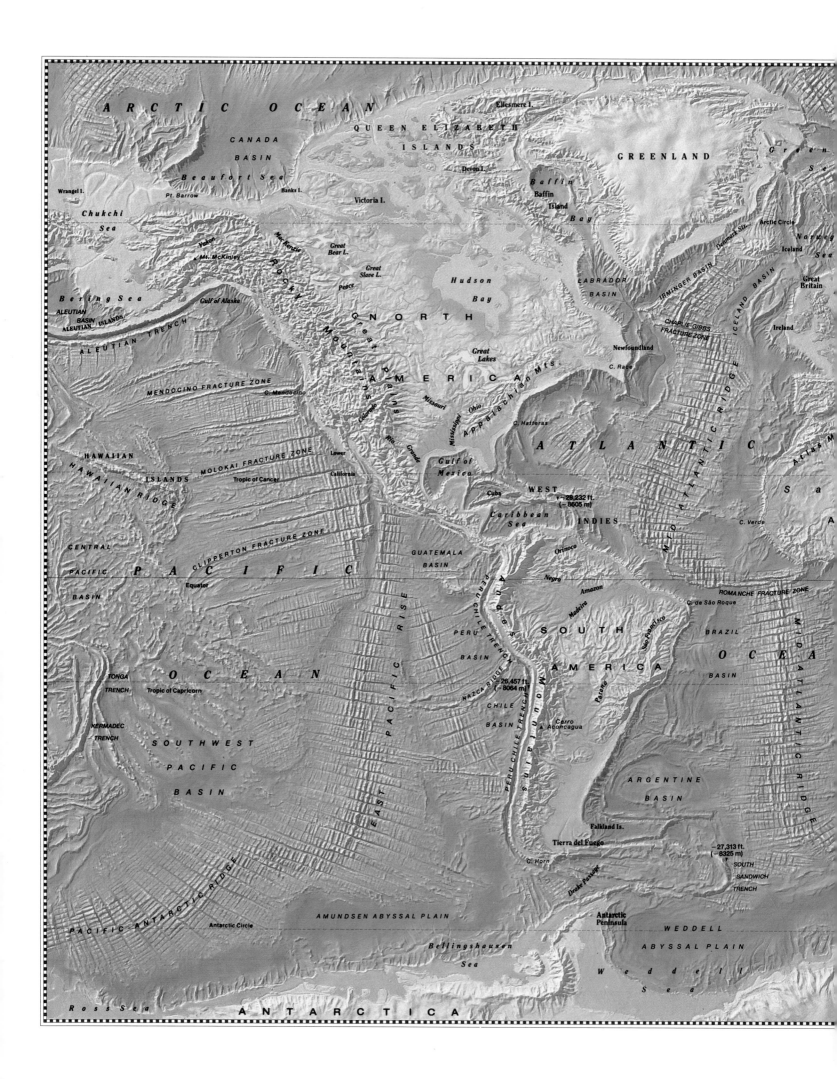

ARCTIC OCEAN

CANADA
BASIN

Beaufort Sea

QUEEN ELIZABETH
ISLANDS

Ellesmere I.

Devon I.

GREENLAND

Green
Se

Wrangel I.

Pt. Barrow

Banks I.

Baffin
Island

Baffin

Bay

Arctic Circle

Chukchi
Sea

Victoria I.

Denmark Str.

Norweg

Iceland

Great
Britain

Yukon

Mackenzie

Great
Bear L.

LABRADOR
BASIN

IRMINGER BASIN

Mt. McKinley

ROCKY

Great
Slave L.

Hudson
Bay

ICELAND BASIN

Ireland

Bering Sea

Peace

Mountains

MID-ATLANTIC RIDGE

Gulf of Alaska

CHARLIE-GIBBS
FRACTURE ZONE

ALEUTIAN
BASIN
ALEUTIAN ISLANDS

NORTH

Newfoundland

ALEUTIAN TRENCH

Great
Plains

Great
Lakes

C. Race

MENDOCINO FRACTURE ZONE

C. Mendocino

Missouri

AMERICA

Ohio

Appalachian Mts.

ATLANTIC

Alibs M

HAWAIIAN

Colorado

C. Hatteras

Sea

MOLOKAI FRACTURE ZONE

Mississippi

ISLANDS

Tropic of Cancer

Lower

Gulf of
Mexico

C. Verde

HAWAIIAN RIDGE

California

WEST

▽ −28,232 ft.
(− 8605 m)

Cuba

CLIPPERTON FRACTURE ZONE

GUATEMALA
BASIN

Caribbean
Sea

INDIES

CENTRAL

Orinoco

PACIFIC

Equator

Negro

ROMANCHE FRACTURE ZONE

BASIN

PACIFIC

Amazon

C. de São Roque

Madeira

SOUTH

São Francisco

BRAZIL

OCEA

PERU-CHILE TRENCH

PERU

EAST

BASIN

AMERICA

BASIN

TONGA
TRENCH

Tropic of Capricorn

NAZCA RIDGE

PACIFIC RISE

▽ −26,457 ft.
(− 8064 m)

Paraná

MID-ATLANTIC RIDGE

OCEAN

CHILE
BASIN

KERMADEC
TRENCH

Cerro
Aconcagua

SOUTHWEST

ARGENTINE

PACIFIC

Andes Mountains

BASIN

BASIN

Falkland Is.

Tierra del Fuego

−27,313 ft.
(− 8325 m)

C. Horn

SOUTH
SANDWICH
TRENCH

Drake Passage

PACIFIC-ANTARCTIC RIDGE

AMUNDSEN ABYSSAL PLAIN

Antarctic
Peninsula

WEDDELL

Antarctic Circle

ABYSSAL PLAIN

Bellingshausen
Sea

W e d d e l l
S e a

Ross Sea

ANTARCTICA

World

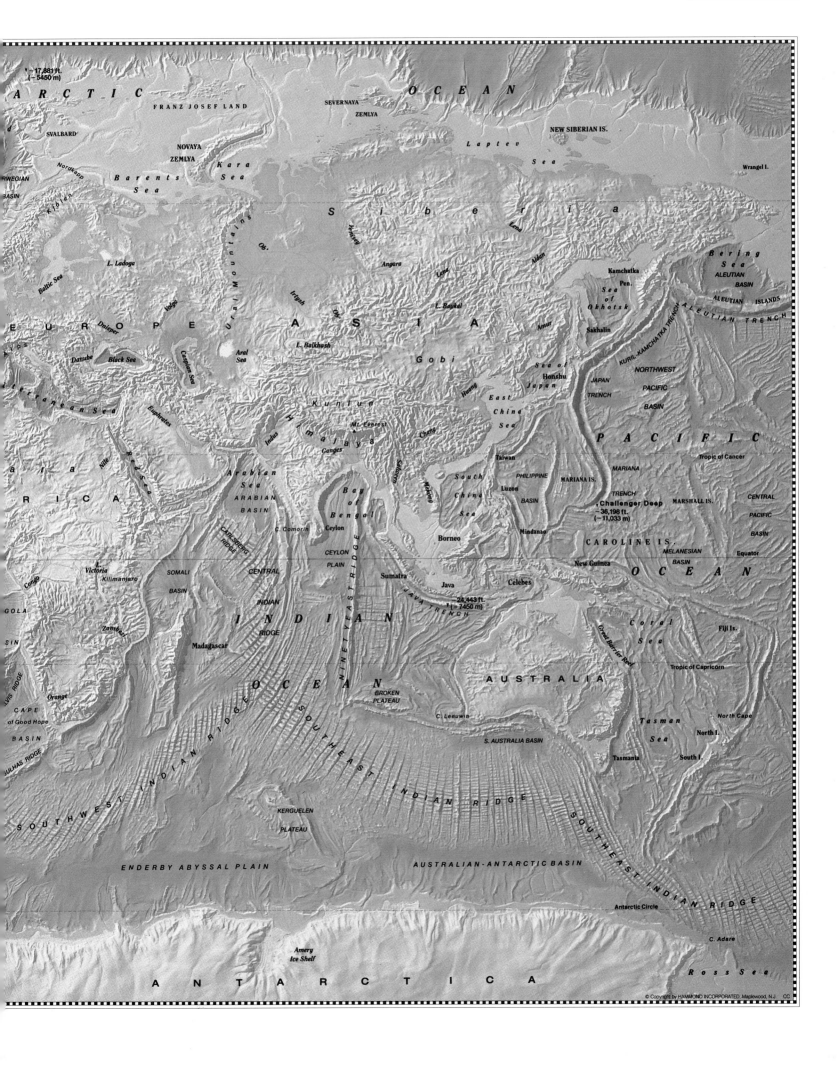

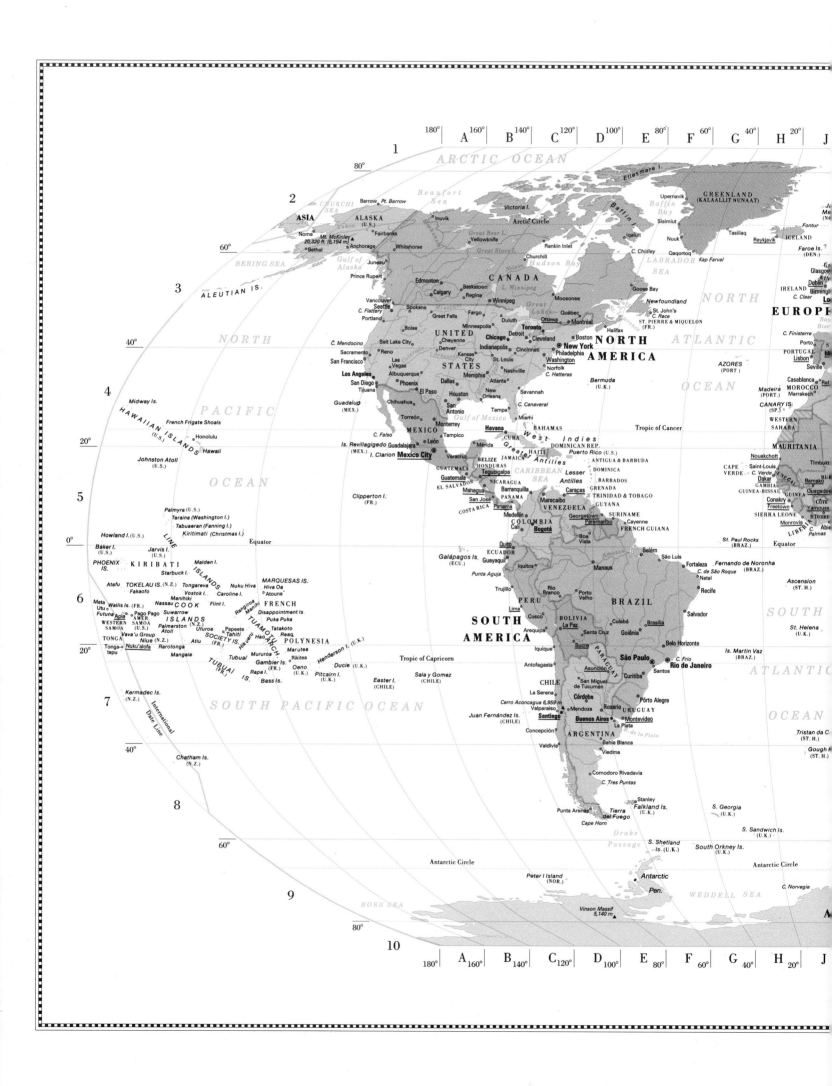

World

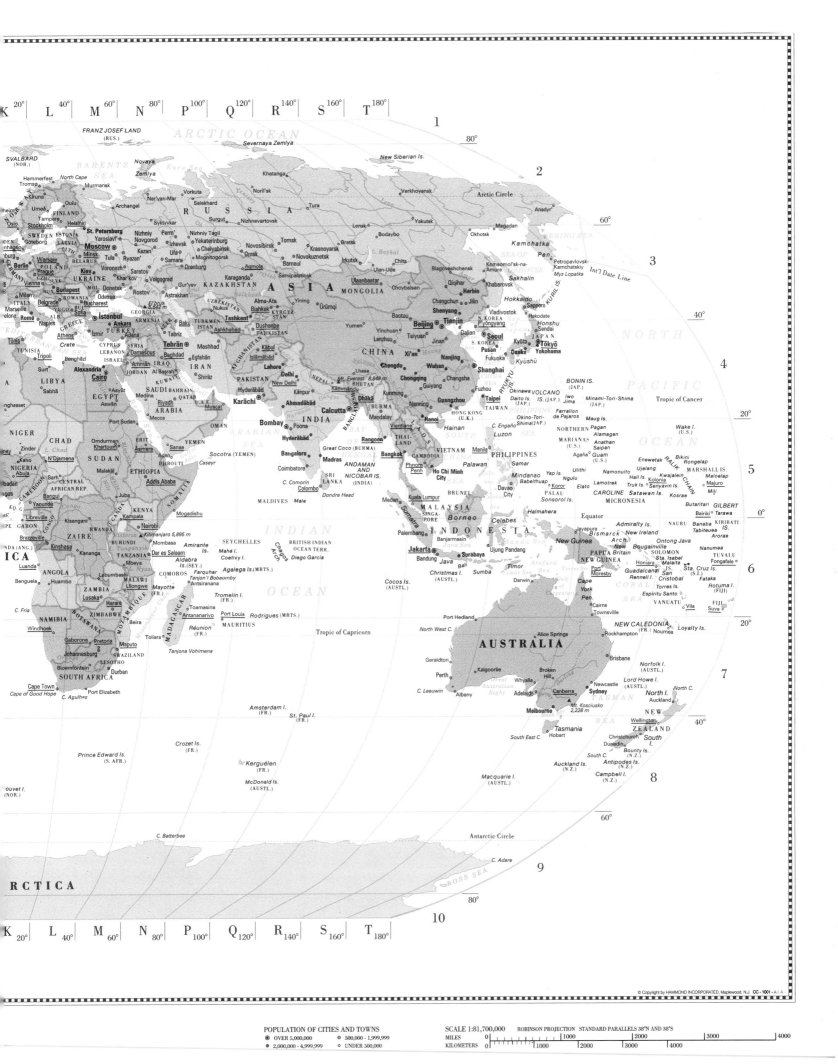

K L M N P Q R S T

1

FRANZ JOSEF LAND (RUS.)

ARCTIC OCEAN

80°

SVALBARD (NOR.)

Severnaya Zemlya

New Siberian Is.

2

BARENTS SEA

Novaya Zemlya

Kara Sea

Khatanga

Hammerfest
Tromsø
North Cape
Murmansk

Kiruna

Nar'yan-Mar

Noril'sk

Verkhoyansk

Aretic Circle

Anadyr

Oulu
FINLAND

Vorkuta
Salekhard

RUSSIA

Tura

60°

Yakutsk

Magadan

BERING SEA

Oslo
SWEDEN
Stockholm
Helsinki
St. Petersburg

Surgut
Nizhnevartovsk

Lensk

Bodaybo

Okhotsk

Kamchatka
Pen.

3

Int'l Date Line

Petropavlovsk-
Kamchatskiy
Komsomol'sk-na-
Amure
Mys Lopatka

KURIL IS.

40°

Göteborg
Moscow
Yaroslavl'
Izhevsk
Yekaterinburg
Novosibirsk
Tomsk
Krasnoyarsk
Bratsk

Chita

Khabarovsk
Sakhalin

Hokkaido
Sapporo

Warsaw
Minsk
BELARUS
Tula
Ryazan'
Kazan
Ufa
Magnitogorsk
Omsk
Novokuznetsk
Irkutsk
Ulan-Ude

Blagoveshchensk

Vladivostok

Hakodate
JAPAN

Berlin
Prague
Kiev
UKRAINE
Voronezh
Saratov
Samara
Orenburg
Barnaul
Semipalatinsk

Ulaanbaatar

Qiqihar
Harbin
N. KOREA
P'yŏngyang

Honshu
Sendai

20°

Vienna
Budapest
MOL.
Donets'k
Gur'yev
KAZAKHSTAN

ASIA
MONGOLIA

Choybalsan

Changchun
Jilin
Shenyang
Seoul
Kyōto
Tōkyō

ROMANIA
Bucharest
Rostov
Astrakhan'
El'brus
8,642 m

Alma-Ata
Yining
Ürümqi

Baotou
Beijing
Tianjin
Dalian
S. KOREA
Pusan
Osaka
Yokohama

Belgrade
Sofia
Istanbul
Ankara
GEORGIA
Baku
UZBEKISTAN
KYRGYZ-
STAN

Yinchuan
Taiyuan
Jinan
Fukuoka
Kyūshū

Rome
Athens
Izmir
TURKEY
Adana
ARMENIA
TURKMEN-
ISTAN
Tashkent

Yumen
Zhengzhou
Xi'an
Nanjing
Shanghai

Tunis
Crete
CYPRUS
SYRIA
Damascus
Tehrān
Mashhad
TAJIKISTAN
Dushanbe

Lanzhou

Chengdu
Chongqing
Wuhan
Changsha

MEDITERRANEAN SEA
LEBANON
ISRAEL
Baghdad
IRAN
Eşfahān
AFGHANISTAN
Kābul
Islāmābād

Lhasa
Mt. Everest 8,848 m
BHUTAN

Kunming
Guiyang

Fuzhou
Taipei

Alexandria
Cairo
JORDAN
Al Başrah
Shīrāz
PAKISTAN
Lahore
NEPAL
Kāthmāndu
BANGLADESH

Nanning
Guangzhou

HONG KONG (U.K.)

TAIWAN

Tropic of Cancer

20°

LIBYA
Sabhā
EGYPT
Asyūt
Aswān
SAUDI
ARABIA
BAHRAIN
Medina
QATAR
U.A.E.
Riyadh
Muscat
Hyderābād
KUWAIT
New Delhi
Kānpur

Delhi
Ahmadābād

Karāchi

INDIA
Calcutta

Dhākā
BURMA
Mandalay

Hanoi

Hainan

PHILIPPINE

NIGER
CHAD
Omdurman
Khartoum
Mecca
OMAN
ARABIAN SEA
Bombay
Poona
Hyderābād

Nagpur

BAY OF BENGAL
Rangoon

LAOS
Vientiane
THAI-
LAND

SOUTH
CHINA
SEA

Luzon
Manila

NORTHERN
MARIANAS
(U.S.)

5

Zinder
Kano
N'Djamena
SUDAN
YEMEN
Sanaa
Aden

Socotra (YEMEN)

Bangalore
Madras

ANDAMAN
AND
NICOBAR IS.
(INDIA)

CAMBODIA
Bangkok
Phnom
Penh
Ho Chi Minh
City

VIETNAM
Palawan

Samar

Agaña
Guam
(U.S.)

NIGERIA
Abuja
ERIT.
Asmera
DJIBOUTI
Caseyr
Coimbatore
C. Comorin
Colombo

SRI
LANKA
Dondra Head

MALDIVES Male

Medan

BRUNEI
Davao
Mindanao

MICRONESIA

CAROLINE

CENTRAL
AFRICAN REP.
Bangui
Yaoundé
ETHIOPIA
Addis Ababa
SOMALIA

MALAYSIA
SINGA-
PORE
Kuala Lumpur

Halmahera

PALAU

Libreville
GABON
EQ. G.
Kisangani
UGANDA
KENYA
Kampala
Nairobi
Mogadishu

Sumatra
Borneo
Celebes

Equator

0°

Brazzaville
Kinshasa
ZAIRE
RWANDA
BURUNDI
Lake Victoria
Kilimanjaro 5,895 m
SEYCHELLES
Amirante
Is.
Mahé I.
Coetivy I.
BRITISH INDIAN
OCEAN TERR.
Diego Garcia

Palembang
INDONESIA

Jakarta
Java
Surabaya
Ujung Pandang

New Guinea
Jayapura

PAPUA
NEW GUINEA
Port
Moresby

Luanda
ANGOLA
Lubumbashi
TANZANIA
Dar es Salaam
Mombasa
Mbeya

Aldabra
Is.(SEY.)
Farquhar
Tanjon'i Bobaomby
Antsiranana
Agalega Is.(MRTS.)

Christmas I.
(AUSTL.)
Bali
Sumba
Timor

Darwin

C. Fria
Benguela
Huambo
ZAMBIA
Lusaka
MALAWI
Lilongwe
Mayotte
COMOROS

Cocos Is.
(AUSTL.)

INDIAN

OCEAN

NAMIBIA
ZIMBABWE
Harare
MADAGASCAR
Antananarivo
Toamasina
Port Louis
Rodrigues (MRTS.)

Windhoek
BOTSWANA
Gaborone
Pretoria
Johannesburg
SWAZILAND
Beira
Réunion
(FR.)
MAURITIUS

Maputo
Toliara
Tanjona Vohimena

Tropic of Capricorn

20°

SOUTH AFRICA
Bloemfontein
LESOTHO
Durban

Cape Town
Cape of Good Hope
Port Elizabeth
C. Agulhas

Amsterdam I.
(FR.)
St. Paul I.
(FR.)

AUSTRALIA
Alice Springs

Rockhampton

7

40°

Crozet Is.
(FR.)

Kerguélen
(FR.)

8

Prince Edward Is.
(S. AFR.)

McDonald Is.
(AUSTL.)

60°

9

Antarctic Circle

C. Batterbee

10

ANTARCTICA

80°

K L M N P Q R S T

POPULATION OF CITIES AND TOWNS

◉ OVER 5,000,000   ⊙ 500,000 - 1,999,999
◉ 2,000,000 - 4,999,999   ○ UNDER 500,000

SCALE 1:81,700,000   ROBINSON PROJECTION   STANDARD PARALLELS 38°N AND 38°S

MILES   0   1000   2000   3000   4000
KILOMETERS   0   1000   2000   3000   4000

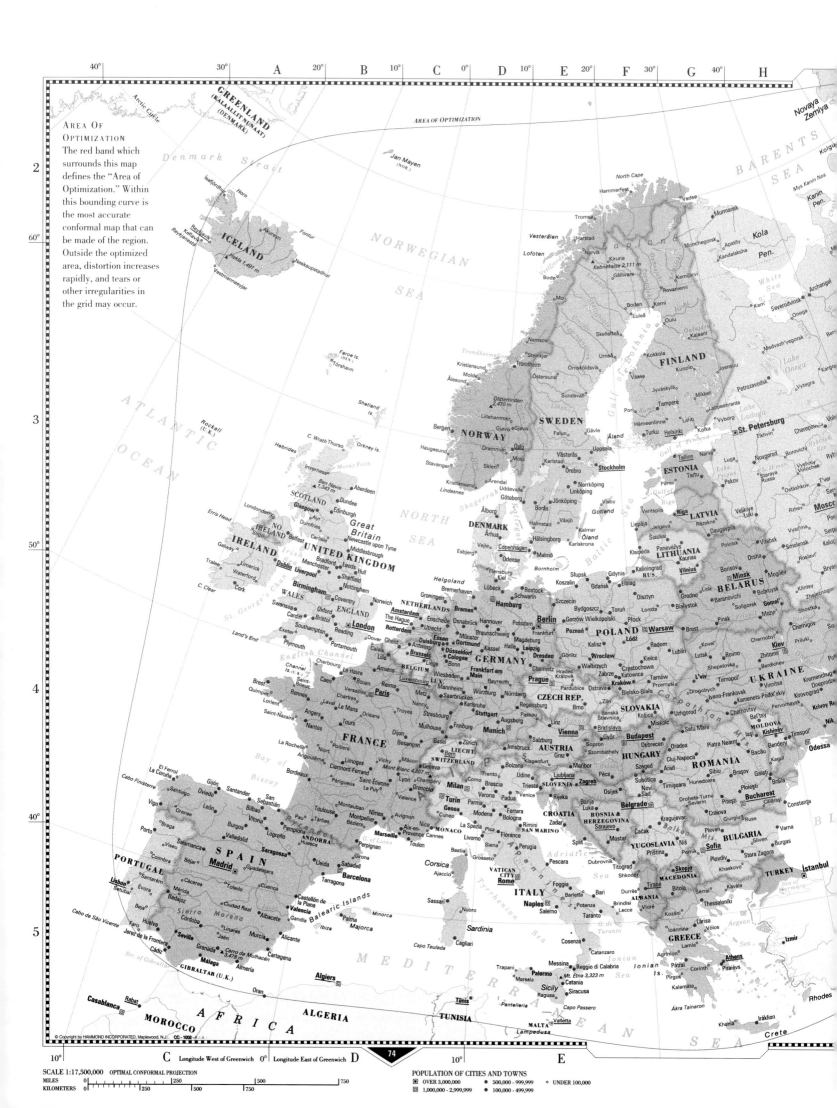

AREA OF
OPTIMIZATION
The red band which
surrounds this map
defines the "Area of
Optimization." Within
this bounding curve is
the most accurate
conformal map that can
be made of the region.
Outside the optimized
area, distortion increases
rapidly, and tears or
other irregularities in
the grid may occur.

AREA OF OPTIMIZATION

SCALE 1:17,500,000   OPTIMAL CONFORMAL PROJECTION

MILES   0   250   500   750

KILOMETERS 0   250   500   750

POPULATION OF CITIES AND TOWNS

▣ OVER 3,000,000   ● 500,000 - 999,999   ○ UNDER 100,000

▣ 1,000,000 - 2,999,999   ● 100,000 - 499,999

© Copyright by HAMMOND INCORPORATED, Maplewood, N.J.   CC - 1002 - A

Longitude West of Greenwich 0° Longitude East of Greenwich

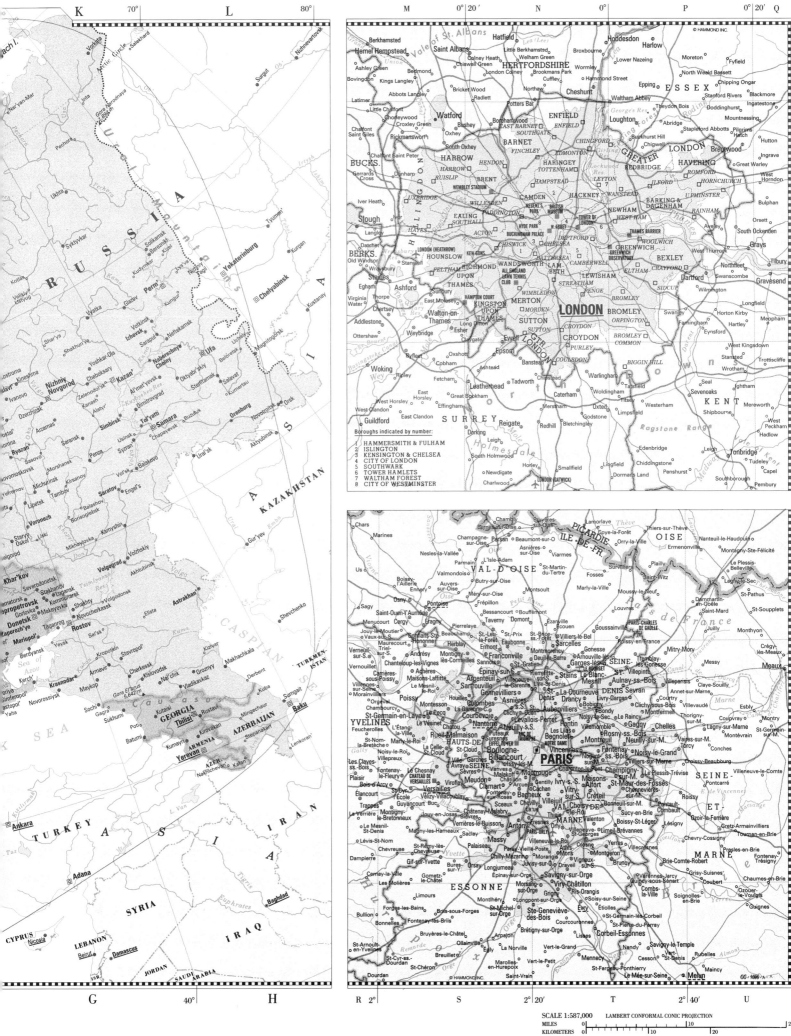

SCALE 1:587,000   LAMBERT CONFORMAL CONIC PROJECTION

Scandinavia and Finland, Iceland

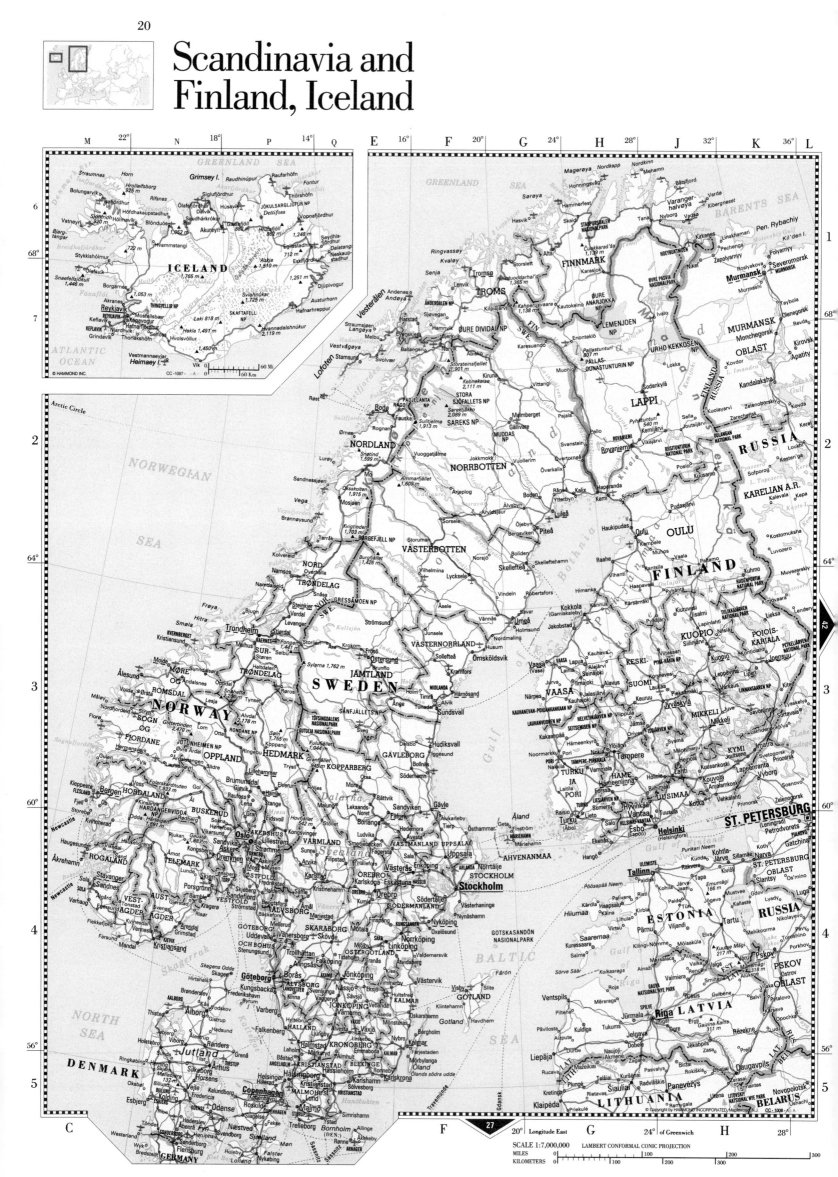

United Kingdom, Ireland

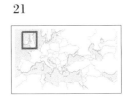

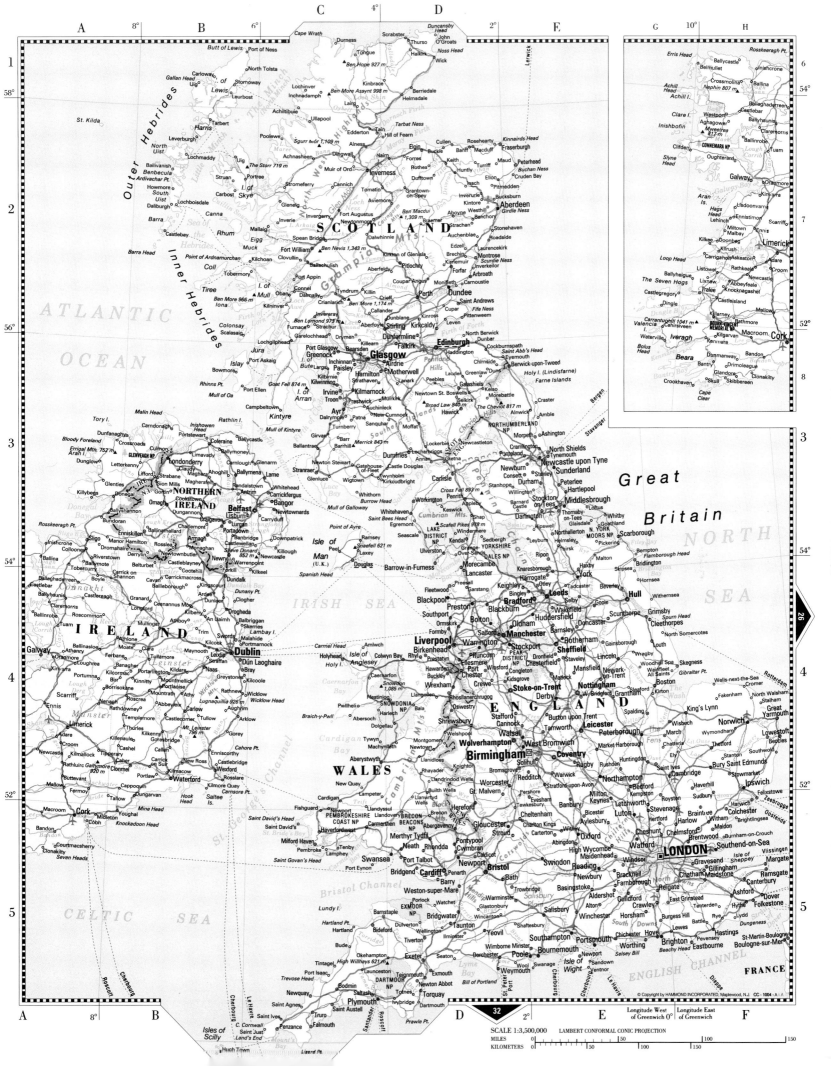

SCALE 1:3,500,000   LAMBERT CONFORMAL CONIC PROJECTION

Longitude West of Greenwich 0° Longitude East of Greenwich

MILES

KILOMETERS

© Copyright by HAMMOND INCORPORATED, Maplewood, N.J.   CC · 1004 · A · A · A

Northeastern Ireland, Northern England and Wales

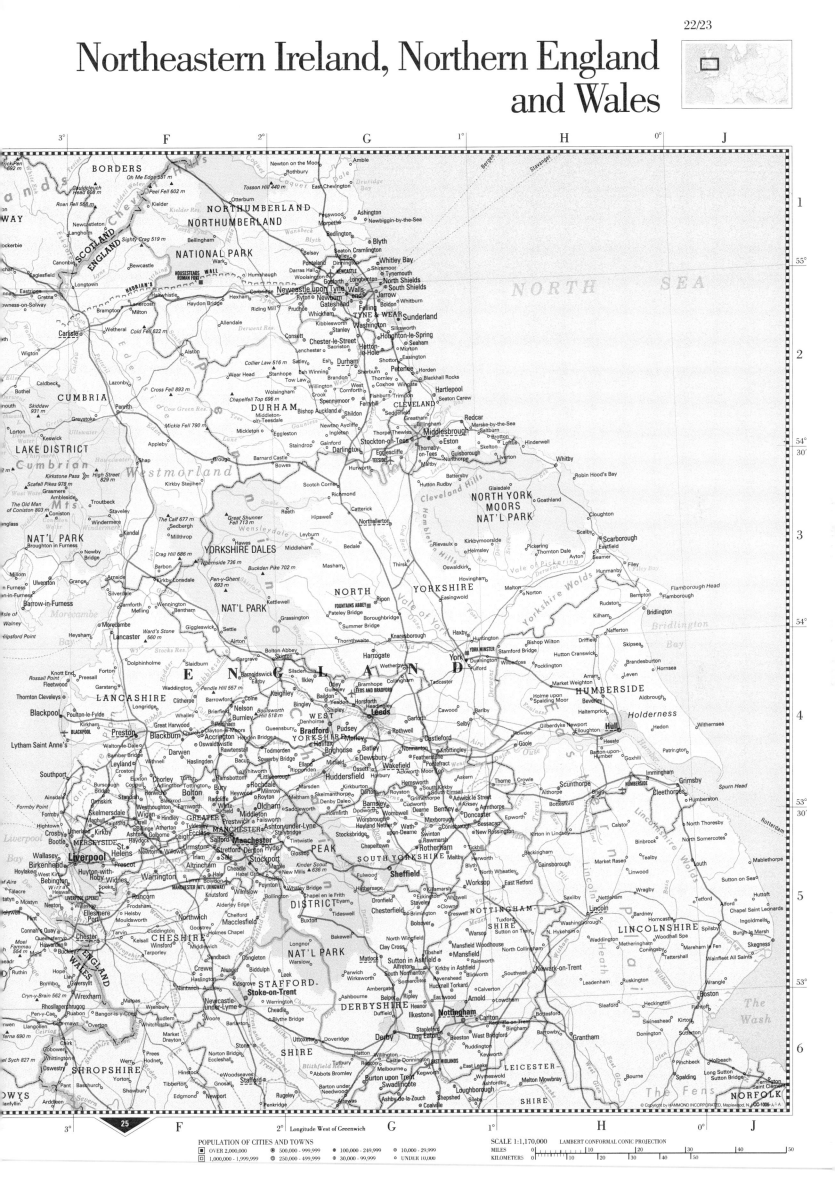

POPULATION OF CITIES AND TOWNS

■ OVER 2,000,000	● 500,000 - 999,999	● 100,000 - 249,999	○ 10,000 - 29,999
□ 1,000,000 - 1,999,999	● 250,000 - 499,999	○ 30,000 - 99,999	○ UNDER 10,000

SCALE 1:1,170,000 LAMBERT CONFORMAL CONIC PROJECTION

MILES

KILOMETERS

Longitude West of Greenwich

Southern England and Wales

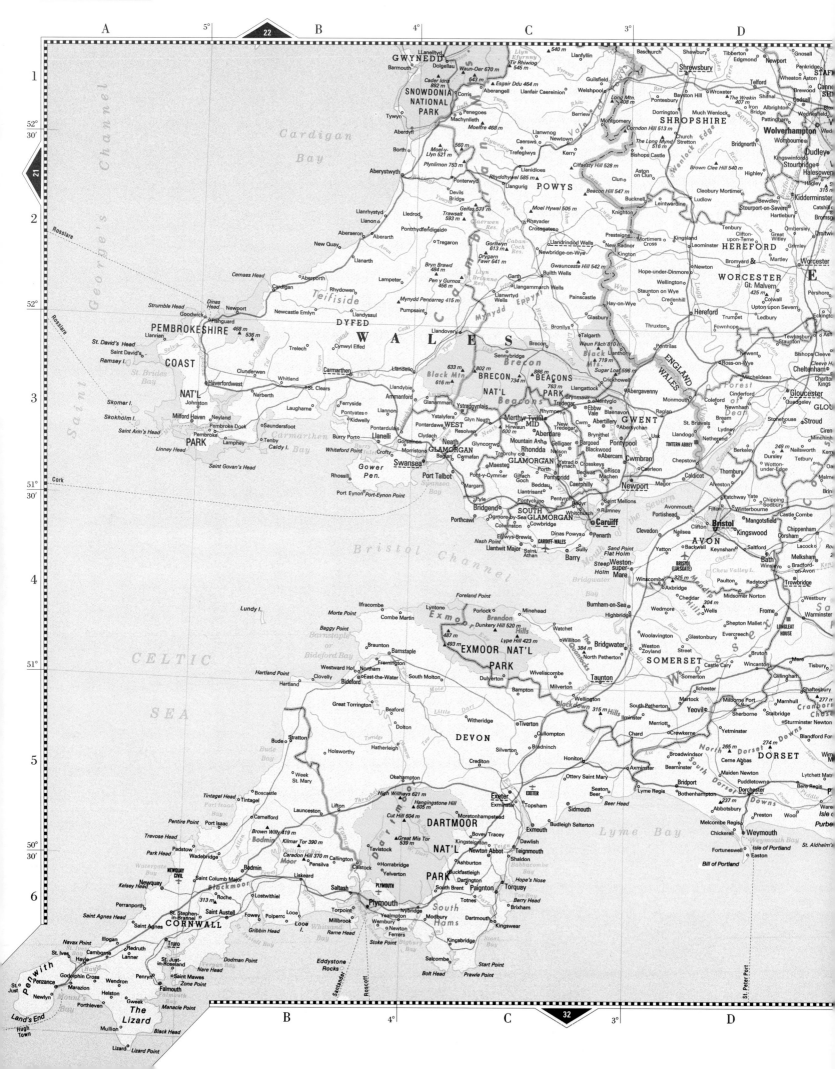

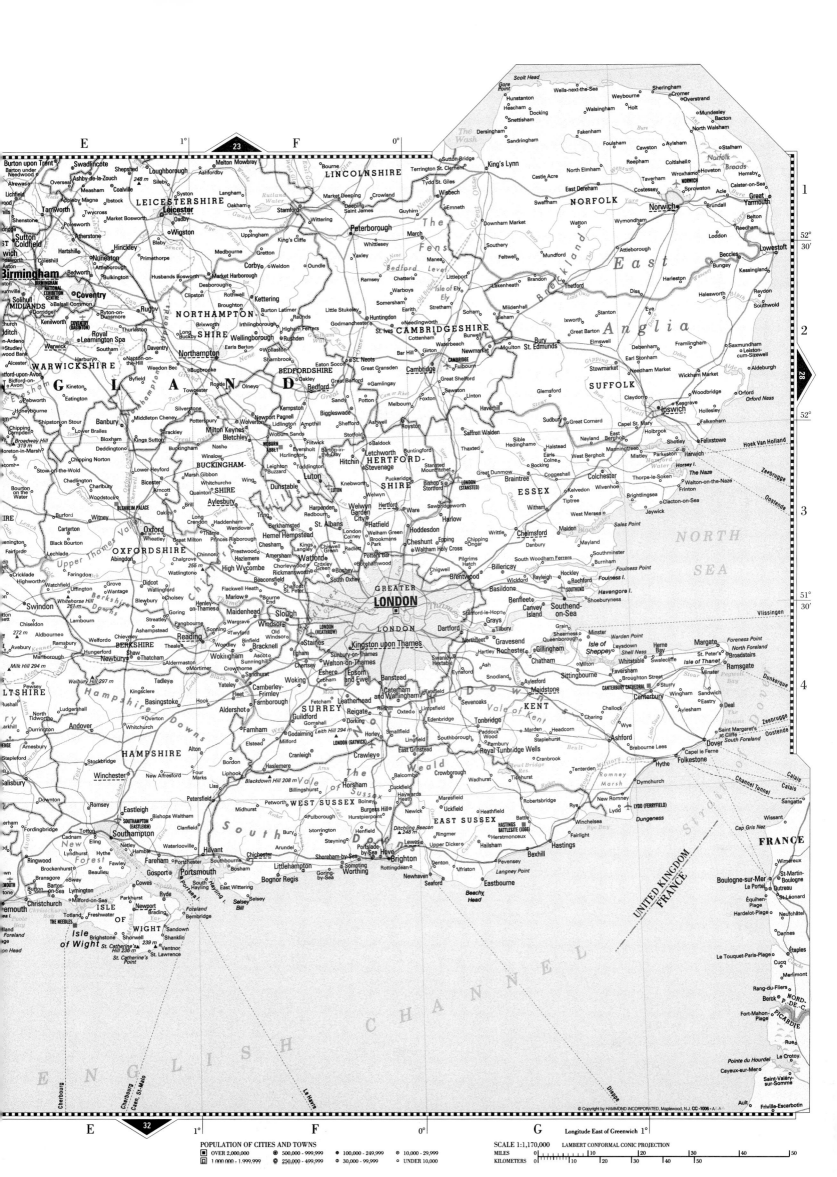

North Central Europe

Netherlands, Northwestern Germany

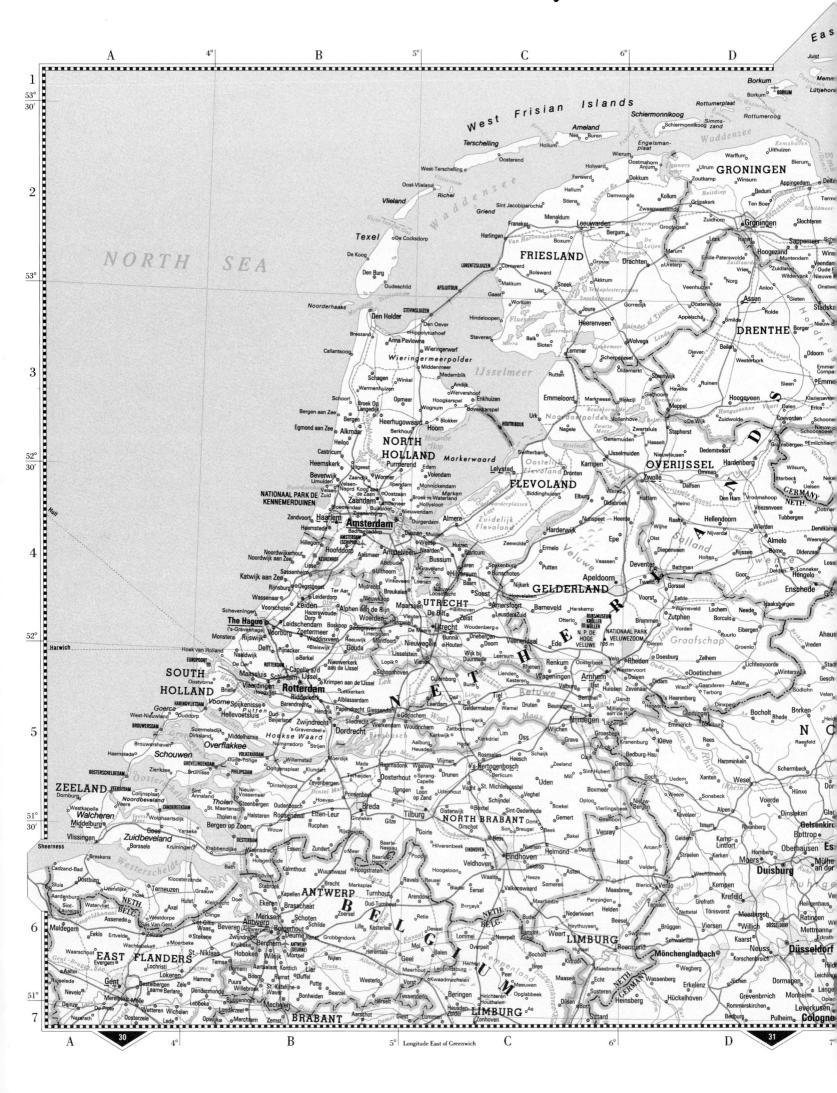

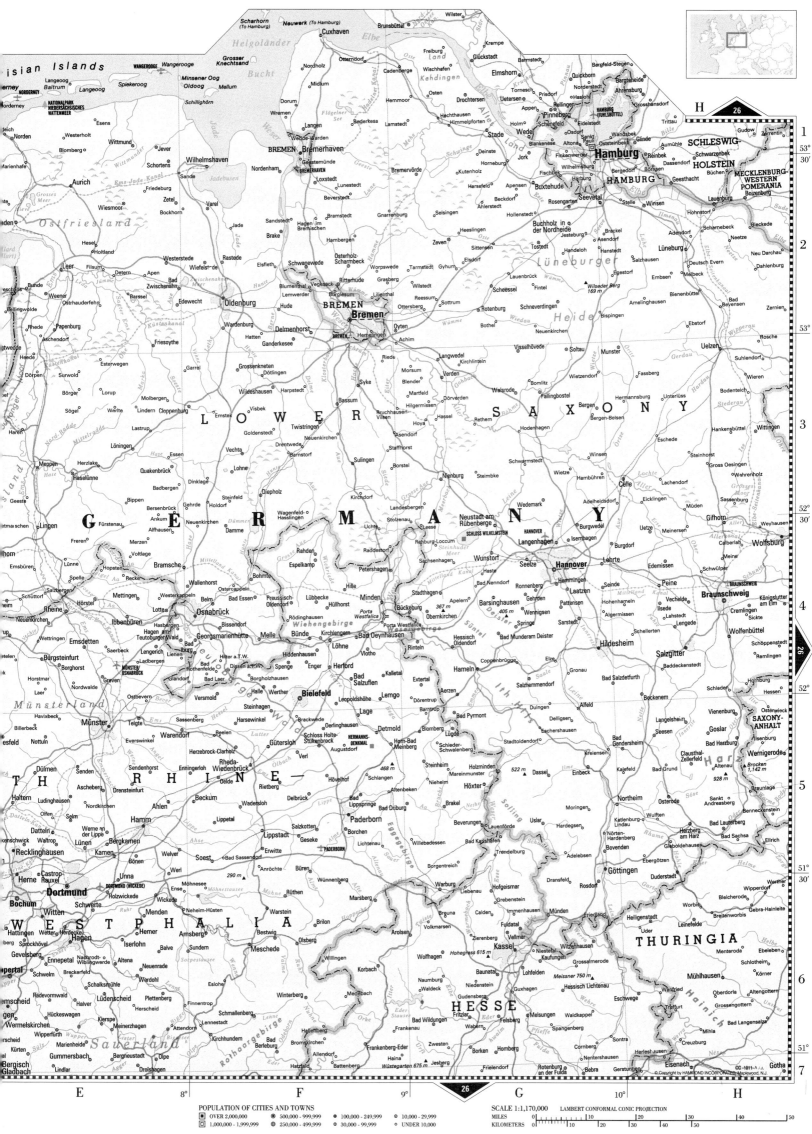

POPULATION OF CITIES AND TOWNS

- ◼ OVER 2,000,000
- ◻ 1,000,000 - 1,999,999
- ● 500,000 - 999,999
- ● 250,000 - 499,999
- ● 100,000 - 249,999
- ● 30,000 - 99,999
- ○ 10,000 - 29,999
- ○ UNDER 10,000

SCALE 1:1,170,000   LAMBERT CONFORMAL CONIC PROJECTION

MILES
KILOMETERS

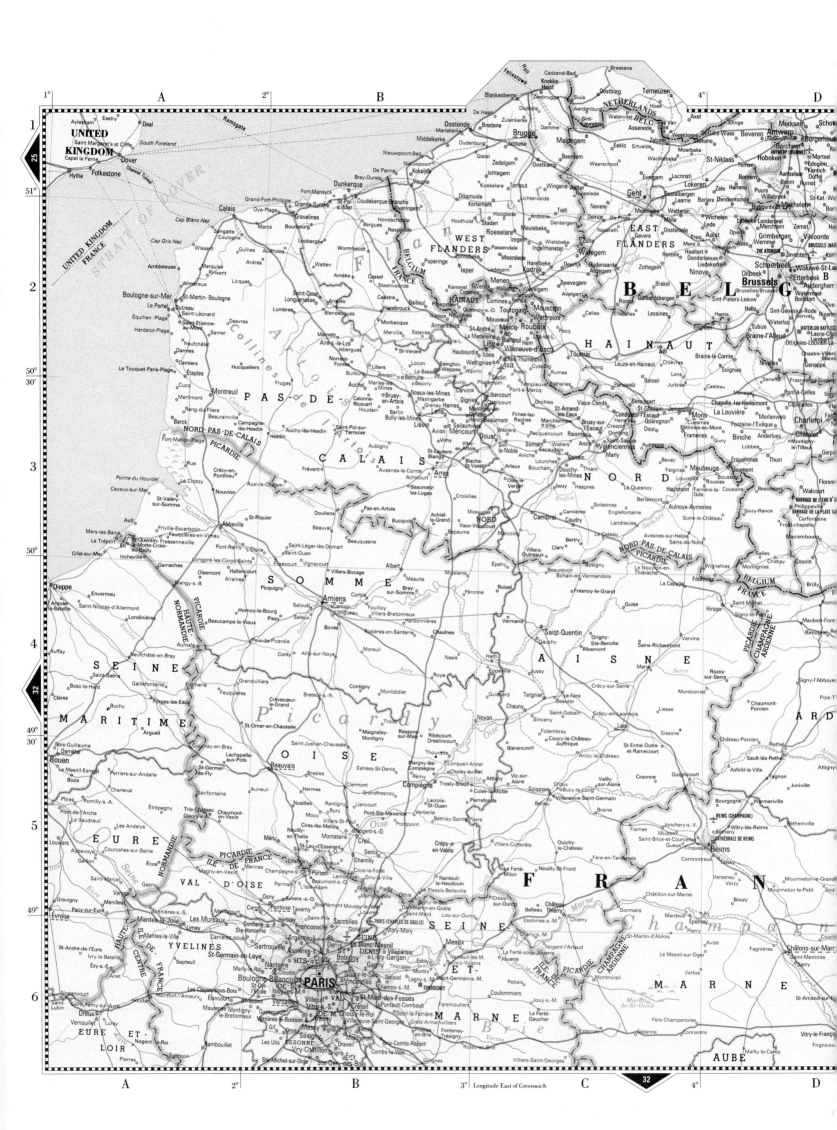

Belgium, Northern France, Western Germany

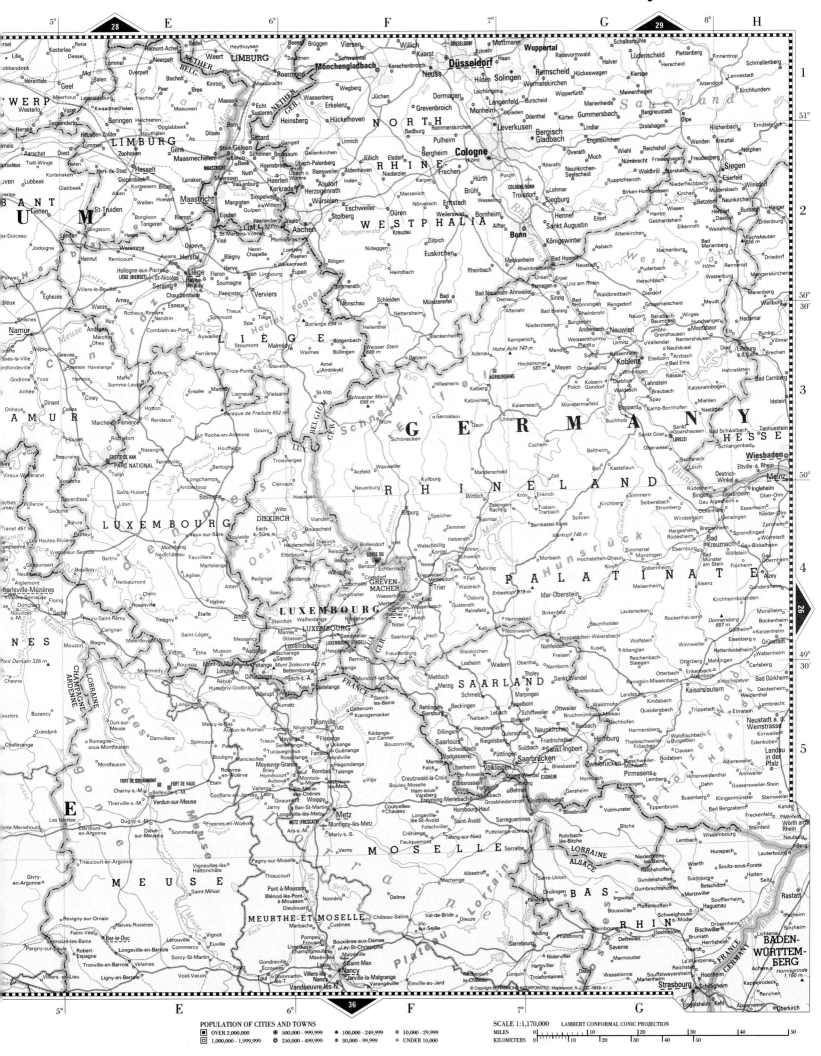

POPULATION OF CITIES AND TOWNS

| ■ OVER 2,000,000 | ● 500,000 - 999,999 | ● 100,000 - 249,999 | ○ 10,000 - 29,999 |
| □ 1,000,000 - 1,999,999 | ● 250,000 - 499,999 | ● 30,000 - 99,999 | ○ UNDER 10,000 |

SCALE 1:1,170,000   LAMBERT CONFORMAL CONIC PROJECTION

MILES 0   10   20   30   40   50

KILOMETERS 0   10   20   30   40   50

West Central Europe

POPULATION OF CITIES AND TOWNS

SCALE 1:3,500,000   LAMBERT CONFORMAL CONIC PROJECTION

Spain, Portugal

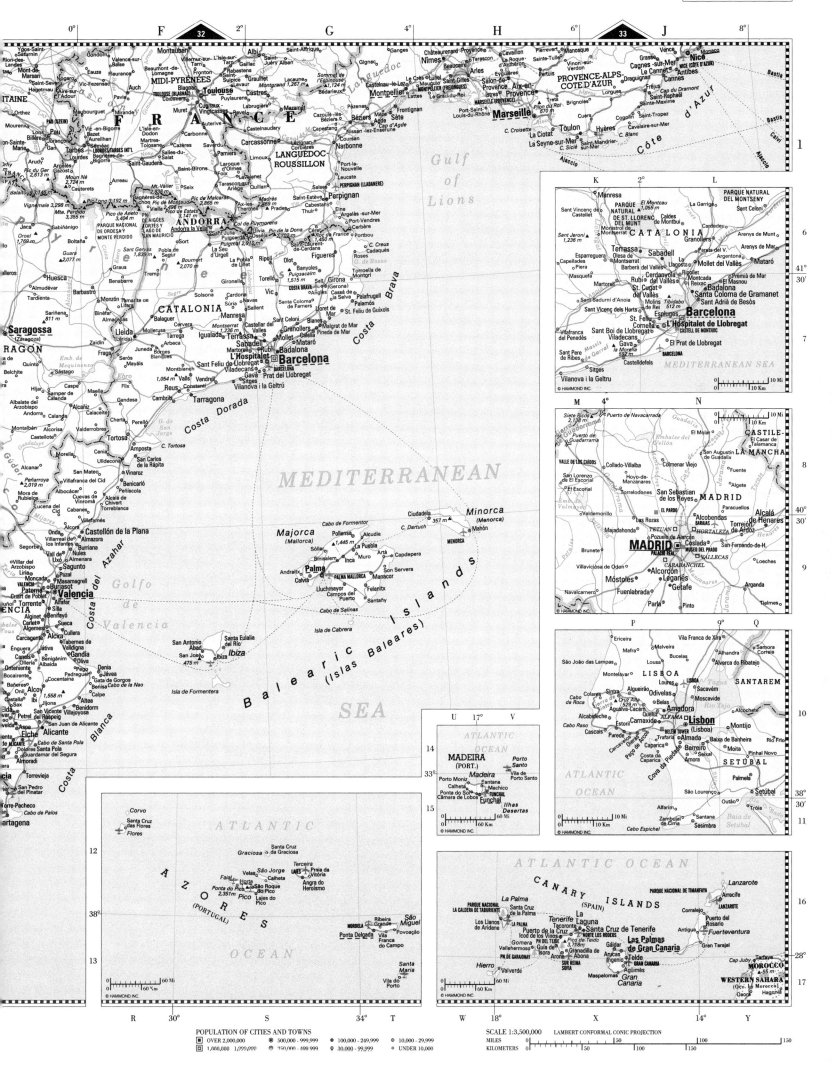

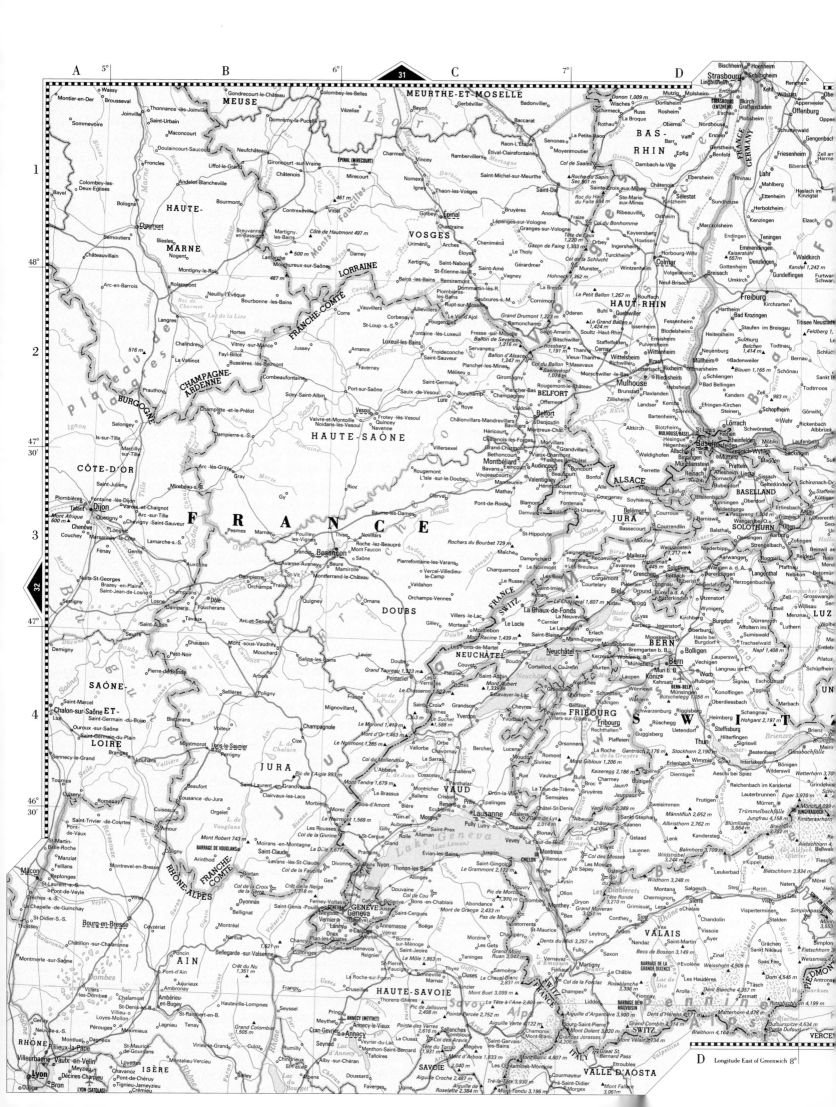

Central Alps Region

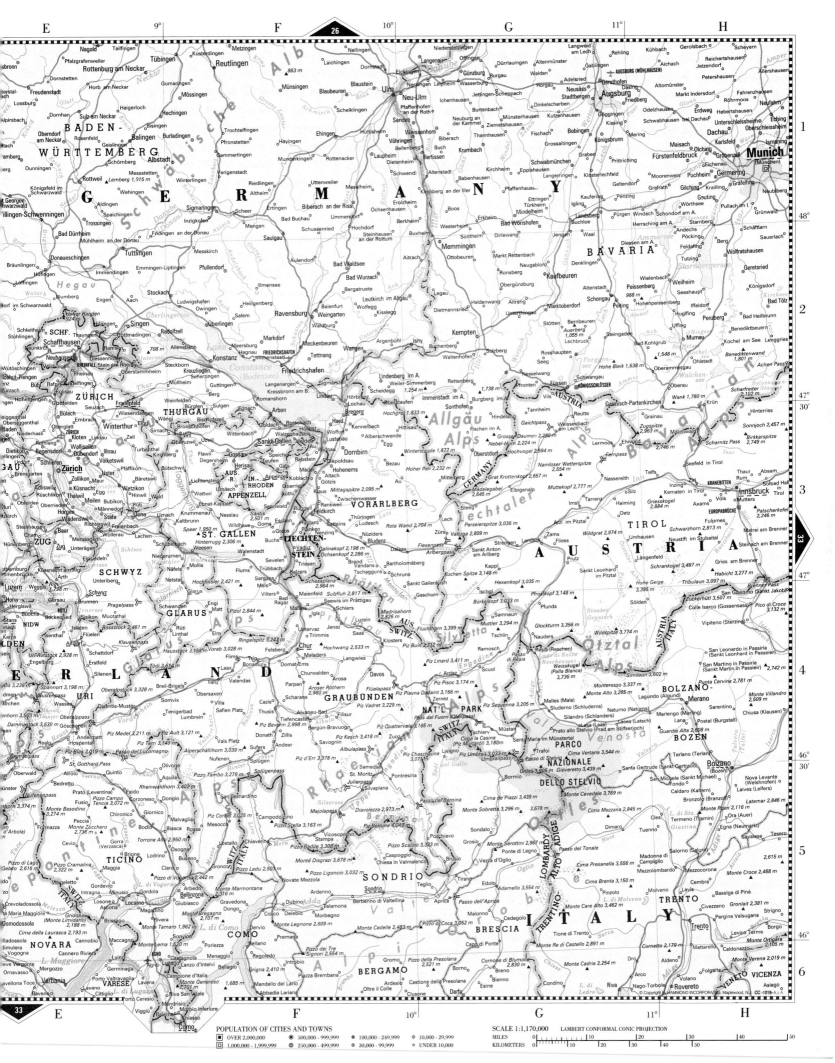

POPULATION OF CITIES AND TOWNS

■ OVER 2,000,000
□ 1,000,000 - 1,999,999
● 500,000 - 999,999
◎ 250,000 - 499,999
● 100,000 - 249,999
○ 30,000 - 99,999
○ 10,000 - 29,999
○ UNDER 10,000

SCALE 1:1,170,000   LAMBERT CONFORMAL CONIC PROJECTION

MILES
KILOMETERS

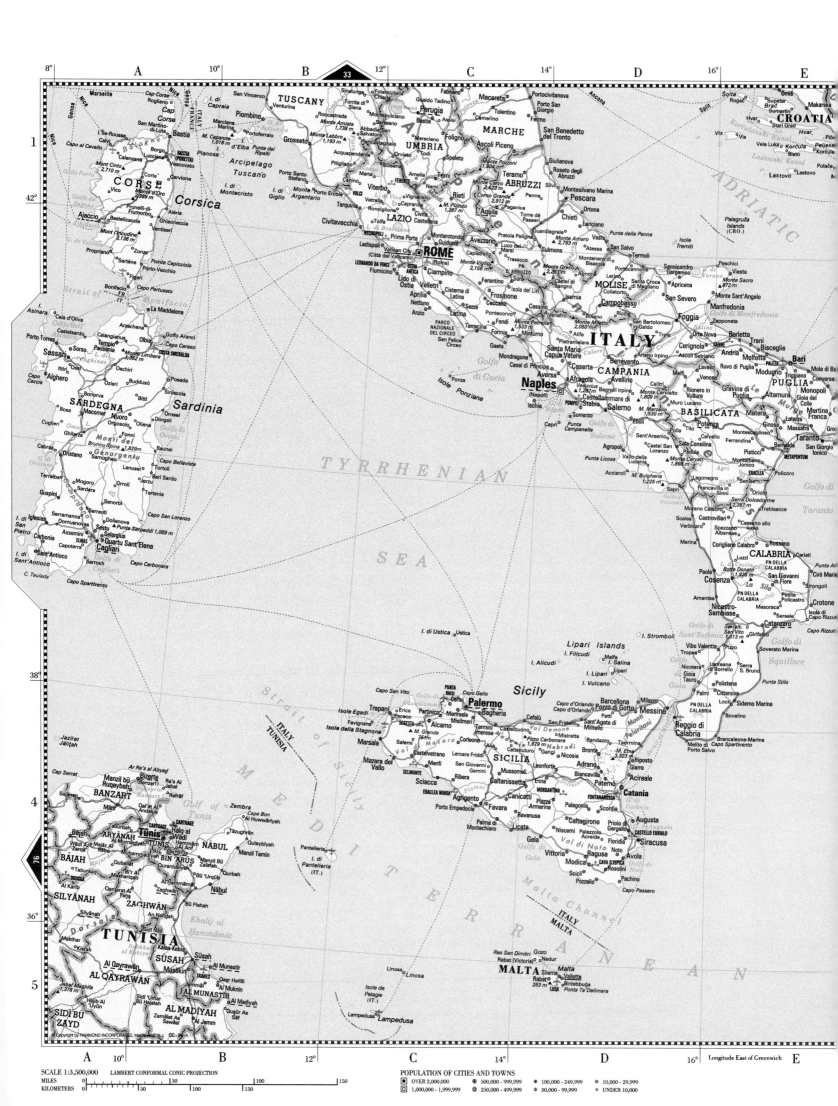

SCALE 1:3,500,000   LAMBERT CONFORMAL CONIC PROJECTION

MILES   0   50   100   150

KILOMETERS   0   50   100   150

POPULATION OF CITIES AND TOWNS

| ■ OVER 2,000,000 | ● 500,000 - 999,999 | ○ 100,000 - 249,999 | ○ 10,000 - 29,999 |
| □ 1,000,000 - 1,999,999 | ● 250,000 - 499,999 | ○ 30,000 - 99,999 | · UNDER 10,000 |

Longitude East of Greenwich

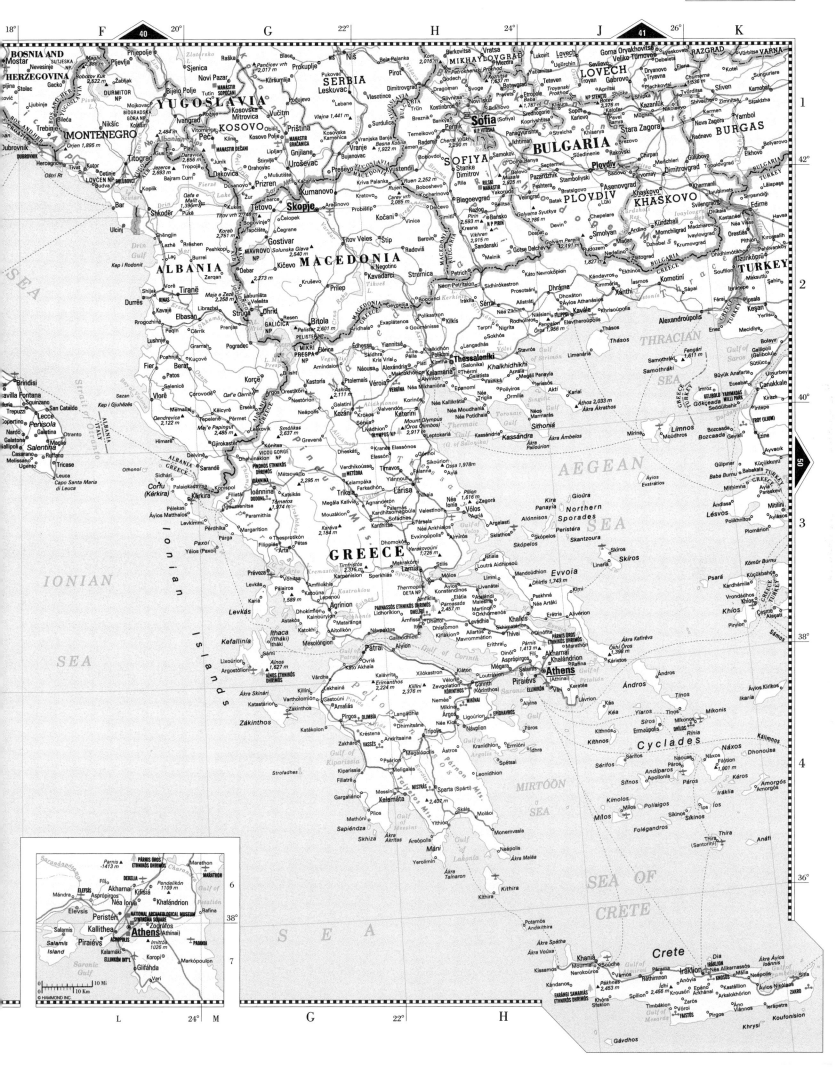

SCALE 1:3,500,000   LAMBERT CONFORMAL CONIC PROJECTION

MILES
KILOMETERS

POPULATION OF CITIES AND TOWNS

■ OVER 2,000,000
◻ 1,000,000 - 1,999,999
● 500,000 - 999,999
● 250,000 - 499,999
● 100,000 - 249,999
● 30,000 - 99,999
○ 10,000 - 29,999
○ UNDER 10,000

* WHILE THERE IS NO OTHER OFFICIALLY RECOGNIZED NAME FOR THE
AREA, THE NAME "MACEDONIA" DERIVES FROM ITS FORMER STATUS AS
A YUGOSLAV REPUBLIC, AND IS NOT RECOGNIZED BY MANY NATIONS.

Hungary, Northern Balkan States

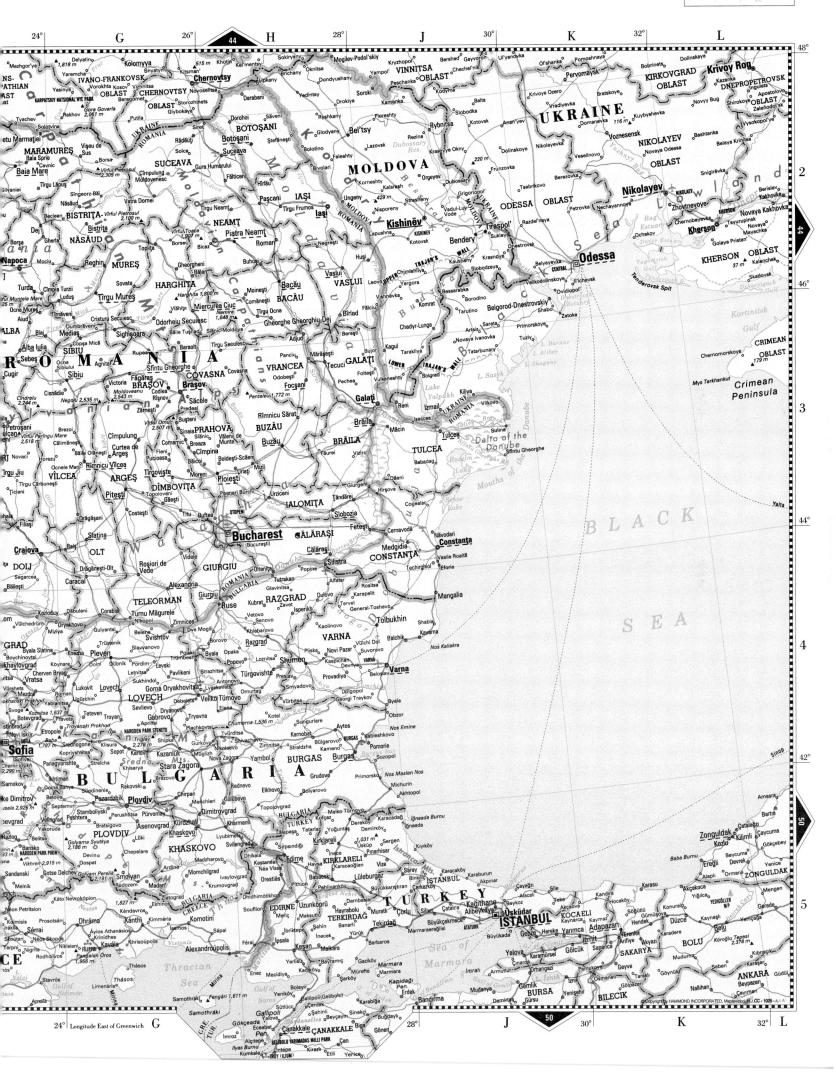

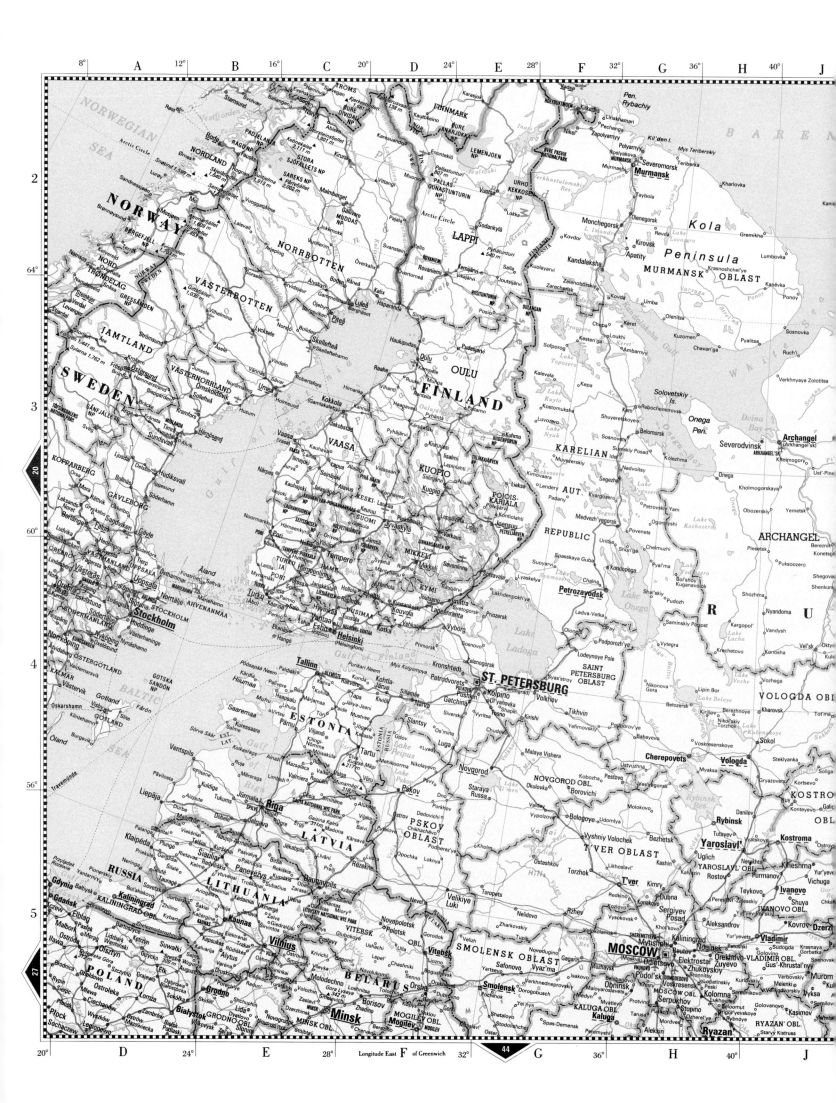

Northeastern Europe

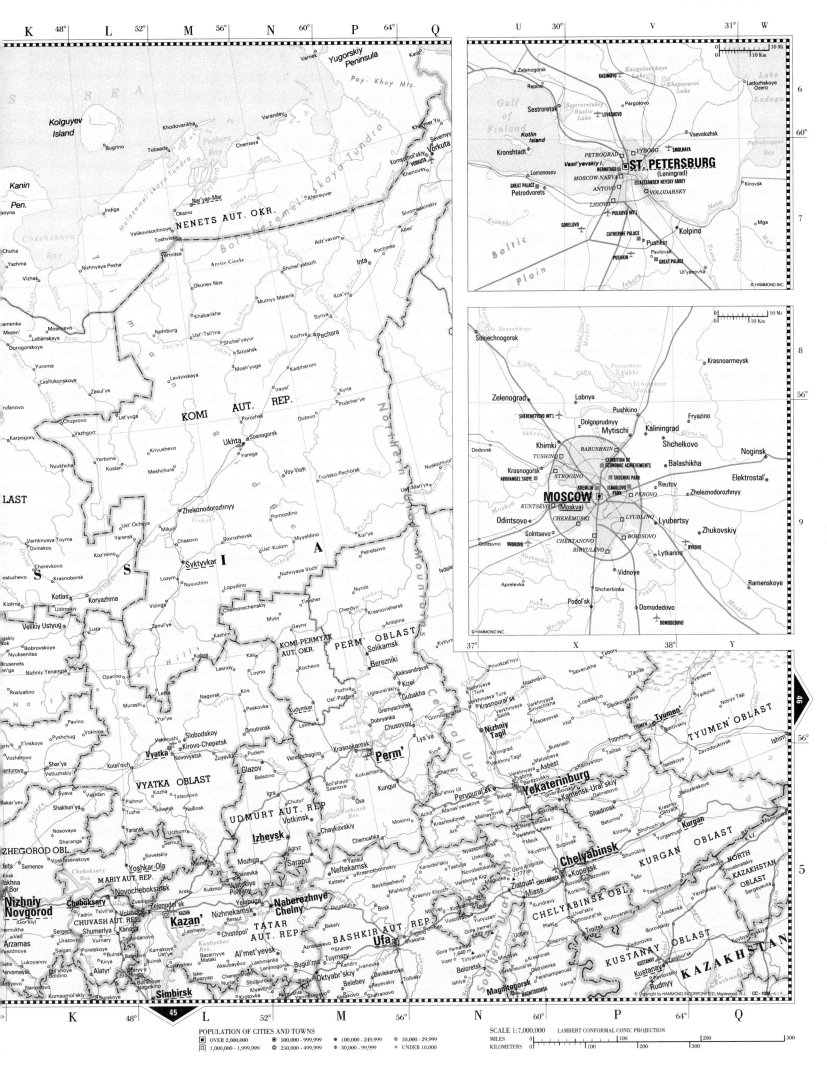

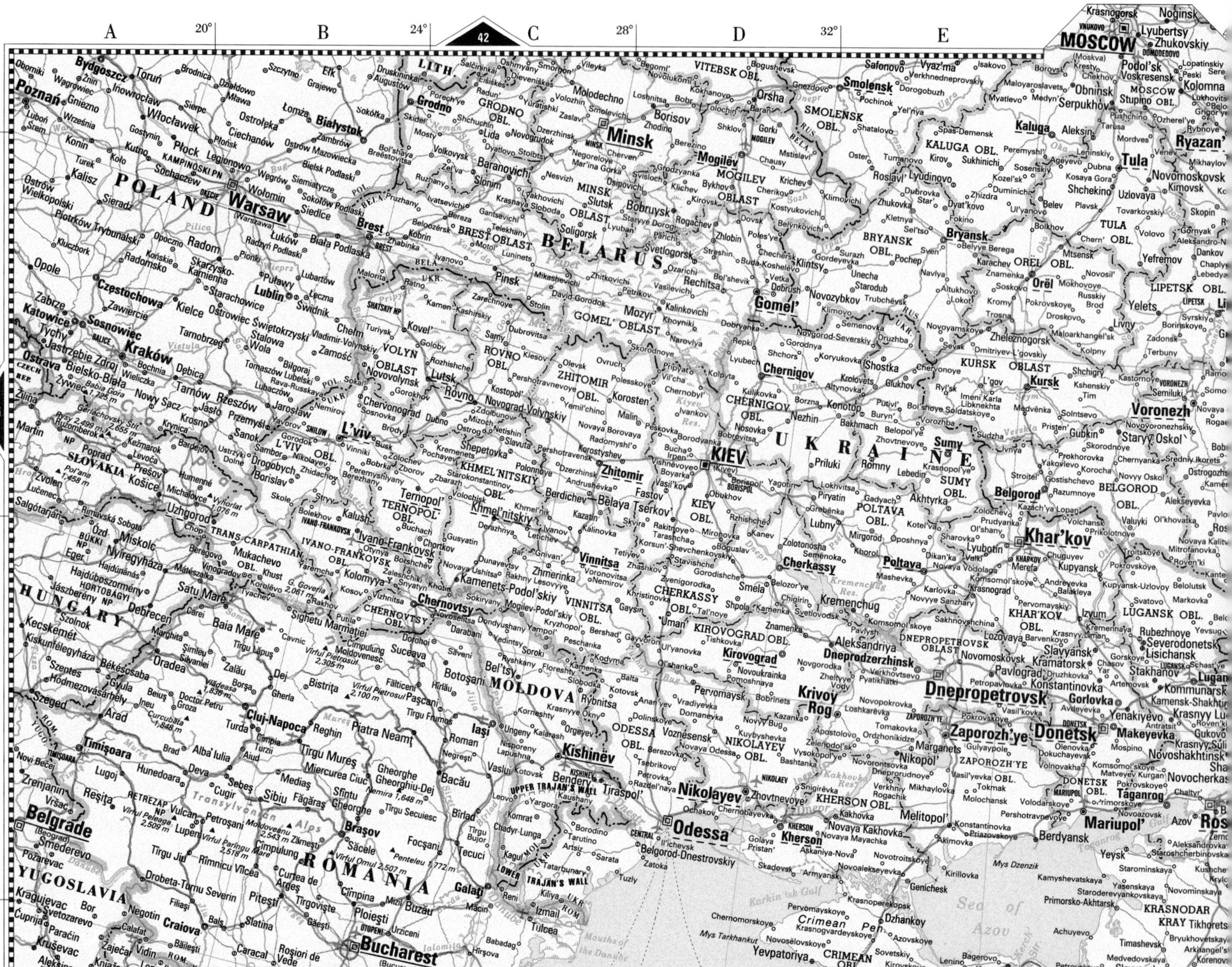

POLAND

BELARUS

UKRAINE

MOSCOW

HUNGARY

SLOVAKIA

ROMANIA

MOLDOVA

YUGOSLAVIA

BULGARIA

GREECE

TURKEY

MACEDONIA

BLACK SEA

Sea of Azov

AEGEAN SEA

Warsaw

Minsk

KIEV

Bucharest

Sofia

Belgrade

Istanbul

Ankara

Athens

Odessa

Kishinëv

Southeastern Europe

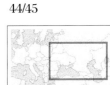

Russia and Neighboring Countries

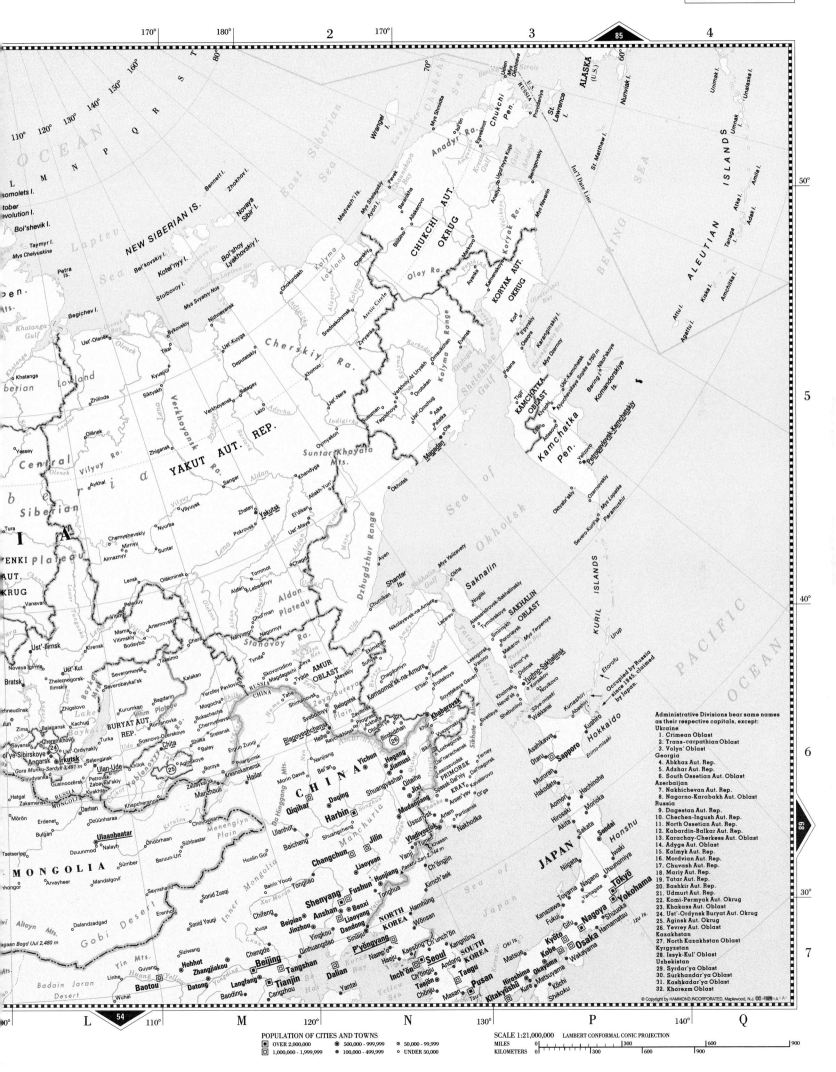

Asia

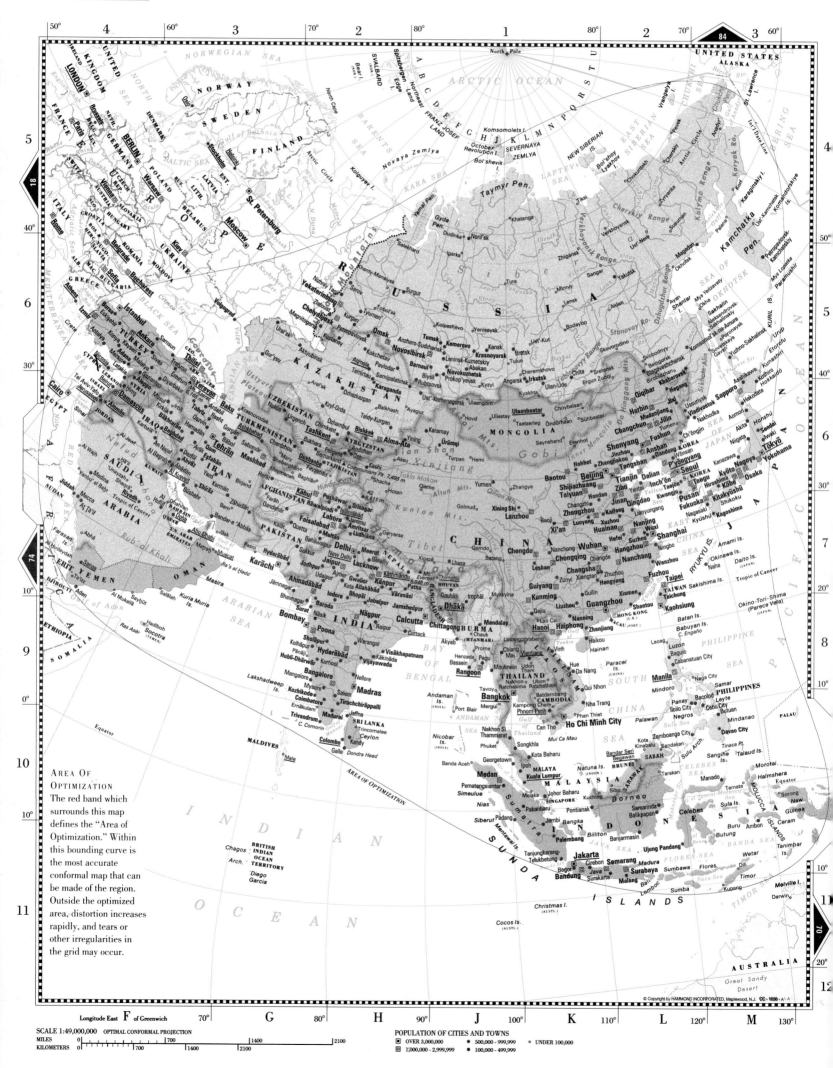

Eastern Mediterranean Region

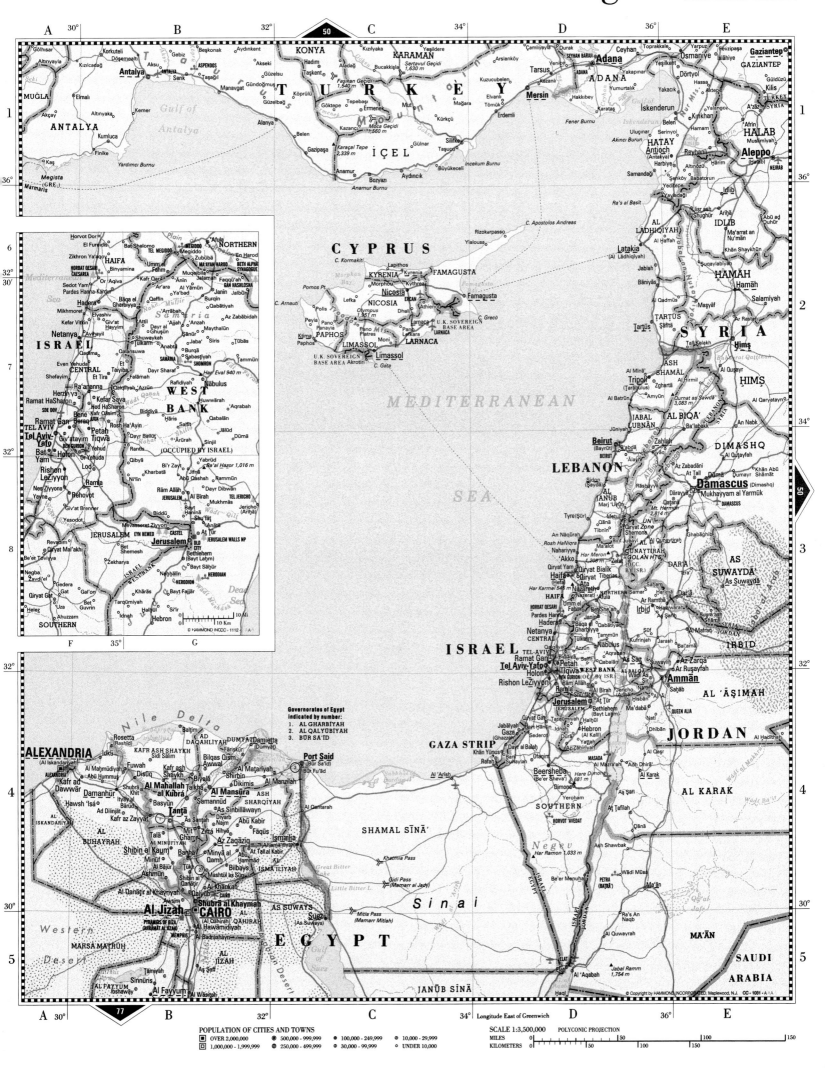

POPULATION OF CITIES AND TOWNS

■ OVER 2,000,000	● 500,000 - 999,999	● 100,000 - 249,999	○ 10,000 - 29,999
▣ 1,000,000 - 1,999,999	● 250,000 - 499,999	● 30,000 - 99,999	○ UNDER 10,000

SCALE 1:3,500,000   POLYCONIC PROJECTION

Longitude East of Greenwich

© Copyright by HAMMOND INCORPORATED, Maplewood, N.J. CC-1081-A-A

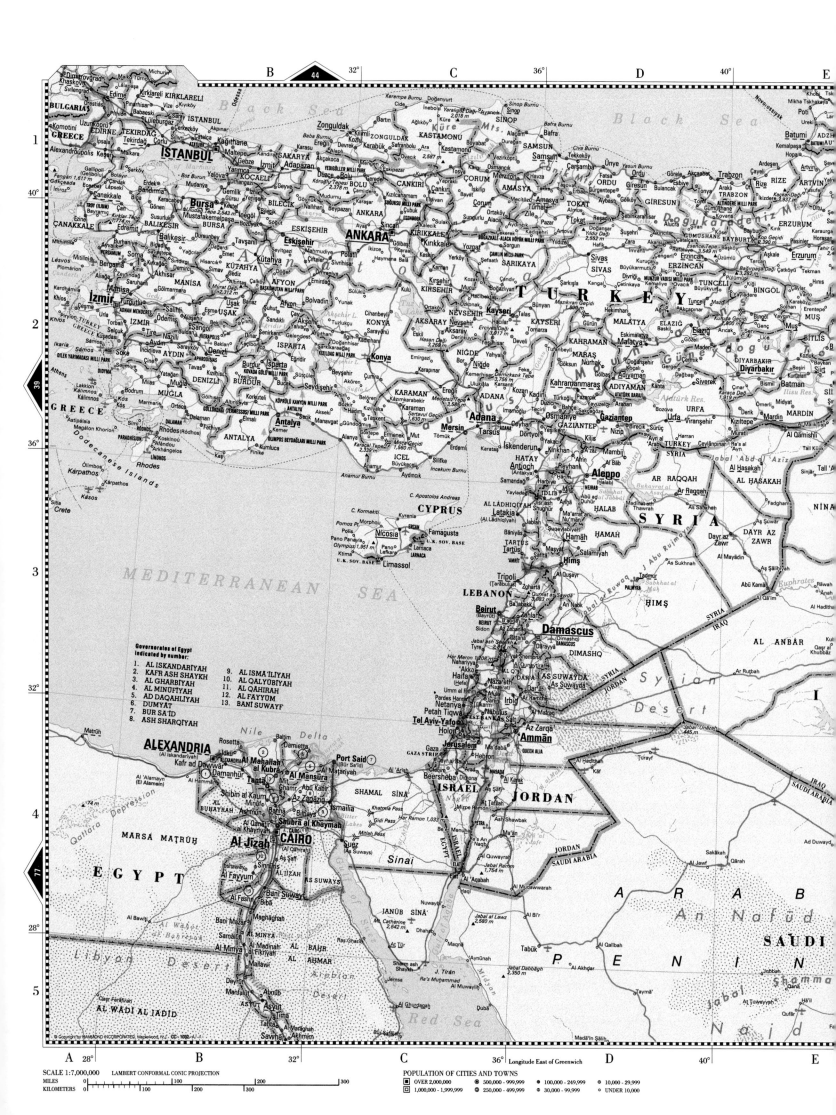

SCALE 1:7,000,000   LAMBERT CONFORMAL CONIC PROJECTION
MILES   0   100   200   300
KILOMETERS 0   100   200   300

POPULATION OF CITIES AND TOWNS
■ OVER 2,000,000   ● 500,000 - 999,999   ● 100,000 - 249,999   ○ 10,000 - 29,999
▫ 1,000,000 - 1,999,999   ◐ 250,000 - 499,999   ● 30,000 - 99,999   ○ UNDER 10,000

Northern Middle East

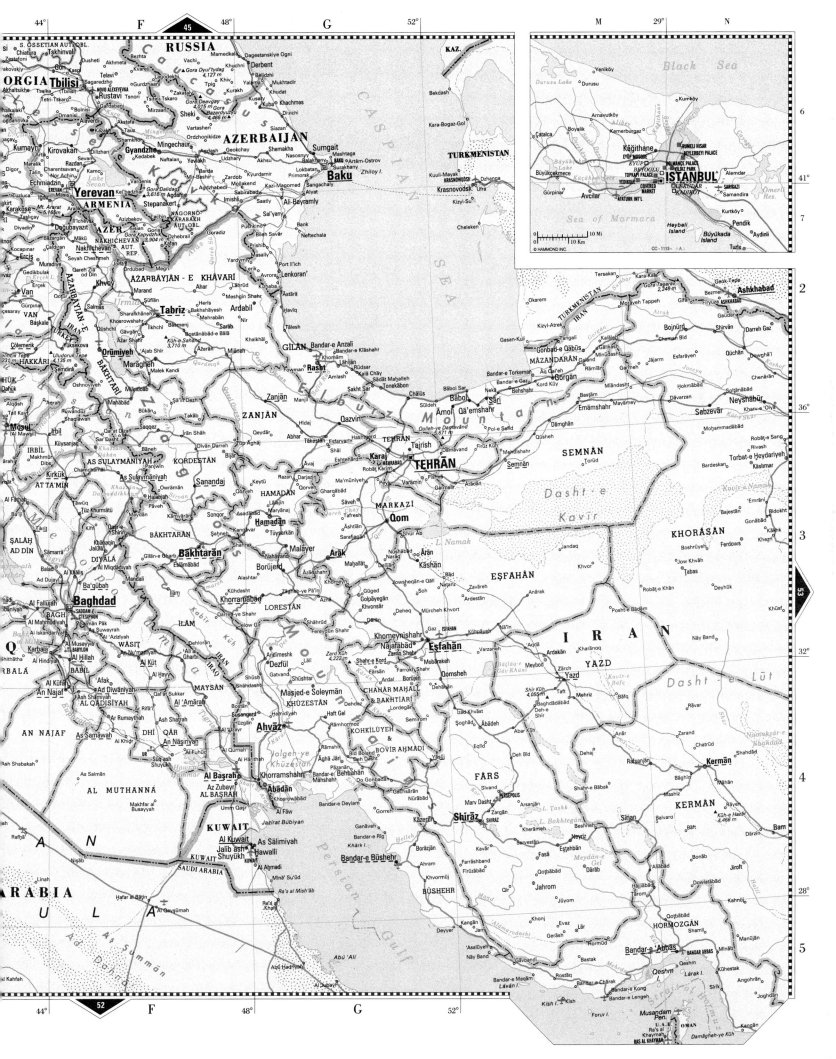

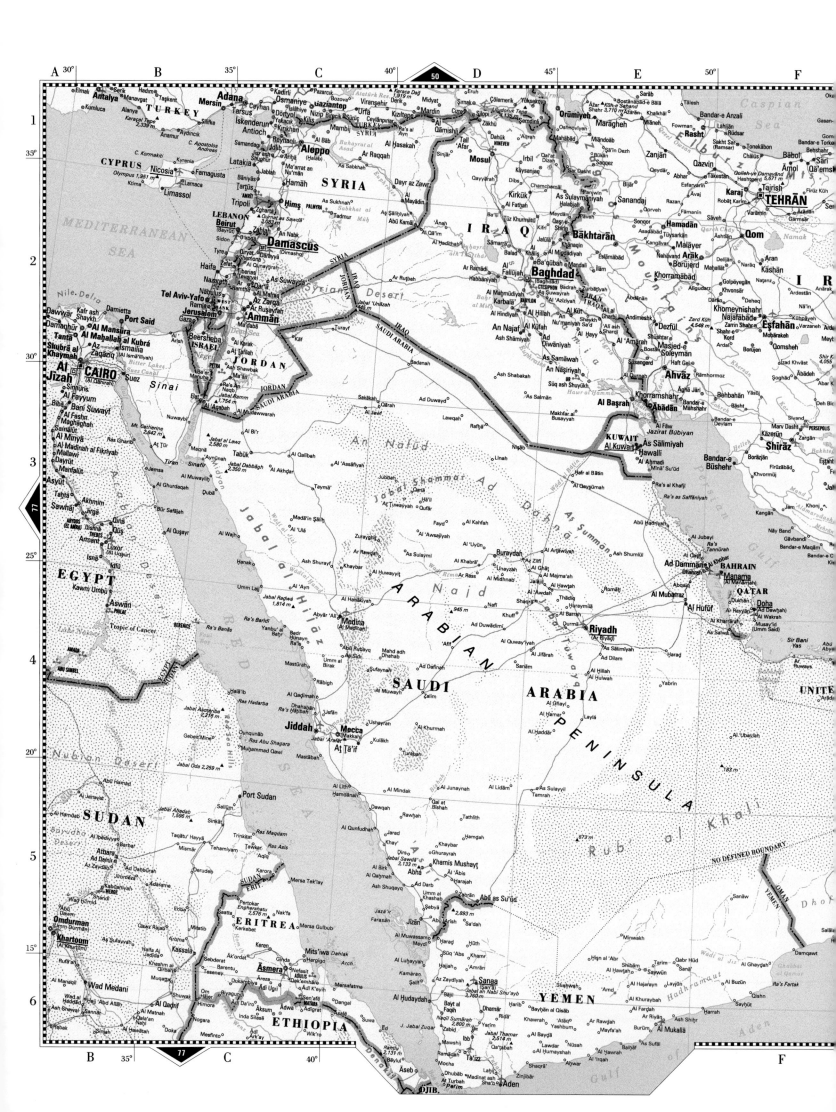

Southwestern Asia

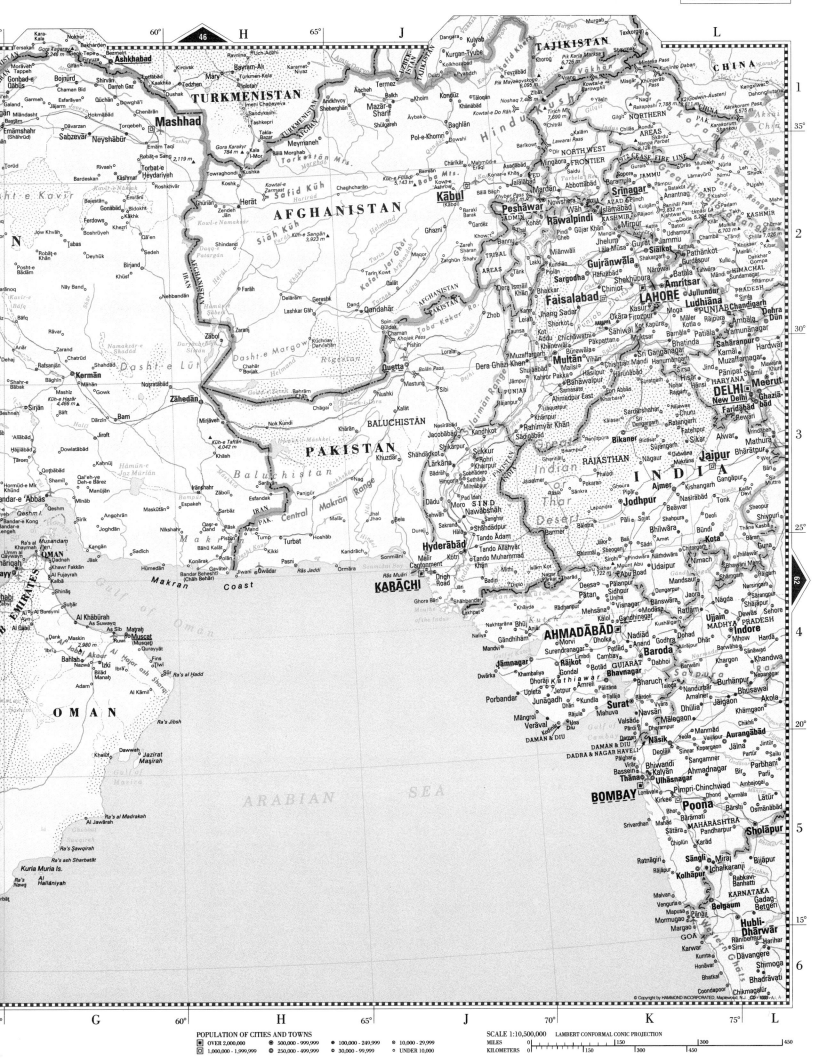

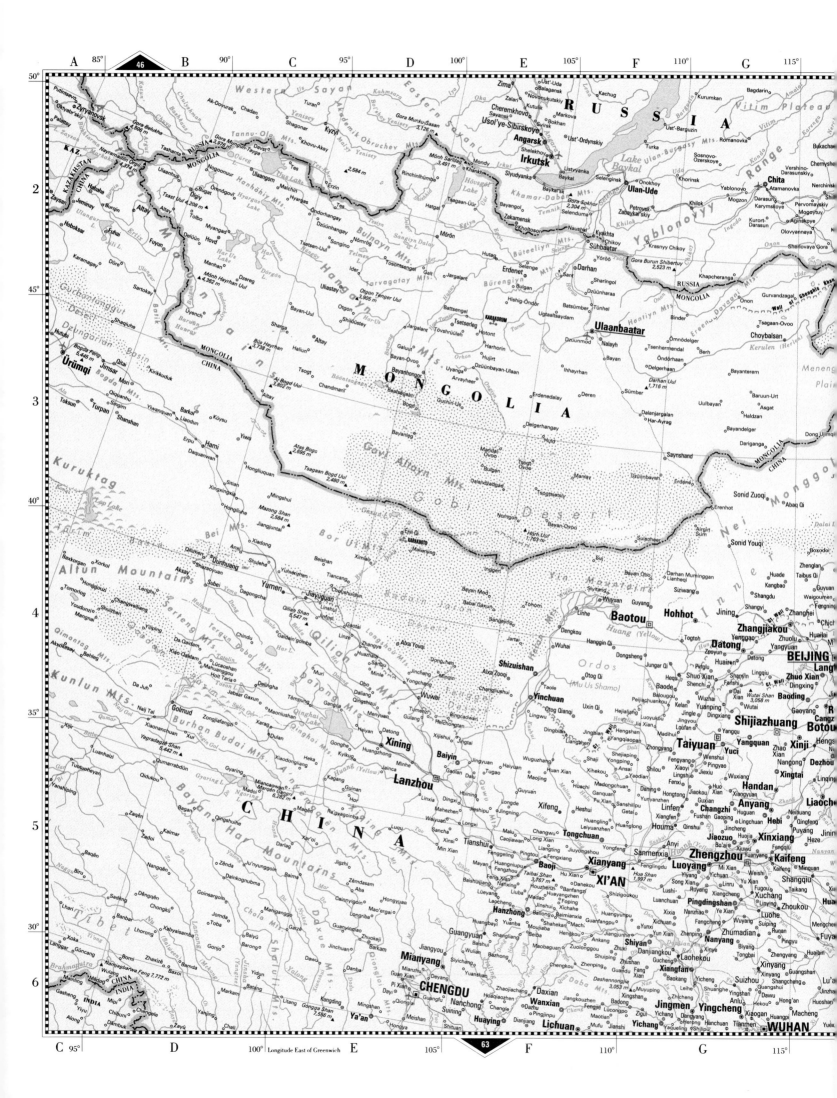

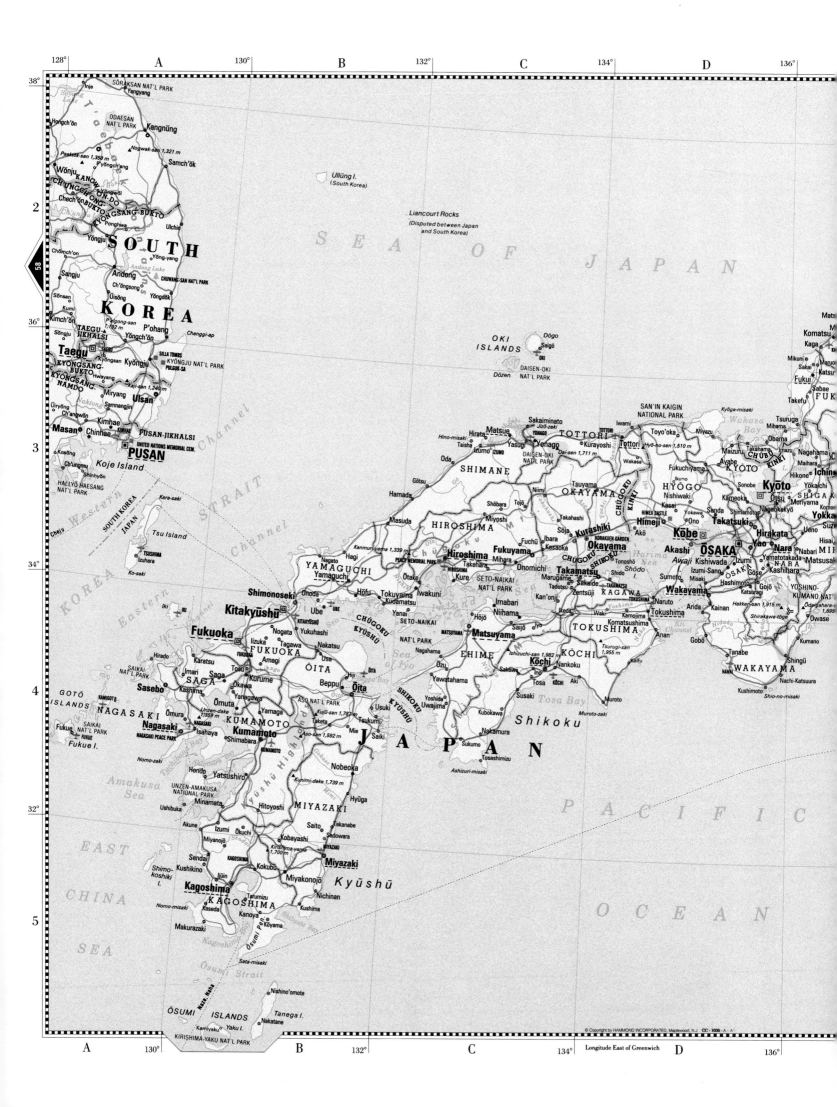

Central and Southern Japan

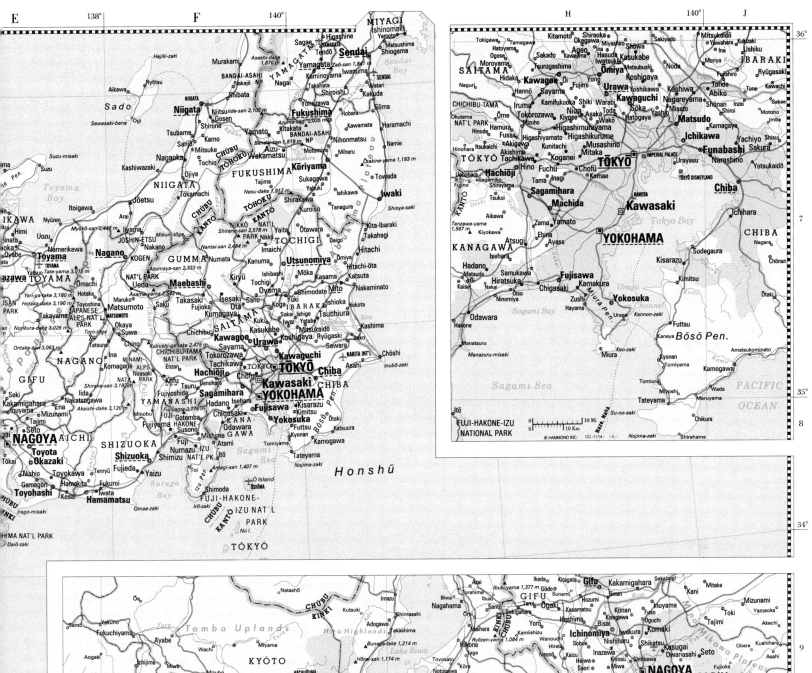

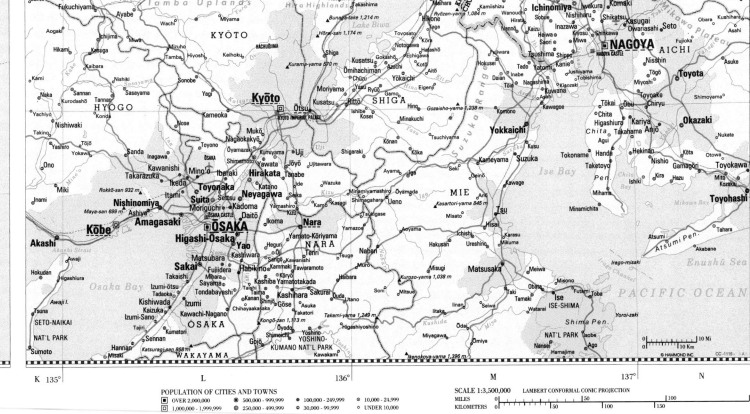

Korea

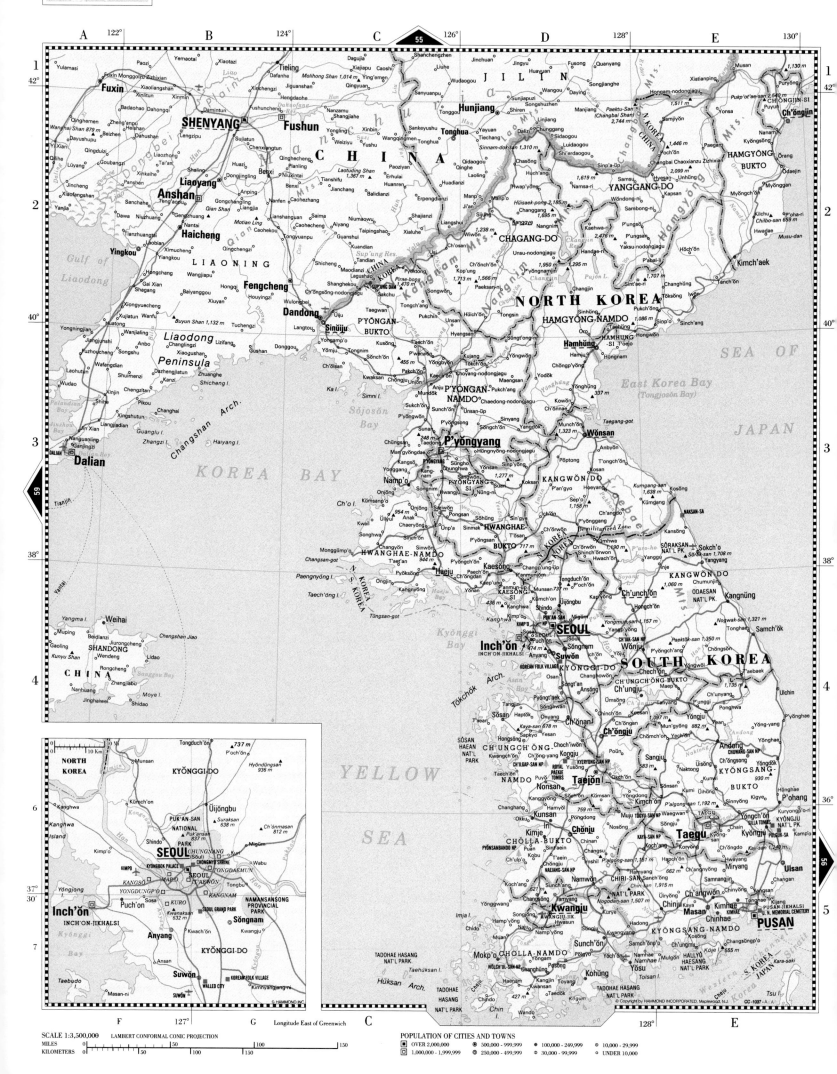

POPULATION OF CITIES AND TOWNS

■ OVER 2,000,000	● 500,000 - 999,999	■ 100,000 - 249,999	● 10,000 - 29,999
▣ 1,000,000 - 1,999,999	● 250,000 - 499,999	● 30,000 - 99,999	○ UNDER 10,000

Northeastern China

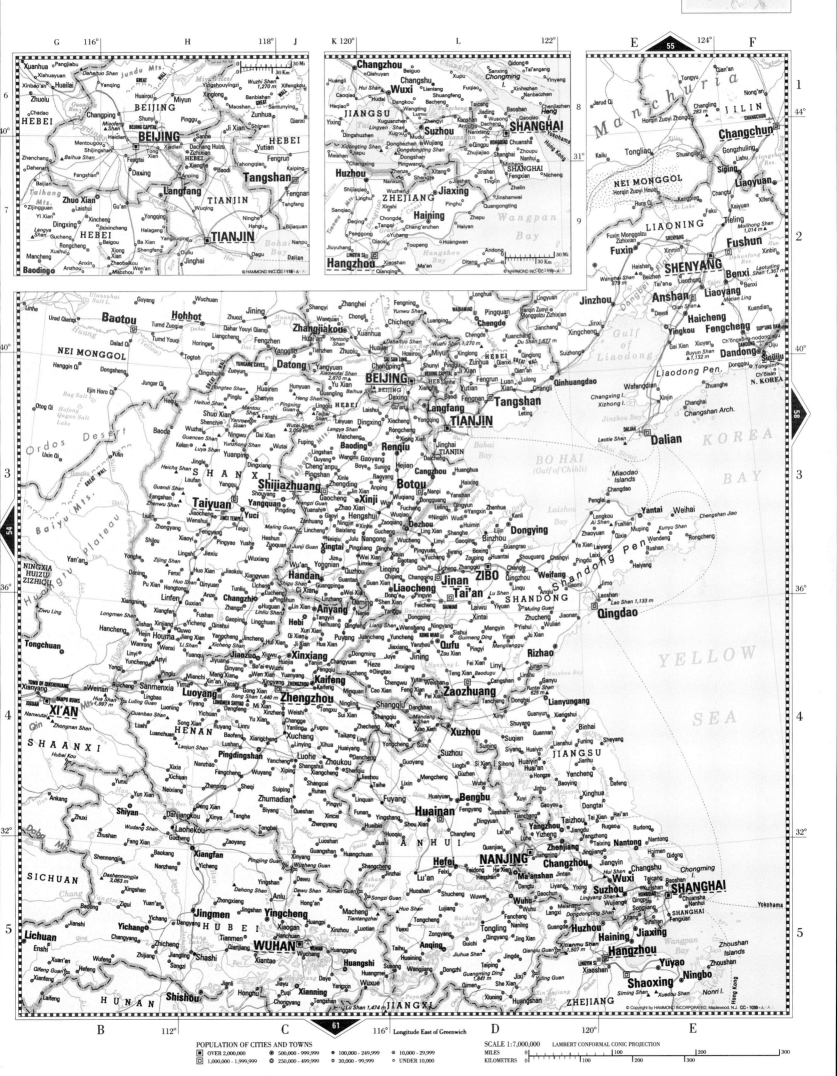

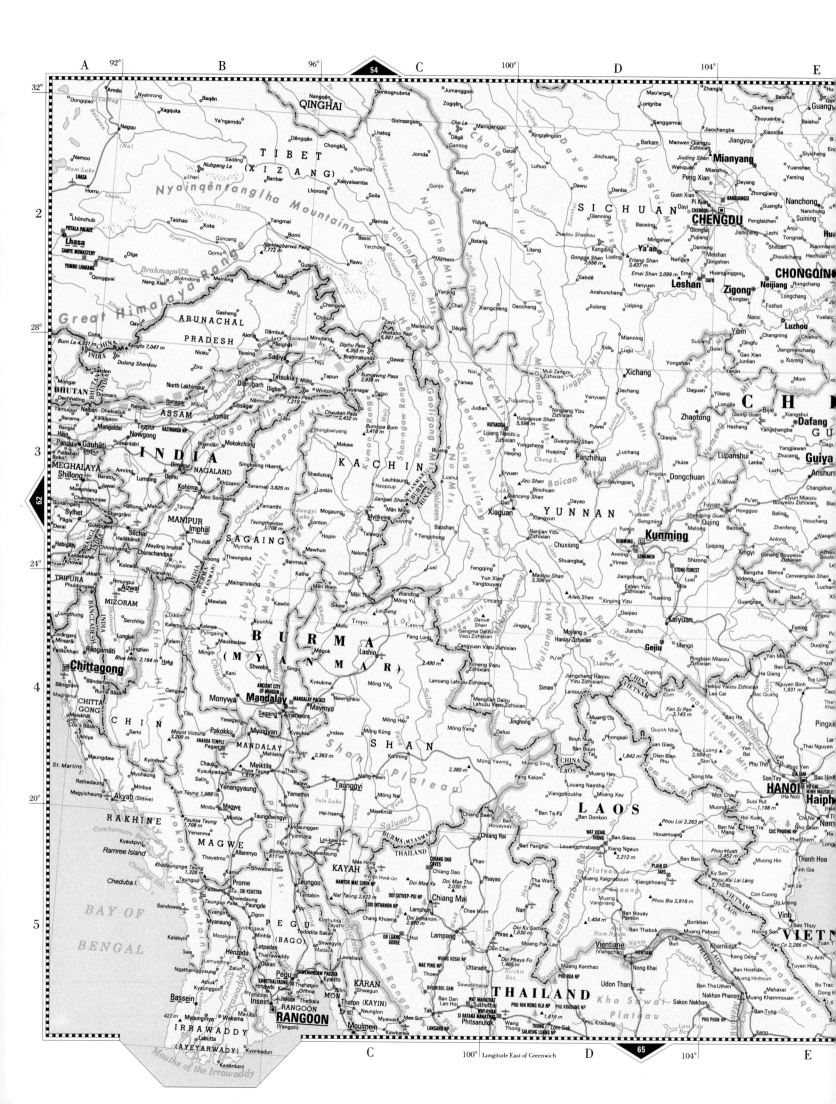

Southeastern China, Burma

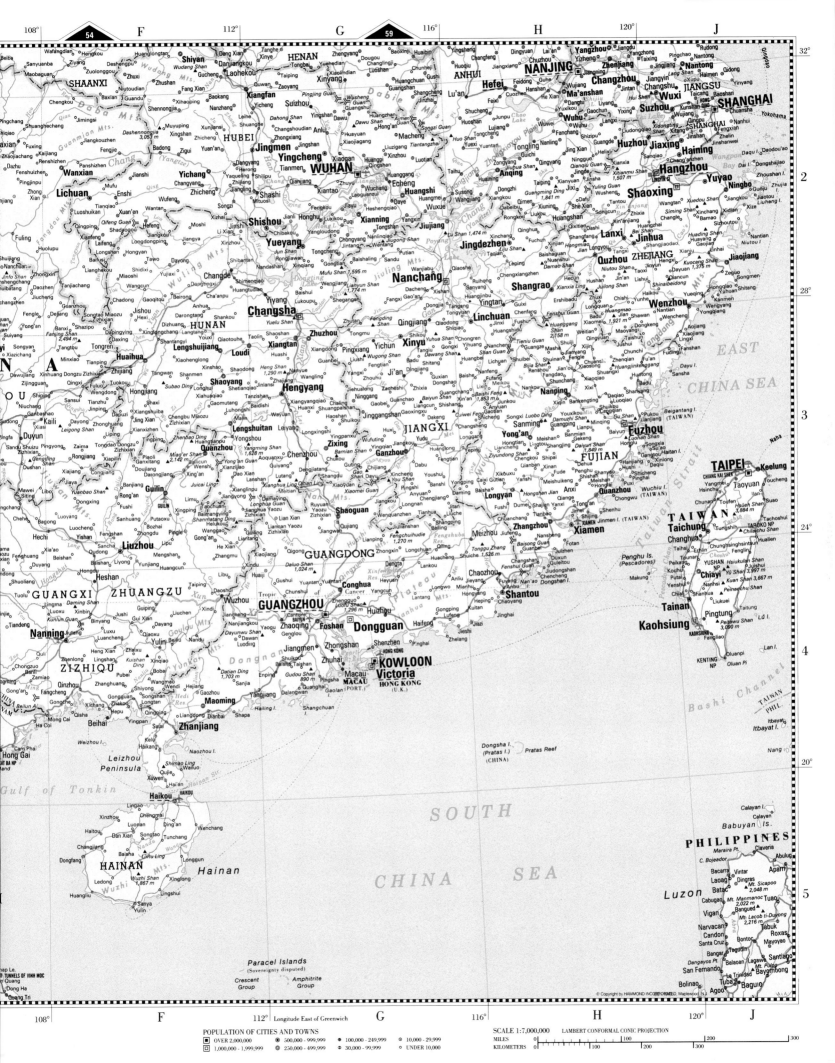

PAKISTAN

PUNJAB   **HARYANA**

DELHI — New Delhi — Faridabad

RĀJASTHĀN   Jaipur   Jodhpur   Ajmer   Bikaner

Great Indian Thar Desert

KARĀCHI   Hyderābād   SIND

Meerut   Morādābād   Bareilly   Shāhjahānpur

UTTAR PRADESH   Āgra   Kānpur   Lucknow   Allahābād   Vārānasi

Gwalior   Jhānsi

TIBET (XIZANG)   **NEPAL**   Kāthmāndu   Mt. Everest 8,848 m

Great Himalaya Range   Sīwālik Range

SIKKIM   **BHUTAN**   Thimphu   Gangtok   Darjiling

BANGLADESH   **DHĀKA**   Khulna

GUJARĀT   **AHMADĀBĀD**   Baroda   Rājkot   Jāmnagar   Bhāvnagar   Surat

Tropic of Cancer

MADHYA PRADESH   Bhopāl   Indore   Ujjain   Jabalpur   Sāgar

BIHĀR   Patna   Gaya   Dhānbād   Ranchi   Jamshedpur

Chota Nāgpur Plateau

WEST BENGAL   **CALCUTTA**   Howrah   Durgāpur   Āsansol   Kharagpur

Satpura Range   Narmada

INDIA

Nāgpur   Amrāvati   Akola   Raipur   Bhilai   Durg

ORISSA   Cuttack   Bhubaneswar   Berhampur   Sambalpur

MAHĀRĀSHTRA   **BOMBAY**   Thāna   Poona   Nāsik   Aurangābād   Sholāpur

Mouths of the Ganges

HYDERĀBĀD   Secunderābād   Warangal

ANDHRA PRADESH   Vijayawada   Guntūr   Visākhapatnam   Rājahmundry   Kurnool

KARNĀTAKA   Belgaum   Hubli-Dhārwār   Gulbarga   Bijāpur

GOA   Pānjī   Mārgao

ARABIAN SEA

BAY OF BENGAL

Lakshadweep Islands   **LAKSHADWEEP**   Kavaratti

Laccadive Sea   Malabar Coast

BANGALORE   Mysore   Mangalore   Salem   Coimbatore   Erode

MADRAS   Kānchipuram   Vellore   **Pondicherry**

Coromandel Coast

KERALA   Kozhikode   Cochin   Trichūr

TAMIL NĀDU   Tiruchchirāppalli   Madurai   Thanjāvur   Tuticorin

Trivandrum   Quilon   Nāgercoil   C. Comorin

SRI LANKA   Ceylon   Jaffna   Trincomalee   Anuradhapura   Kandy   **Colombo**   Galle   Matara   Dondra Head

Gulf of Mannar   Palk Strait

MALDIVES   Maldive Islands   Eight Degree Channel

INDIAN OCEAN

Southern Asia

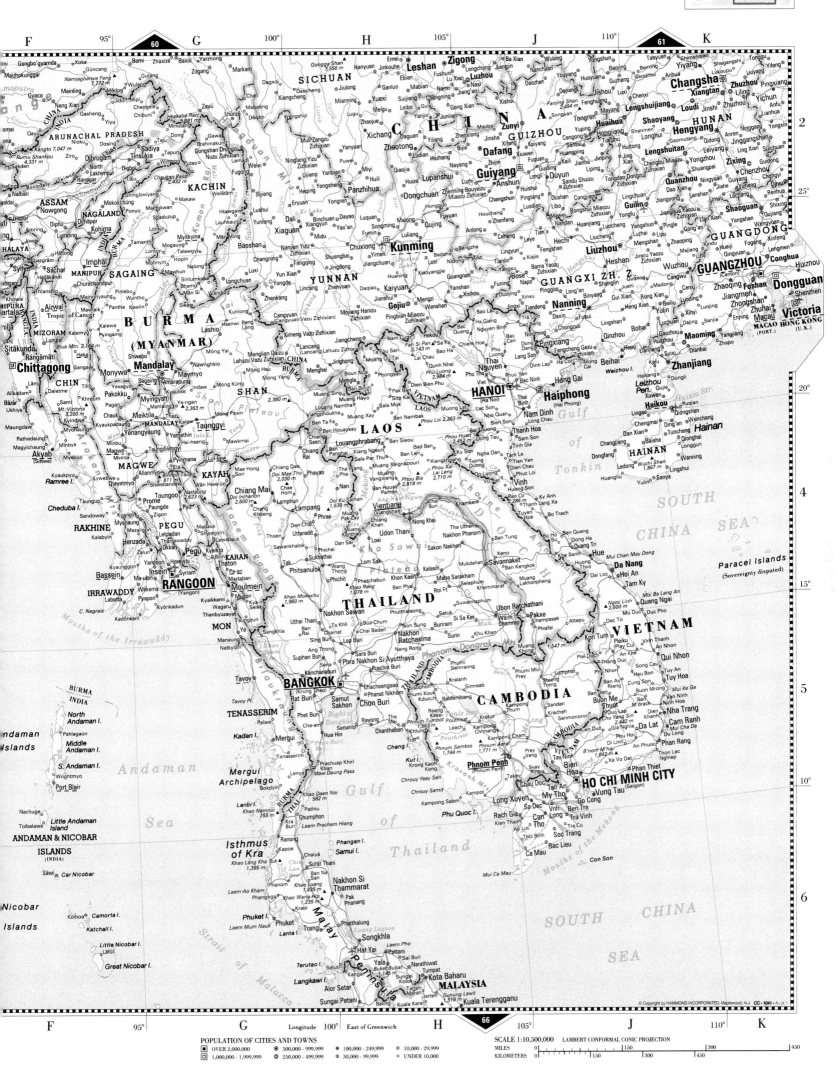

Punjab Plain, Southern India

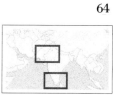

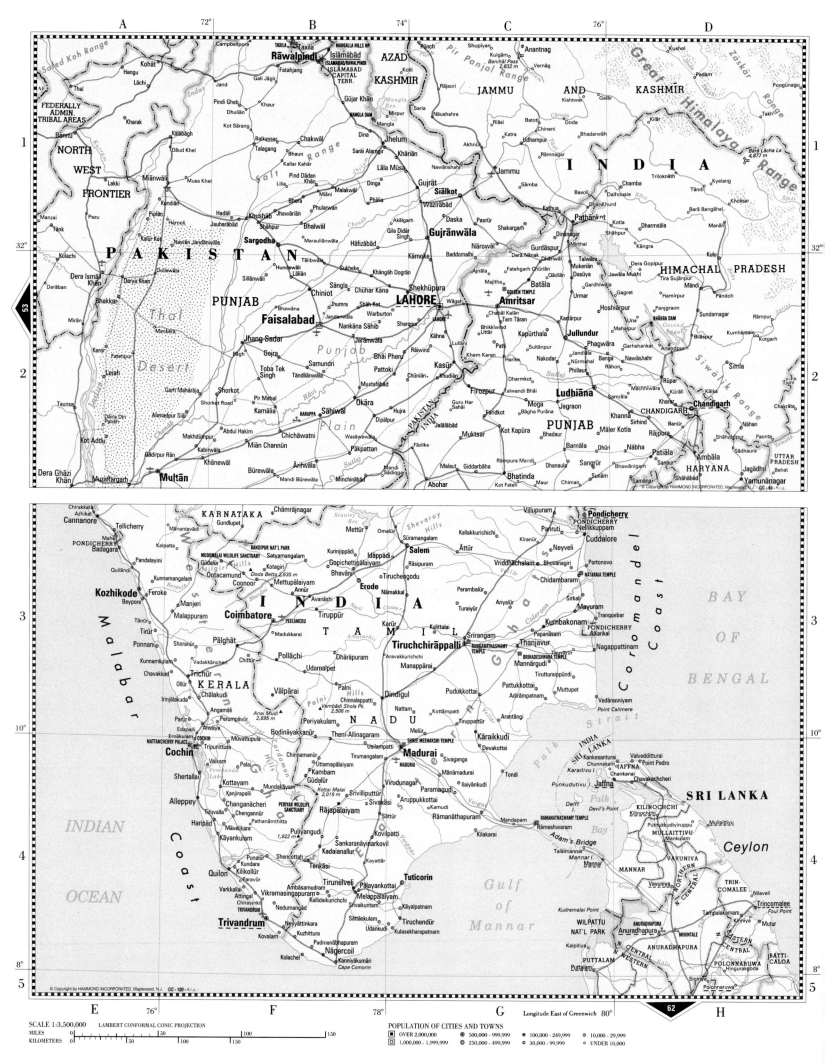

Eastern Burma, Thailand, Indochina

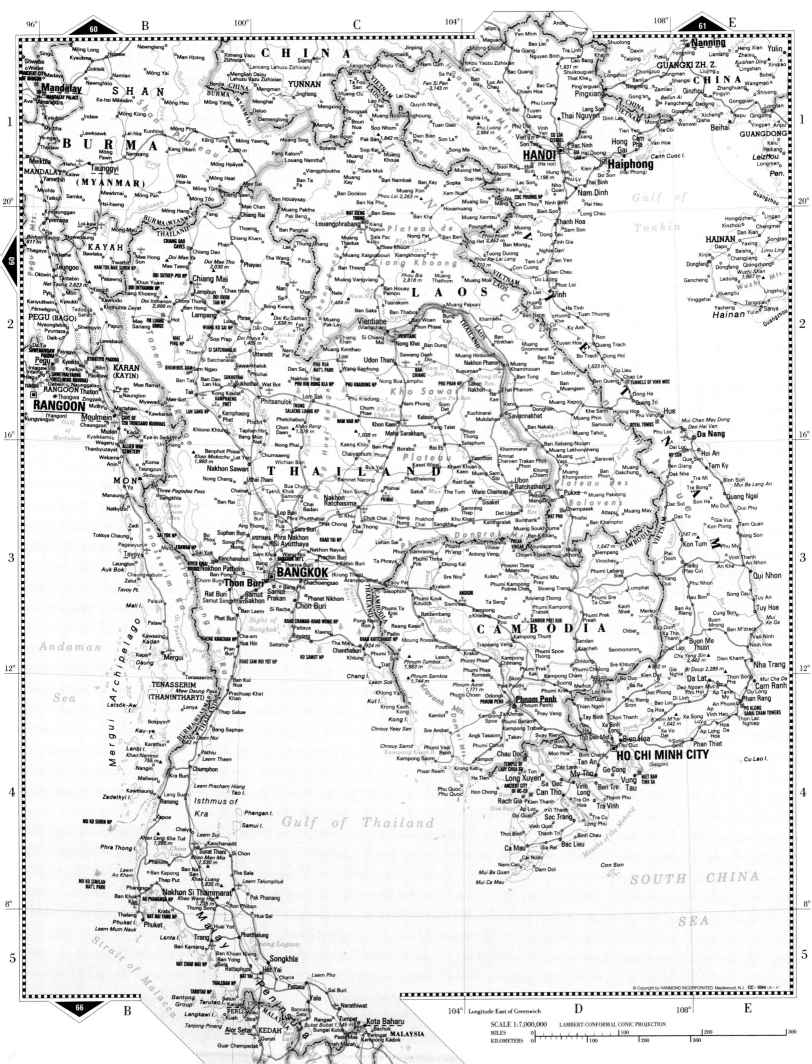

SCALE 1:7,000,000   LAMBERT CONFORMAL CONIC PROJECTION

MILES 0   100   200   300

KILOMETERS 0   100   200   300

© Copyright by HAMMOND INCORPORATED, Maplewood, N.J. CC-1044-A-A

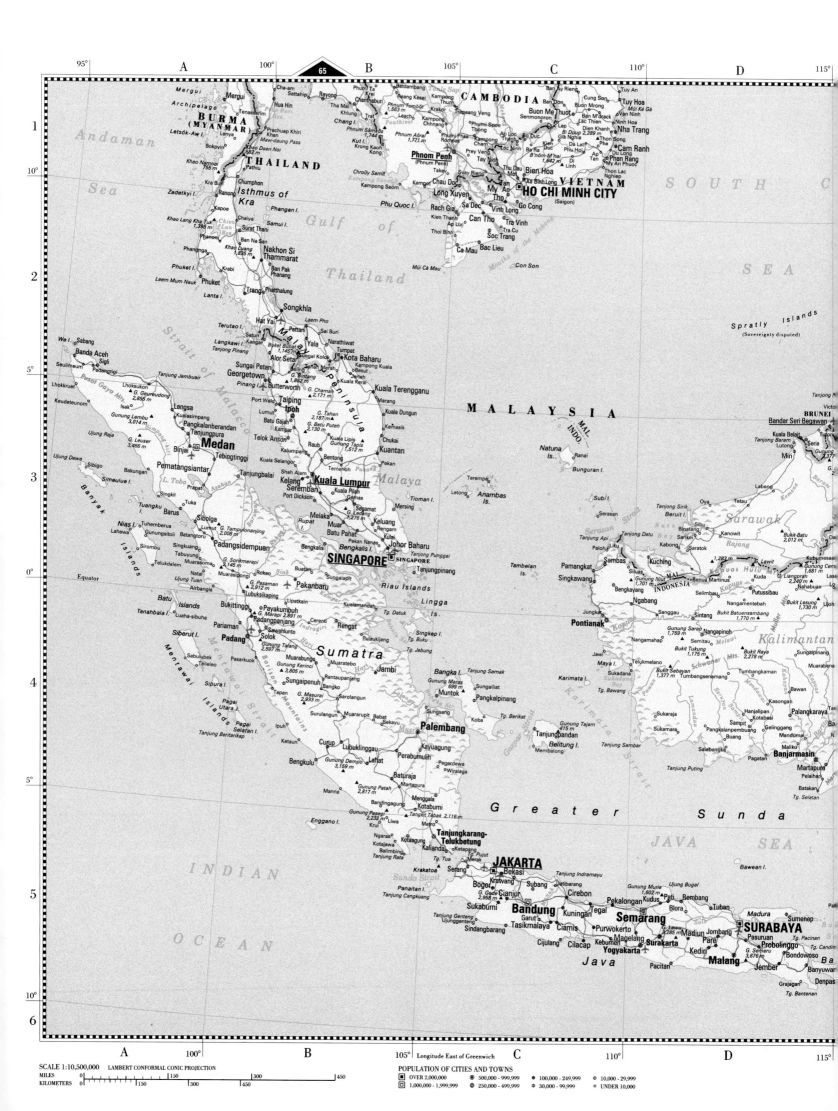

A 95° · 100° **B** 105° **C** 110° **D** 115°

Mergui
Archipelago
Mergui
Cha-am
Sattahip
Tonle Sap
Ban Ay Rieng
Cung Son
Tuy An

BURMA
(MYANMAR)
Hua Hin
Rayong
Chanthaburi
Phum Ta Krei
Phum Tumbot
1,563 m
Battambang
Ban Don
Buon Mrong
Tuy Hoa
Mui Ke Ga
Van Ninh

CAMBODIA

THAILAND
Phetchaburi
Khao Daen Noi
582 m

Phnom Penh
(Phnum Penh)

VIETNAM

HO CHI MINH CITY
(Saigon)

MALAYSIA

Andaman
Sea

Gulf
of

Thailand

SOUTH
C

SEA

Spratly Islands
(Sovereignty disputed)

Malay
Peninsula

Kuala Terengganu

MALAYSIA

MAL.
INDO.
Natuna
Is.

BRUNEI
Bandar Seri Begawan

Medan

Kuala Lumpur

Malaya

Anambas
Is.

Sarawak

Kalimantan

SINGAPORE
SINGAPORE

INDONESIA

Pontianak

Sumatra

Palembang

Banjarmasin

INDIAN

Greater   Sunda

JAVA   SEA

JAKARTA

OCEAN

Bandung

Semarang

SURABAYA

Java

Malang

A 100° **B** 105° Longitude East of Greenwich **C** 110° **D** 115°

SCALE 1:10,500,000   LAMBERT CONFORMAL CONIC PROJECTION
MILES   0   150   300   450
KILOMETERS 0   150   300   450

POPULATION OF CITIES AND TOWNS
■ OVER 2,000,000   ● 500,000 - 999,999   ● 100,000 - 249,999   • 10,000 - 29,999
▣ 1,000,000 - 1,999,999   ⊡ 250,000 - 499,999   • 30,000 - 99,999   • UNDER 10,000

Southeastern Asia

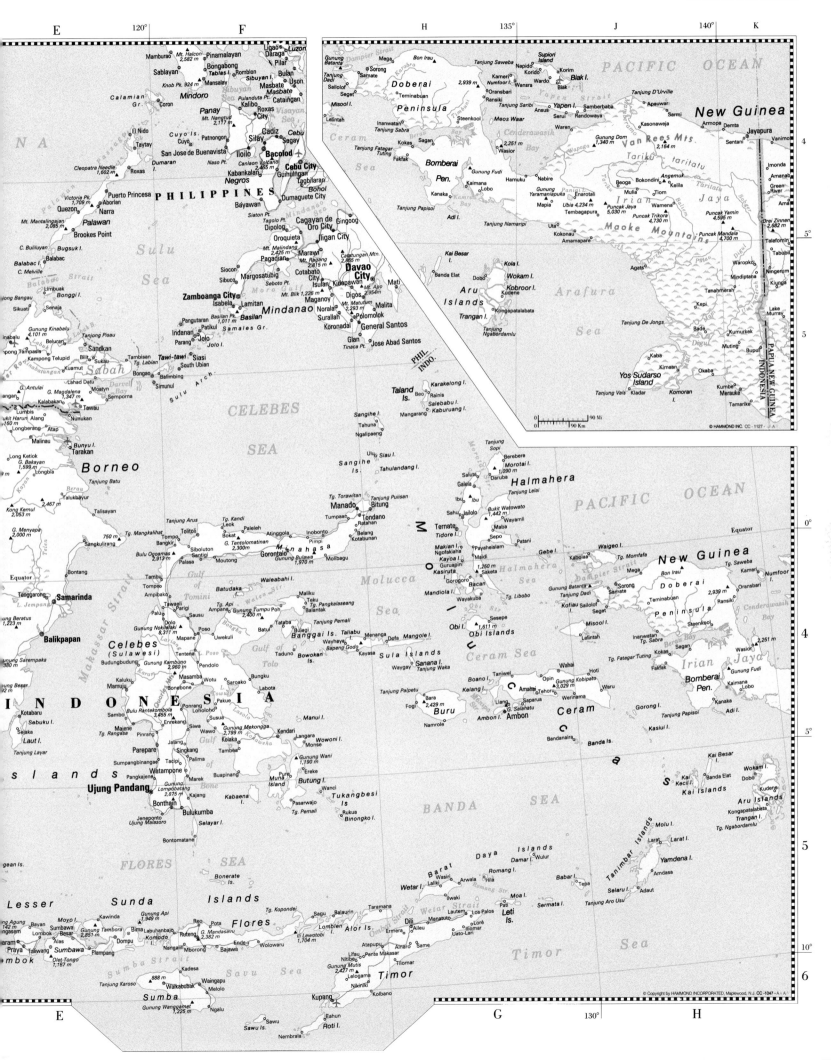

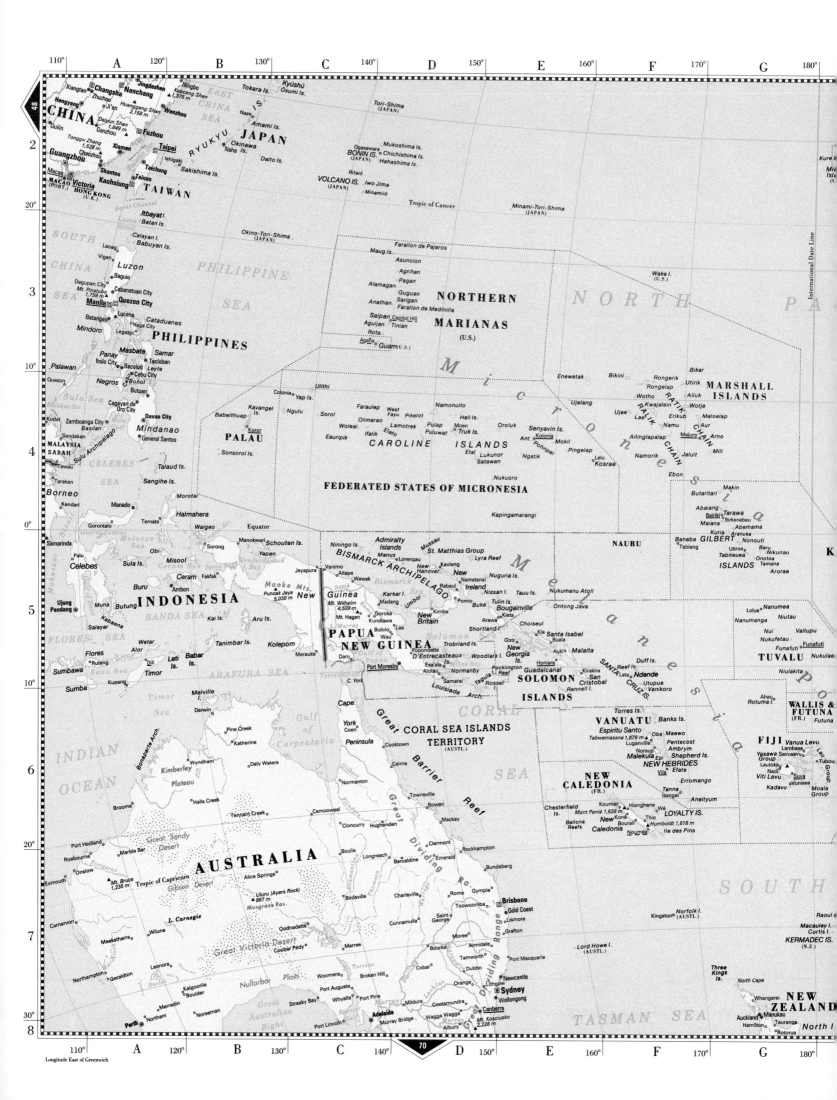

Central Pacific Ocean

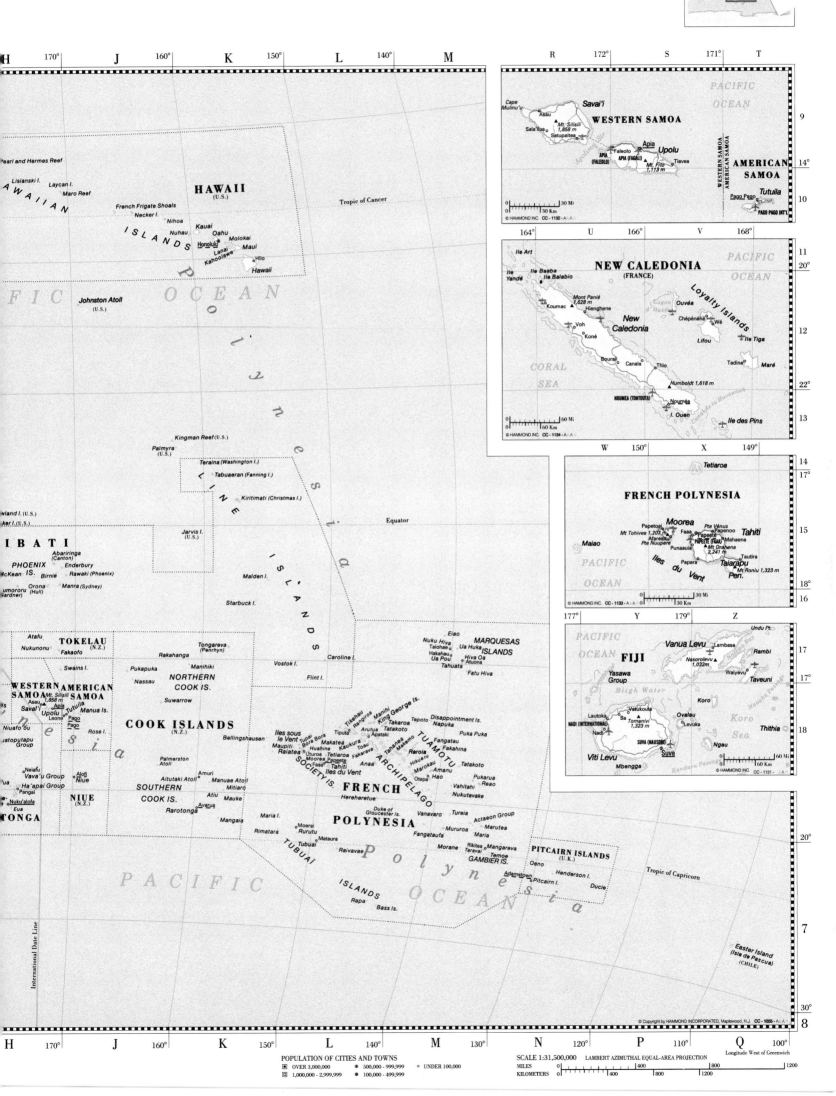

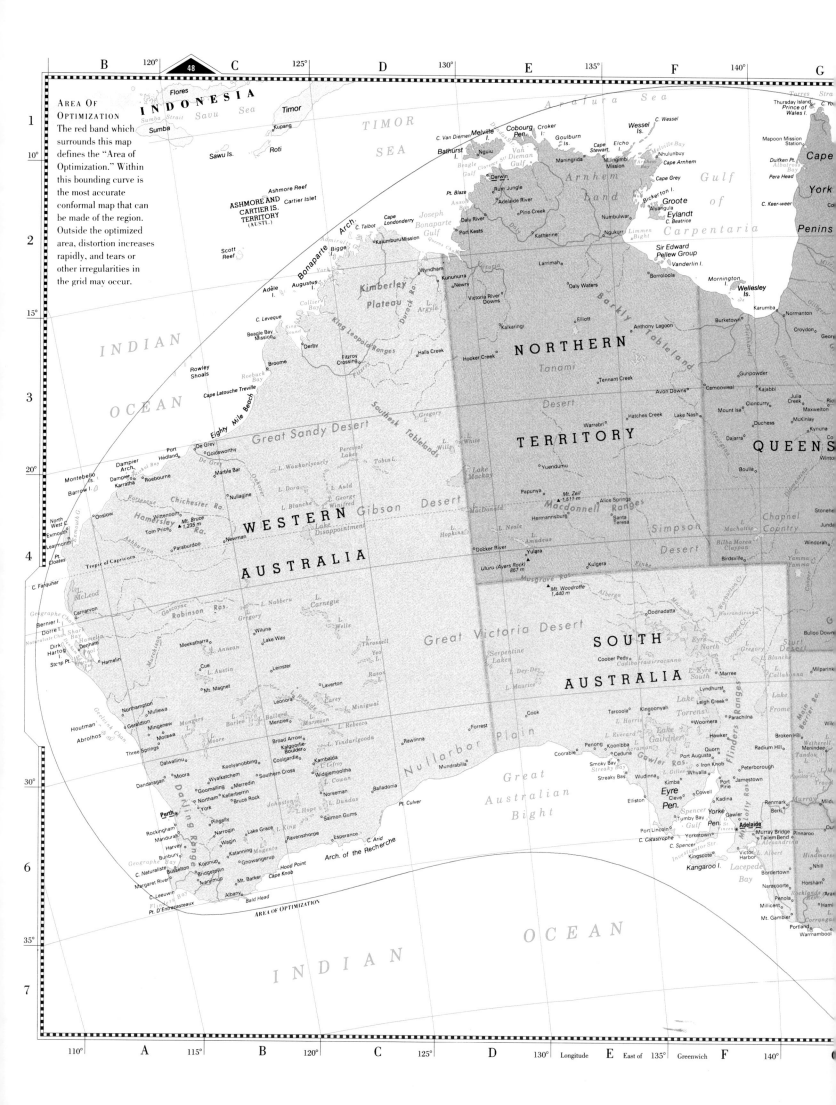

AREA OF OPTIMIZATION
The red band which surrounds this map defines the "Area of Optimization." Within this bounding curve is the most accurate conformal map that can be made of the region. Outside the optimized area, distortion increases rapidly, and tears or other irregularities in the grid may occur.

INDONESIA

Flores

Timor

Sumba Strait *Savu Sea*

Sumba *Kupang*

Sawu Is. *Roti*

TIMOR

SEA

Arafura Sea

Thursday Island
Prince of Wales I.
C. Ya

C. Wessel

C. Van Diemen Melville Cobourg Croker
I. Pen. I.

Bathurst Nguiu Goulburn Cape Elcho
I. Is. Stewart I.

Mapoon Mission
Station

Duifken Pt.
Albatross
Bay

Pera Head

Cape

York

Penins

Wessel
Is.

Melville Bay
Nhulunbuy

Maningrida Milingimbi
Mission Cape Arnhem

Darwin Arnhem Cape Grey

Rum Jungle Land

Pt. Blaze Adelaide River Bickerton I.
Alyangula

Pine Creek Groote
Eylandt
C. Beatrice

Numbulwar

Daly River Katherine Ngukurr Limmen
Bight

Port Keats

Sir Edward
Pellew Group

Vanderlin I.

Larrimah

Borroloola Mornington
I.

Wellesley
Is.

Wyndham Newry Victoria River
Downs

Kununurra Daly Waters

Gulf

of

Carpentaria

Karumba

Normanton

Kalkaringi Elliott Anthony Lagoon

Burketown

Croydon

ASHMORE AND
CARTIER IS.
TERRITORY
(AUSTL.)

Ashmore Reef Cartier Islet

Scott
Reef

Cape
Londonderry

Joseph
Bonaparte
Gulf

Bonaparte
Arch.

C. Talbot

Kalumburu Mission

Adèle
I.

Augustus
I.

Bigge

Collier
Bay

Kimberley

Plateau

Durack Ra.

L.
Argyle

NORTHERN

Tanami

TERRITORY

Hooker Creek

Tennant Creek

Barkly Tableland

Gunpowder

Avon Downs Camooweal

Warrabri Hatches Creek Lake Nash

Kajabbi

Mount Isa Cloncurry

Julia
Creek

Maxwelton

McKinlay

Kyuna

Duchess

Dajarra

Ris

QUEENS

Winto

C. Leveque

Beagle Bay
Mission

Derby

Halls Creek

Hooker Creek

King Leopold Ranges

Fitzroy
Crossing

Broome Southesk
Tablelands

Southesk
Tablelands

Gregory

L.
Wills

L. White

Desert

Yuendumu

Boulia

INDIAN

Rowley
Shoals

OCEAN

Cape Latouche Treville

Eighty Mile Beach

Great Sandy Desert

Percival
Lakes

Tobin L.

L. Mackay

Papunya Mt. Zeil
1,511 m

MacDonnell Ranges

Alice Springs

Chapnel

Macka

Country

Stoneher

Dampier
Arch.

Port
Hedland

De Grey
Goldsworthy

De Grey

L. Waukartycarly

L. Dora

L. Blanche L. George
Winifred

Hermannsburg

Santa
Teresa

Simpson

Bilba Morea
Claypan

Windorah

Montebello
Is.

Barrow I.

Dampier Roebourne
Karratha

Marble Bar

Nullagine

L. Auld

MacDonald

L. Neale

Desert

Birdsville

Yamma
Yamma

North
West C.

Exmouth
Learmonth

Onslow Witterloom
Tom Price Mt. Bruce
1,235 m

Hamersley

Newman

WESTERN

Gibson Desert

Lake
Disappointment

L.
Hopkins

AUSTRALIA

L.
Amadeus

Docker River

Yulara

Uluru (Ayers Rock)
867 m

Kulgera

Flinke

Pt.
Cloates

Fortescue

Chichester Ra.

Ra.

Ashburton

Paraburdoo

Mt. Woodroffe
1,440 m

Alberga

Oodnadatta

Warrandirrin

C. Farquhar

McLeod

Robinson Ras.

Gascoyne

L. Nabberu

Gregory

L.
Carnegie

Musgrave Ras.

Carnarvon

Wiluna

L.
Wells

Great Victoria Desert

SOUTH

L.
North

L.
Gregory

Desert

L.
Blanche

Milparin

Bernier I.
Dorre I.

Denham

Meekatharra

L. Annean

Threshell

Yeo

L.

Serpentine
Lakes

AUSTRALIA

Coober Pedy

Cadibarrawirracanna

L. Eyre
North

Marree

L.
Callahonna

Shark
Bay

Dirk
Hartog
I.

Hamelin
Pool

Cue Mt. Austin

Leinster

L.
Rason

L. Maurice

L. Dey-Dey

L. Eyre
South

Leigh Creek

Lyndhurst

Lake
Frome

Stop Pt.

Hamelin

Mt. Magnet

Laverton

Lake
Torrens

Flinders Ranges

Parachilna

Tarcoole Kingoonya

Woomera

Hawker

Broken Hill

Northampton
Mullewa

Leonora Roseid

Carey

L. Minigwal

Cook

Forrest

L. Harris

Radium Hill

Geraldton

Mingenew Morawa

Three Springs

Moore

L.
Barlee

Menzies

Marmion

L. Rebecca

Rawlinna

Mundrabilla

Nullarbor Plain

Coorabie

Penong Kooniba
Ceduna

Smoky Bay
Streaky Bay

Koonibba

Port Augusta

Quorn

Peterborough

Jamestown

Menindee

Tandou

Houtman
Abrolhos

Dalwallinu

Moora

Dandaragan

Broad Arrow
Kalgoorlie
Boulder

Coolgardie

L. Yindarlgooda

L.
Cowan

Kambalda

Widgiemooltha

Balladonia

Great

Australian

Bight

Streaky Bay Wudinna

Kimba

Iron Knob

Eyre
Pen. Cleve

Cowell

Whyalla

L. Gilles

Kadina

Port
Pirie

Port Lincoln

Elliston

Wetherell

Wyalkatchem

Merredin
Goomalling

Southern Cross

Narrogin

York

Bruce Rock

Johnston

L. Dundas

Pt. Culver

Kingscote

Spencer
Gulf

Yorke
Pen.

Renmark

Berri

Murray

Mildi

Perth

Rockingham
Mandurah

Harvey

Northam
Kellerberrin

Pingelly

Lake Grace L. King

Norseman

C. Spencer

Tumby Bay

Port
Augusta

Gawler

Adelaide

Pinnaroo

Murray Bridge

Bunbury

Busselton
Bridgetown

Kojonup
Gnowangerup

Katanning Magenta

Ravensthorpe

Esperance

C. Arid

Arch. of the Recherche

C. Catastrophe

Kingscote

Victor
Harbor

L. Albert

Alexandrina

Hindmarsh

Nhill

Bordertown

Naracoorte

Horsham

C. Naturaliste

C. Leeuwin

Margaret River

Nannup Mt. Barker Cape Knob

Hood Point

Kangaroo I. Lacepede
Bay

Penola

Millicent

Ara

Hami

Geographe Bay

Albany

Bald Head

Pt. D'Entrecasteaux

Mt. Gambier

Portland

Corrang

Flinders Bay

AREA OF OPTIMIZATION

OCEAN

Warrnambool

INDIAN

OCEAN

Tropic of Capricorn

Australia; New Zealand

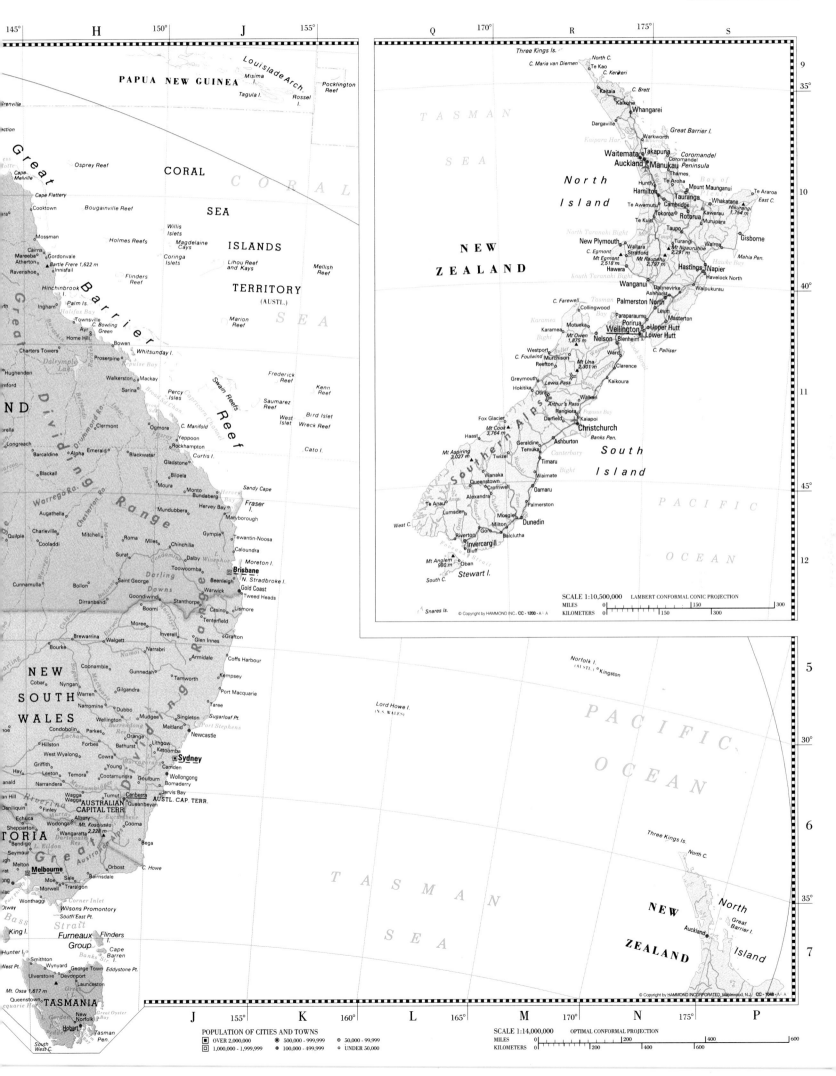

Northeastern Australia

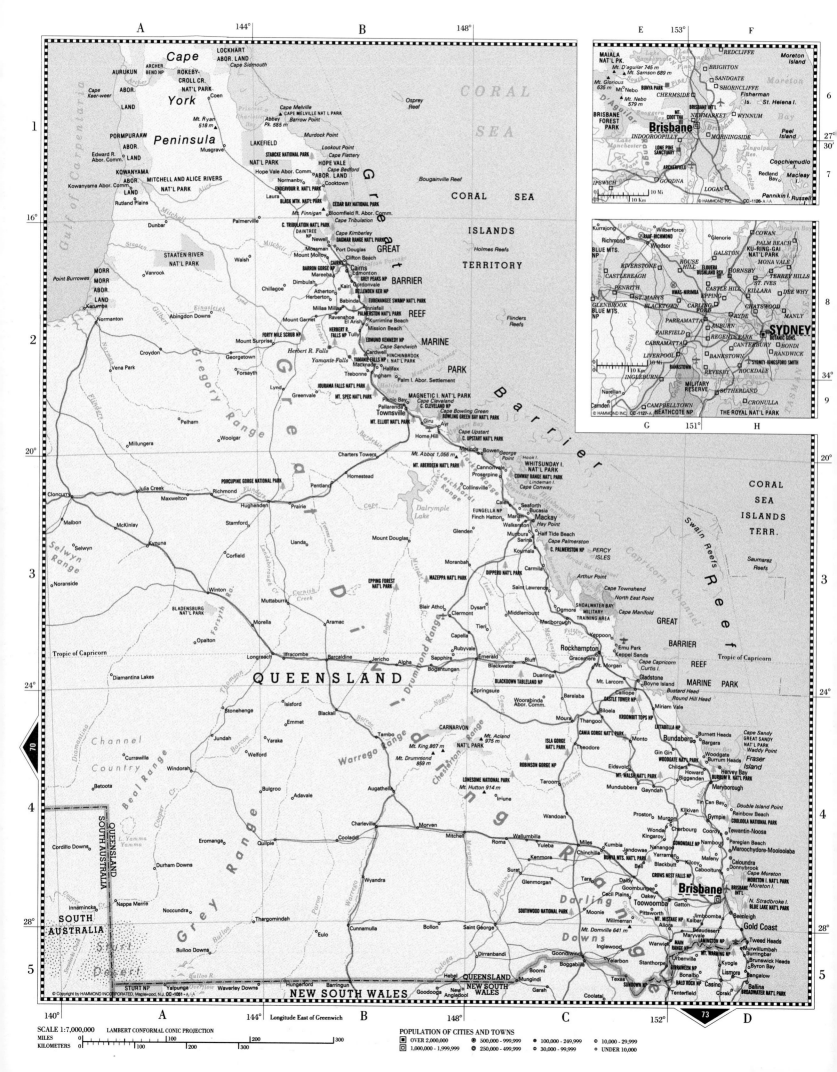

Southeastern Australia

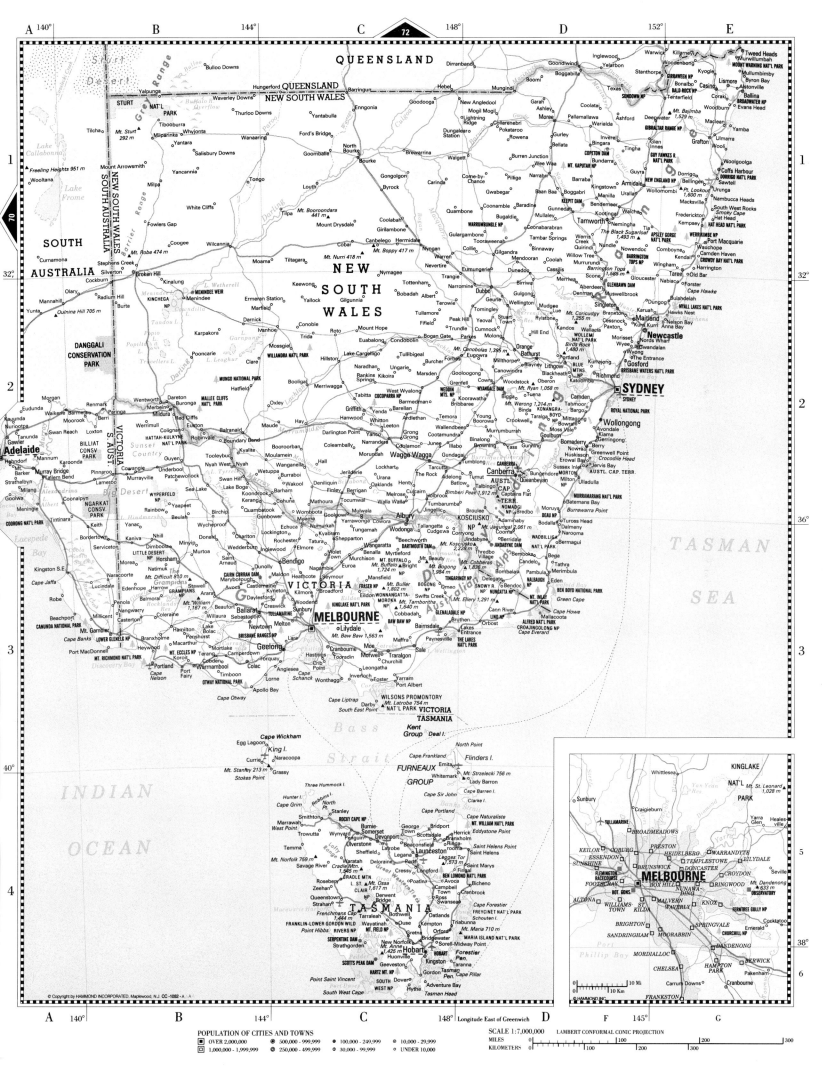

A 140°   **B**   144°   **C**   148°   **D**   152°   **E**

QUEENSLAND

QUEENSLAND
NEW SOUTH WALES

SOUTH
AUSTRALIA

NEW
SOUTH
WALES

SYDNEY

Adelaide

VICTORIA

MELBOURNE

TASMANIA

Hobart

INDIAN
OCEAN

TASMAN
SEA

Bass Strait

FURNEAUX
GROUP

MELBOURNE (inset)

KINGLAKE
NAT'L
PARK

MELBOURNE

KEILOR   COBURG   PRESTON
ESSENDON
SUNSHINE

BROADMEADOWS

TULLAMARINE

Port
Phillip Bay

FRANKSTON

A 140°   **B**   144°   **C**   148°   **D**   Longitude East of Greenwich   **F**   145°   **G**

POPULATION OF CITIES AND TOWNS

| ■ OVER 2,000,000 | ● 500,000 - 999,999 | ● 100,000 - 249,999 | ○ 10,000 - 29,999 |
| □ 1,000,000 - 1,999,999 | ● 250,000 - 499,999 | ● 30,000 - 99,999 | ○ UNDER 10,000 |

SCALE 1:7,000,000   **LAMBERT CONFORMAL CONIC PROJECTION**

MILES 0   100   200   300
KILOMETERS 0   100   200   300

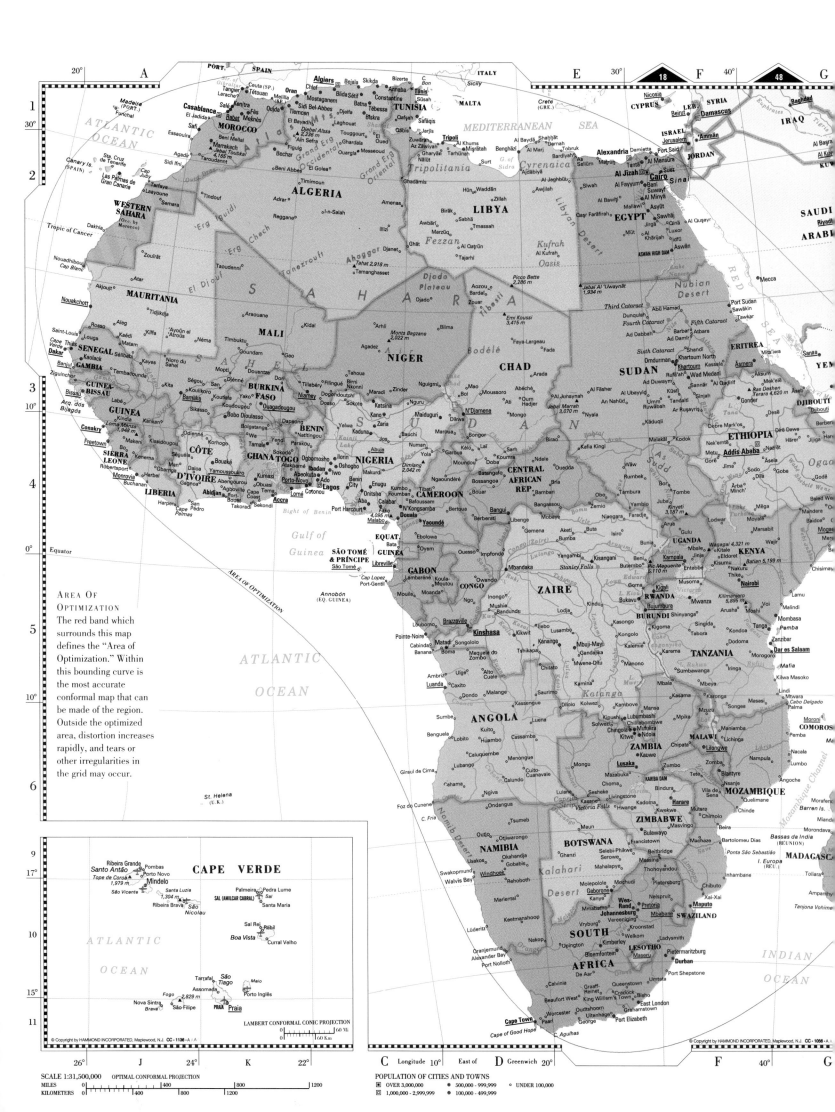

Area Of Optimization
The red band which surrounds this map defines the "Area of Optimization." Within this bounding curve is the most accurate conformal map that can be made of the region. Outside the optimized area, distortion increases rapidly, and tears or other irregularities in the grid may occur.

CAPE VERDE

LAMBERT CONFORMAL CONIC PROJECTION

SCALE 1:31,500,000   OPTIMAL CONFORMAL PROJECTION

MILES   0   400   800   1200
KILOMETERS 0   400   800   1200

POPULATION OF CITIES AND TOWNS
☒ OVER 3,000,000   ● 500,000 - 999,999   ○ UNDER 100,000
☐ 1,000,000 - 2,999,999   ● 100,000 - 499,999

Africa

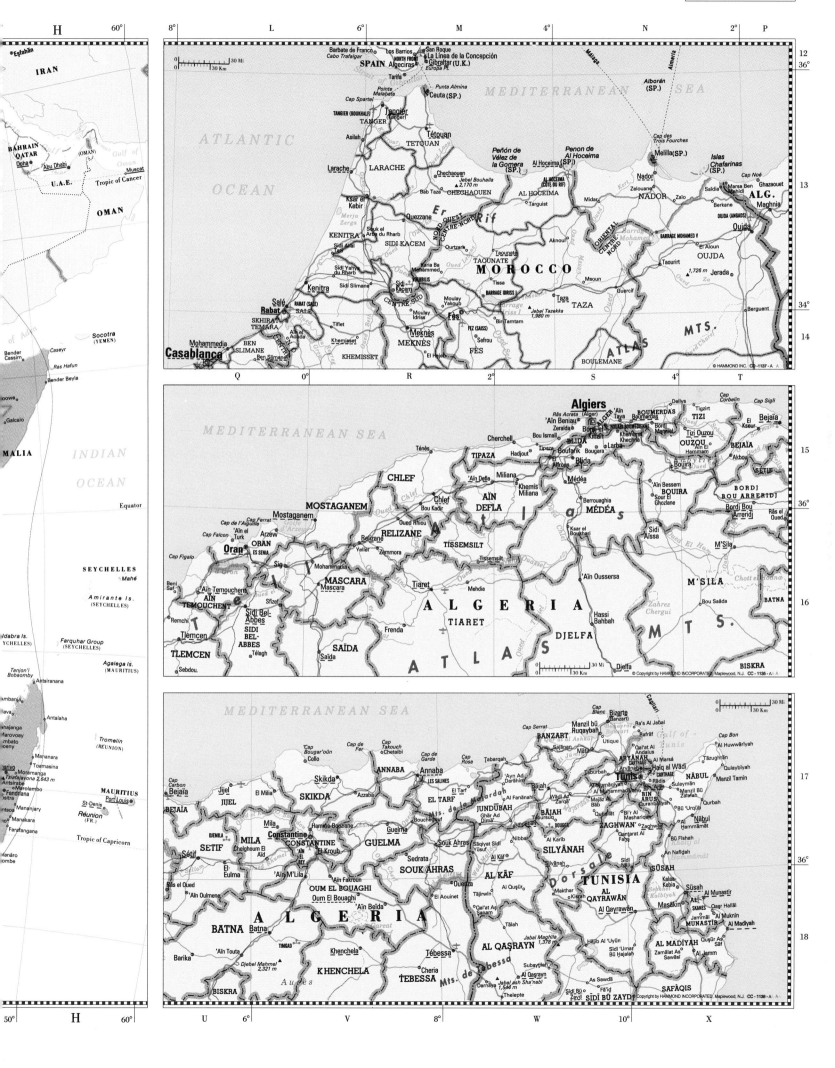

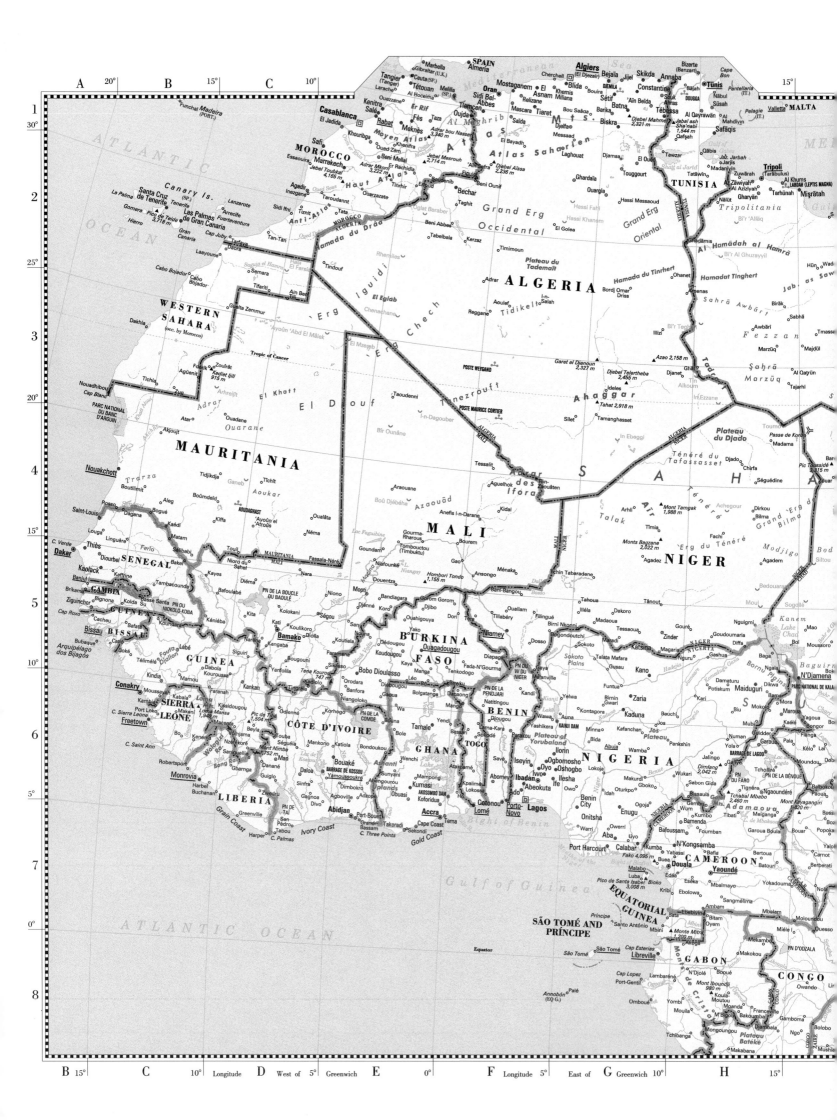

Northern Africa

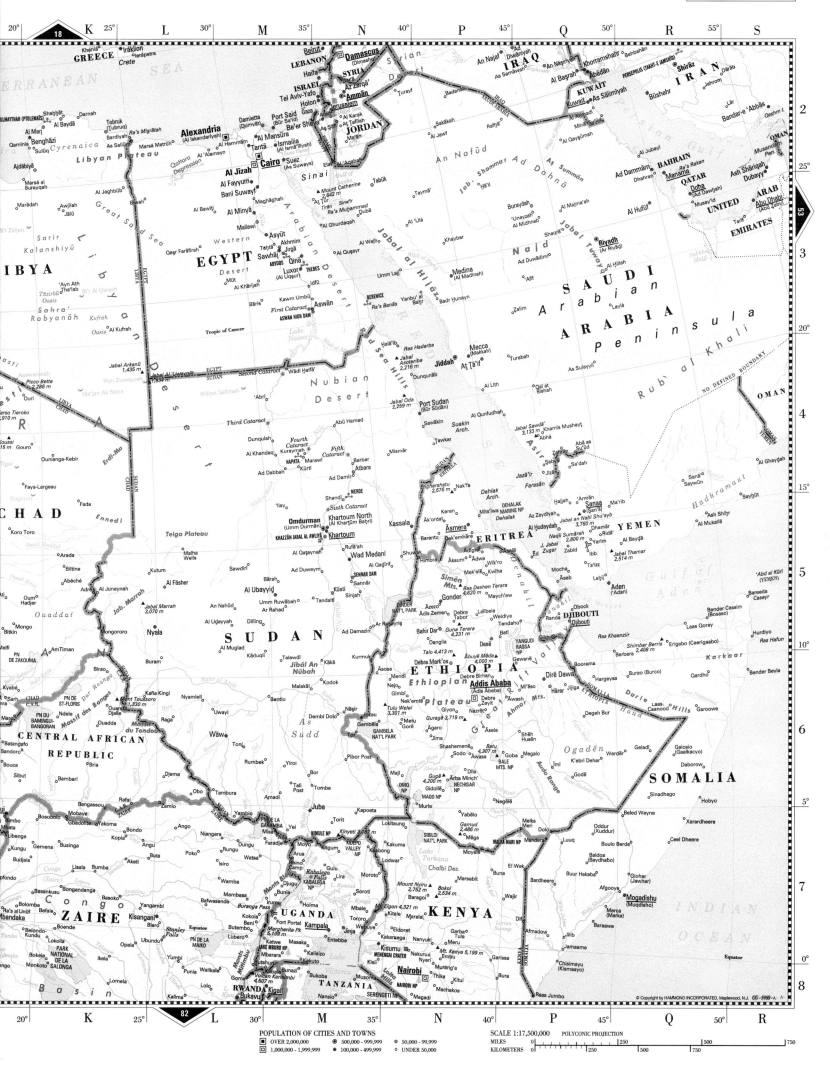

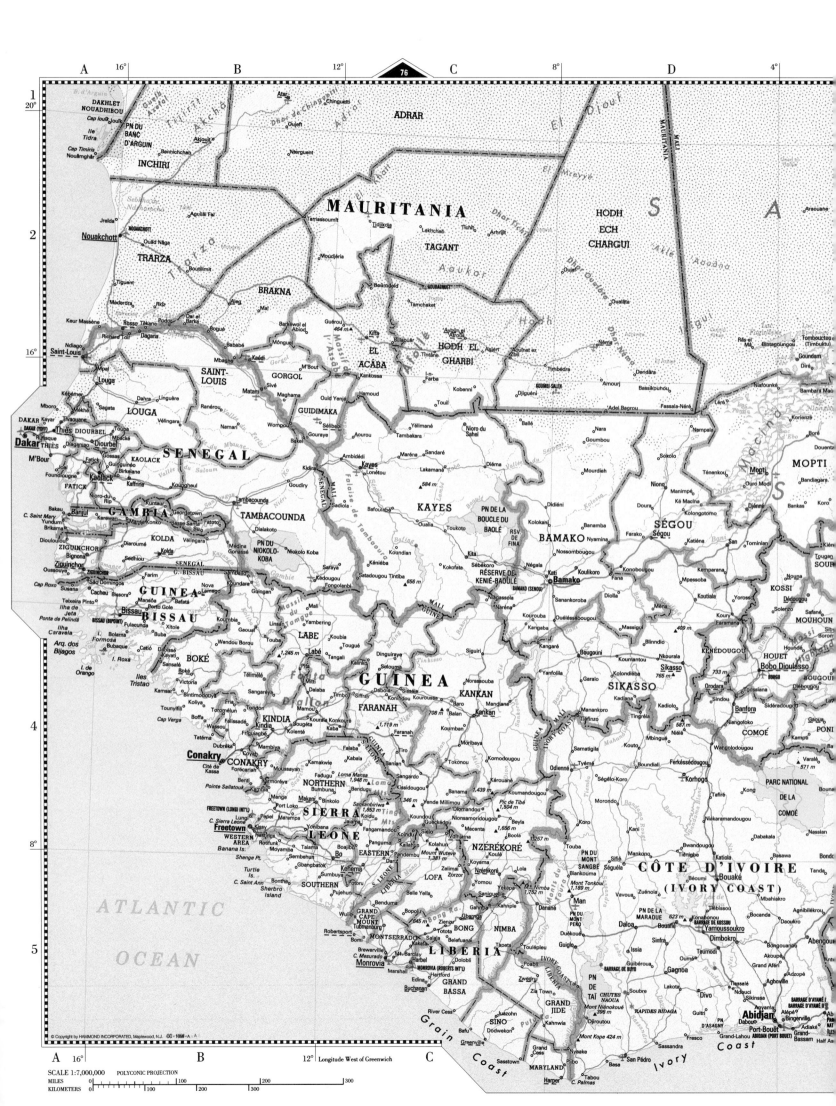

A 16°   B 12°   C 8°   D 4°

1
20°

B. d'Arguin

DAKHLET
NOUADHIBOU

Cap Iouik
Ile
Tidra

Cap Timiris
Nouâmghâr

PN DU
BANC
D'ARGUIN

INCHIRI

Atar

Chinguetti

Oujeft

ADRAR

Dhar de Chinguetti

ADRAR

Tirirt

Akchar

El Djouf

SA

MALI-MAURITANIA

Araouane

2

Nouakchott

NOUAKCHOTT

Jreïda

Aguilal Fai

Tarrassoumit

Tidjikdja

Tichtt

Arhrijit

HODH
ECH
CHARGUI

S

A

TRARZA

Ouâd Nâga

Boutilimit

Moudjéria

TAGANT

Aoukar

Oujaft

MAURITANIA

BRAKNA

Aleg

Mal

Beumdeld

AOUDAGHOST

Tamchaket

Dhar Tichit

Néma

Oualâta

Ras el
Ma

Blintagoungou
(Timbuktu)

Tombouctou
(Timbuktu)

Goundam

Tiguent

Mederdra

Rkiz

Dar el
Barka

Guérou

464 m

Kiffa

Aÿoûn el
Atroûs

Agjert

Zohii

Achilhet ez
Zbil

Timbédra

Dendâra

Amourj

Fassala-Néré

Niafounké

Diré

Bambara-Néré

16°

Keur Massène

Rosso
Richard Toll

Tékane

Dagana

Podor

Bogué

Bababé

Mbagne

Kaédi

Guidimaka

Monguel

Mal

M'Bout

Kankossa

EL
ACÂBA

Billaouar

Tintâne

HODH EL
GHARBI

i-n-Farba

Koumbi Saleh

Djiguéni

'Adel Bagrou

Kobenni

Touil

Léré

Diré

Doupitz

Saint-Louis

Ndiago

Ndiaye

Mpal

Dahra

Linguère

Maghama

Matam

Sivé

GORGOL

Hamoud

Yélimané

Nioro du
Sahel

Ballé

Nampala

Boré

Nara

Goumbou

Sokolo

Niono

Ké-Macina

Ténenkou

Ouro Modi

Mopti

Banguiara

MOPTI

LOUGA

Louga

Kébémer

Mbro

Mékhé

Sagata

Saint-Louis

SAINT-
LOUIS

Namari

Ranérou

Vélingara

Wompou

Sélibabi

Aourou

Tambakara

Maréna

Sandaré

Diéma

Lakamané

Mourdiah

Didiéni

Doura

Manimpé

Kolongotomo

Djénné

Bankas

DAKAR
DAKAR (YOFF)

Thiès
Diourbel

Thiès

Rufisque

Dakar

DIOURBEL

Mbacké

Diagniao

Gossas

Fatick

M'Bour

Joal

Guinguinéo

Birkelane

Touba

Koungheul

KAOLACK

Goudiry

Kidira

Kayes

Lonétou

584 m

KAYES

Bafoulabé

Toukoto

Oualia

Kolokani

Banamba

Nyamina

SÉGOU

Ségou

Katiéna

San

Tominian

SÉGOU

Nouna

Tougan

SOUR

KOSSI

Foundiougne

Kaolack

Nioro-du-
Rip

KAOLACK

Kaffrine

Koumpentoum

SENEGAL

Tambacounda

TAMBACOUNDA

Maka

Sadiola

Sébékoro

Kita

Kati

PN DE LA
BOUCLE DU
BAOLÉ

RSV
DE
FINA

RÉSERVE DE
KENIÉ-BAOULÉ

Kokofata

Nossombougou

Négala

BAMAKO

Koulikoro

Fana

Konobougou

Mpessoba

Koutiala

Yorosso

Dédougou

MOUHOUN

Siby

Boron

Bakau
Banjul
C. Saint Mary
Yundum
Brikama

GAMBIA

Kerewan

Manduar
Konko

Georgetown

Basse Santa
Su

Fatoto

Dialakoto

Médina
Gonassé

PN DU
NIOKOLO-
KOBA

Niokolo Koba

Saraya

Kéniéba

656 m

Kangaba

Narena

Bamako

BAMAKO (SENOU)

Dioila

Sanankoroba

Ouéléssébougou

Bougouni

Garalo

Kolondiéba

Faramana

Sikasso

765 m

SIKASSO

KÉNÉDOUGOU

HOUET

Bobo Dioulasso

Bamako

Koury

KOSSI

BOUGOU

Diébougou

Ziguinchor

Bignona

ZIGUINCHOR

Oussouye

Cap Roxo

Susana

Cacheu
Bissora
Mansôa
Bafatá

Teixeira Pinto
Ilha de
Jeta

Ponta de Pelindé

Ilha
Caravela

Arq. dos
Bijagos

I. Bolama
Formosa

Bubaque

I. Roxa

Iles
Tristao

Cap Verga

Nova
Lamego

Buba

Xitole

KOLDA

Sedhiou

Farim

Kolda

Vélingara

Sambailo

Koumbia

Gaoual

Koundara

Wendou Borou

Kounloun

Satadougou

Fongolanbi

Tintiba

MALI
GUINEA

Nagassola

Kouroussa

708 m

Siguiri

Kankan

Kangaré

Baro

KANKAN

Mandiana

Kouroussa

Tingréla

Kadiana

587 m

Kouto

Tiéfinzo

Mahandiana

BANFORA

Banfora

Sindou

Orodara

Sidéradougou

COMOÉ

Niangoloko

Gaoua

POTI

GUINEA-
BISSAU

BISSAU

BISSAU (BIPONT)

Fulacunda

Catió

Dabissé
Kayati

Sansalé

Boké

Victoria

Boffa

BOKÉ

Bintimodou

Tounyiré

Télimélé

Fria

Tondon

Linsan

Mali

Dalaba

Pita

Labé

LABÉ

1,245 m

Mamou

Tangali

Dinguiraye

Kalinko

Selouma

Dabola

Koninuou

Siguiri

Norassouba

Balan

Faranah

708 m

Kouroussa

Banian

Komodougou

Odienné

Tiéme

Samatiguila

Tienigbé

Boundiali

IVORY COAST

Ferkéssédougou

Korhogo

PARC NATIONAL

DE LA

COMOÉ

Kong

Nassian

Conakry

CONAKRY

Cité de
Kassa

Forécariah

Coyah

Benti

Pointe Sallatouk

Dubréka

Tatéma

Kindia

KINDIA

Friguiagbé

Moussayah

Fadugu

Kamakwie

Kolenté

Sougéta

Kaba

Faranah

1,119 m

GUINEA

SIERRA
LEONE

Kabala

Falaba

Banian

Sangardo

Kissidougou

1,346 m

Yende Milimou

Pic de Tibé
1,504 m

1,439 m

Koundougou

Macenta

Beyla

1,656 m

Nzérékoré

Touba

1257 m

PN DU
MONT
SANGBE

Biankouma

Séguéla

Vavoua

Daloa

CÔTE D'IVOIRE

(IVORY COAST)

Bouaké

Béoumi

Katiola

Basawa

Bondo

4

Conakry

Freetown

LUNGI INT'L

NORTHERN

Bumbuna

Makeni

Port Loko

Binkolo

Marampa

Sankanbiriwa
1,853 m

Koidu

Fangamandou

Koyama

Nionsamoridougou

Gbékédou

Boola

Koyama

Kahnple

Lola

Danané

Man

Mt. Nimba
1,752 m

Mont Tonkoui
1,189 m

Duékoué

Sinfra

Gagnoa

Bocanda

Agnibilékrou

Daoukro

Dimbokro

Bongouanou

Akoupé

Abengourou

8°

C. Sierra Leone

Freetown

WESTERN
AREA

Banana Is.

Rotifunk

Moyamba

Songo

Bo

Yonibana

Taiama

Bauya

EASTERN

Pujehun

Pendembu

Kailahun

Mount Wuteve
1,381 m

Zelima

Zorzor

Yomou

Zienzu

Saniquelie

Yekepa

Ganta

Kahnple

PN DU
MONT
PÉKO

Zuénola

Gbanga

PN DE LA
MARAOUE

623 m

Konahouan

BARRAGE DE KOSSOU

Yamoussoukro

Bouaflé

Tiassalé

Toumodi

Divo

Lakota

Issia

Oumé

Tanda

Bondoukou

Shenge Pt.

Turtle
Is.

C. Saint Ann

Sherbro
Island

SOUTHERN

Sumbuya

Gbangbatok

Bonthe

Bendumbu

GRAND
CAPE
MOUNT

645 m

Tubmanburg

Robertsport

Bomi

Brewerville

C. Mesurado

Monrovia

Edina

Marshall

MONROVIA (ROBERTS INT'L)

Buchanan

GRAND
BASSA

Belle Yella

Bopolu

Gbarnga

NIMBA

BONG

Tapeta

Toulépleu

Guiglo

LIBERIA

Dolobli

Tai

PN
DE
TAI

Zwedru

Zia Town

CHUTES
NAOUA

IVORY
COAST

Mont Niénokoué
396 m

RAPIDES BIDAGA

BARRAGE DE BUYO

Soubré

Gagnoa

Guitri

Sassandra

PN

D'ASSAGNY

Grand-Lahou

Abidjan

ABIDJAN (PORT BOUET)

Port-Bouët

Grand-
Bassam

BARRAGE D'AYAMÉ I
BARRAGE D'AYAMÉ II

Aboisso

5

ATLANTIC

OCEAN

River Cess

Juazohn

SINO

Dodwekro

GRAND
JIDE

Kahnwia

Mont Kope 424 m

Pibo

Djiroutou

Grain

Coast

Bafu

Greenville

Grand
Cess

Sasstown

MARYLAND

Tabou

C. Palmas

Harper

Basa

San Pédro

Fresco

Ivory

Coast

Coast

Abidjan

Half

© Copyright by HAMMOND INCORPORATED, Maplewood, N.J.   CC-1068-A

A 16°   B   12° Longitude West of Greenwich   C

SCALE 1:7,000,000   POLYCONIC PROJECTION
MILES   0   100   200   300
KILOMETERS   0   100   200   300

West Africa

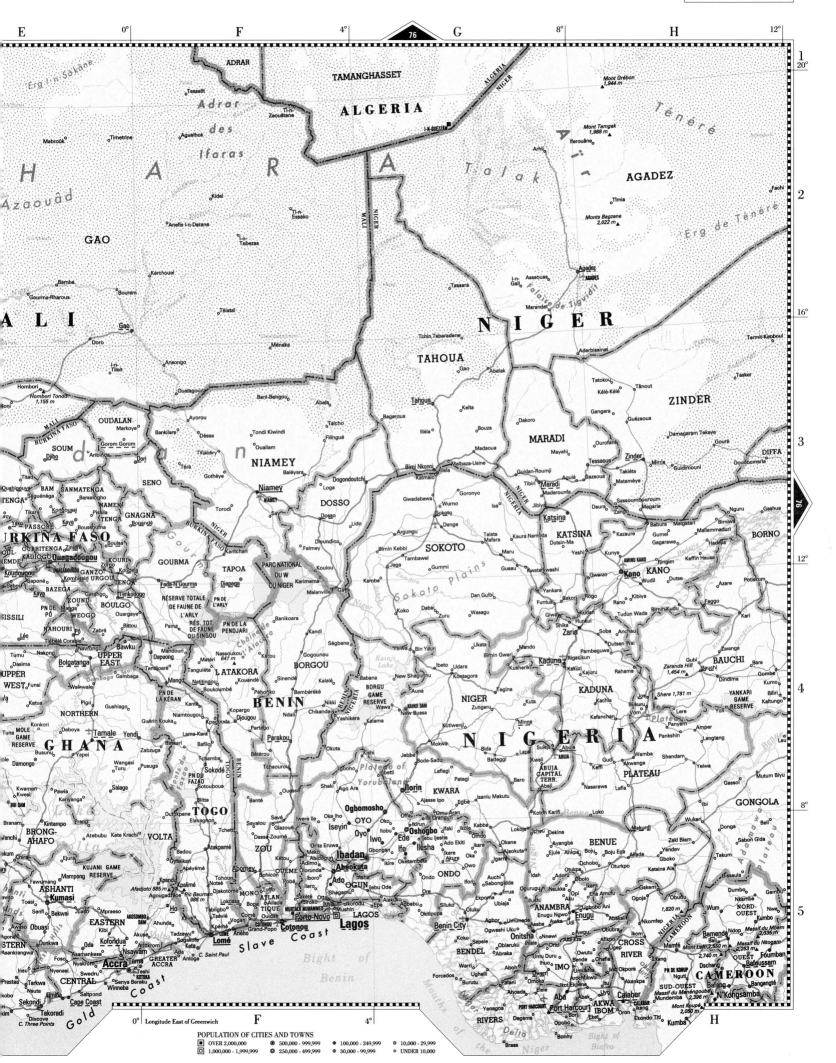

POPULATION OF CITIES AND TOWNS

| ■ OVER 2,000,000 | ● 500,000 - 999,999 | ○ 100,000 - 249,999 | ○ 10,000 - 29,999 |
| □ 1,000,000 - 1,999,999 | ● 250,000 - 499,999 | ○ 30,000 - 99,999 | ○ UNDER 10,000 |

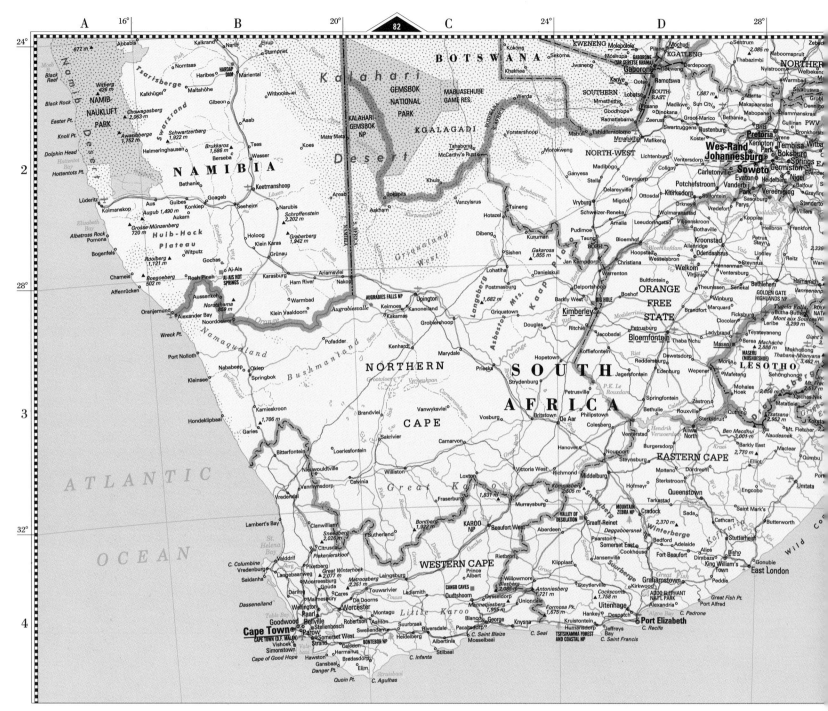

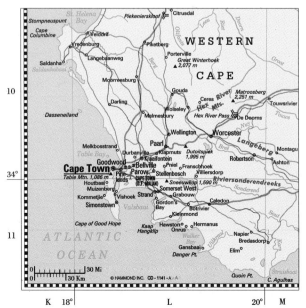

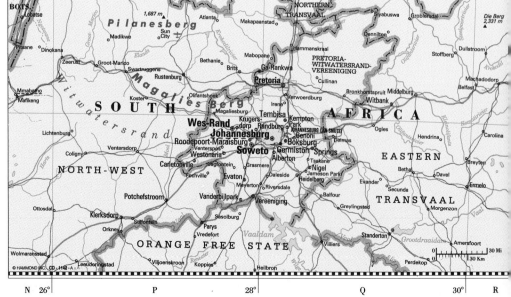

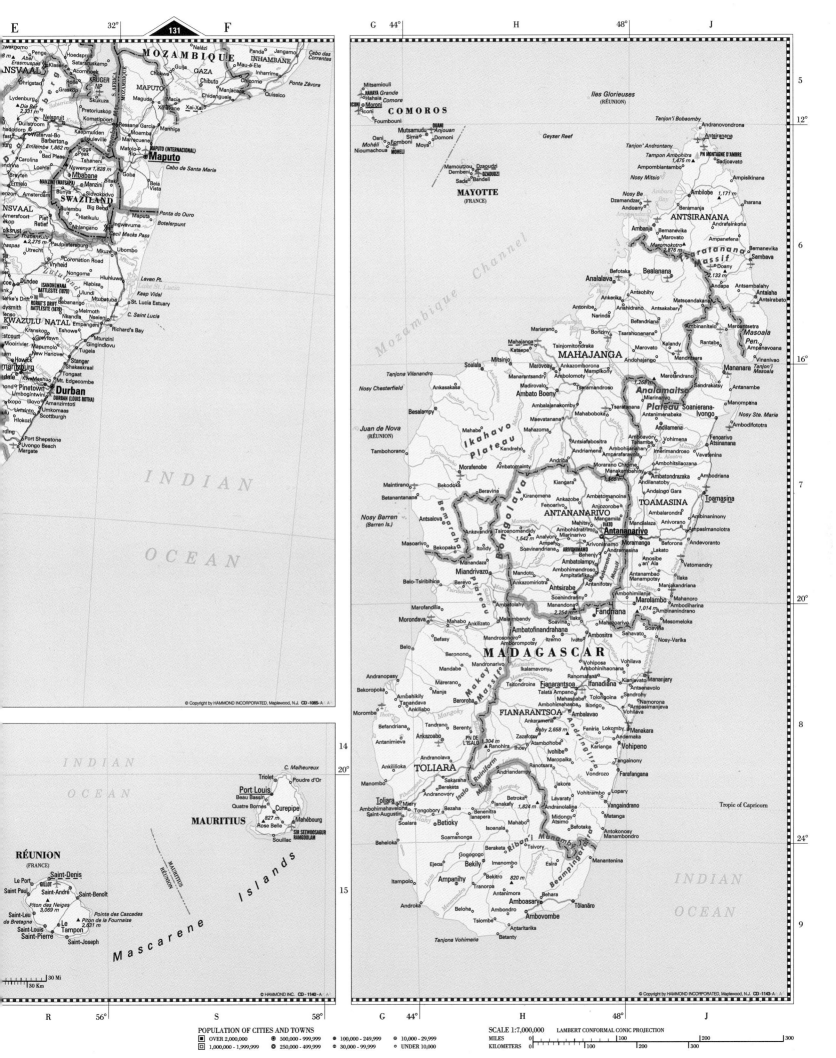

Southern Africa

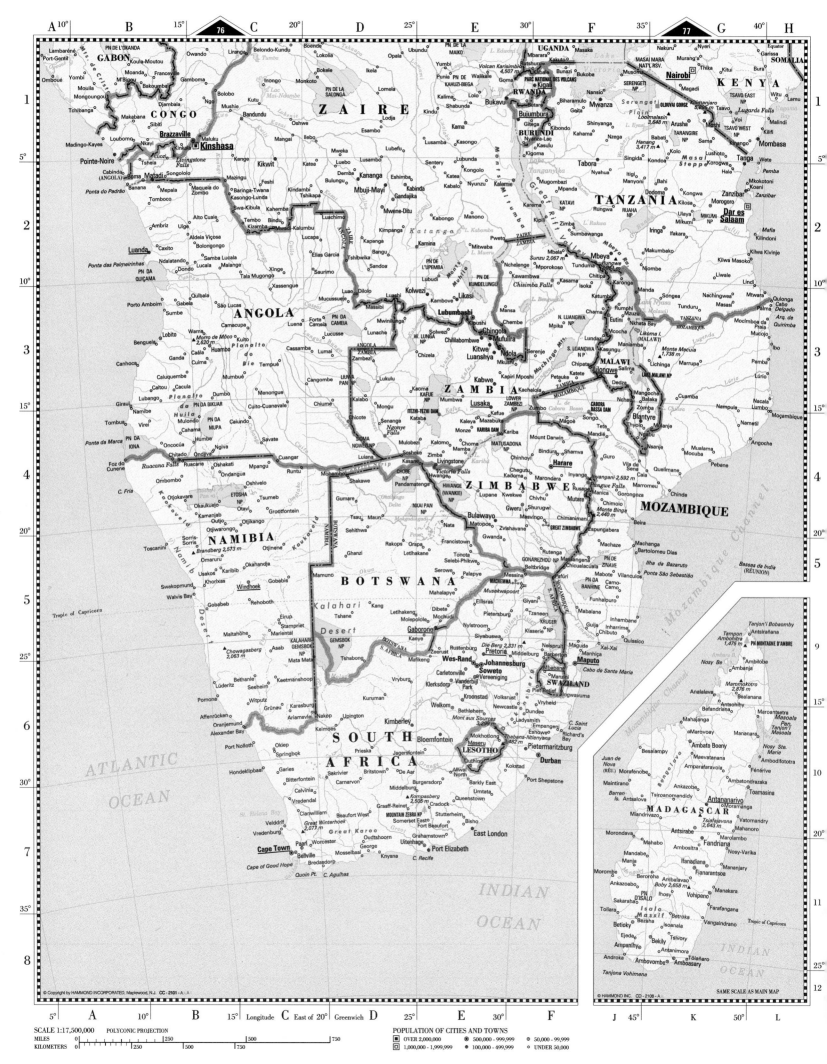

GABON
PN DE L'OKANDA
Lambaréné
Port-Gentil
Omboué
Yombi
Mouila
Mongoungou
Tchibanga
Madingo-Kayes
Pointe-Noire
Cabinda (ANGOLA)
Boma
Matadi

CONGO
Koula-Moutou
M'Bigou
Bakoumba
Moanda
Franceville
Makabana
Loubomo
Nkayi
Tsuozi
Tshela

Brazzaville
Kinshasa
Maluku
Kinkala
Songololo

Owando
Liranga
Belondo-Kundu
Bolobo
Mushie
Bandundu
Kutu
Kikwit
Feshi

ZAIRE
Boende
Lokolia
Ikela
Lodja
Esambo
Kananga
Mbuji-Mayi
Tshikapa

Ubundu
Opala
Yumbi
Punia
Kindu
Kama
Kasongo
Lubefu

PN DE LA MAIKO
Walikale
Goma
Bukavu

RWANDA
Kigali
BURUNDI
Bujumbura
Gitega

Mbarara
Kabale
Kakuto
Bunazi

UGANDA
Masaka
Nakuru
Murang'a
Nyeri
Garissa

KENYA
Nairobi
Thika
Kitui

SOMALIA

TANZANIA
Dar es Salaam

ANGOLA
Luanda
Benguela
Lobito
Lubango
Namibe

ZAMBIA
Lusaka
Lubumbashi
Kitwe
Ndola

MALAWI
Lilongwe
Blantyre
LAKE MALAWI NP

MOZAMBIQUE
Beira

NAMIBIA
Windhoek
Walvis Bay
Swakopmund
Lüderitz

BOTSWANA
Gaborone
Francistown

ZIMBABWE
Harare
Bulawayo
GREAT ZIMBABWE

SOUTH AFRICA
Pretoria
Johannesburg
Soweto
Bloemfontein
Cape Town
Durban
Port Elizabeth
East London

LESOTHO
Maseru

SWAZILAND
Mbabane
Manzini
Maputo

ATLANTIC OCEAN
INDIAN OCEAN
Tropic of Capricorn

MADAGASCAR
Antananarivo
Toamasina
Mahajanga
Fianarantsoa
Toliara

SCALE 1:17,500,000
POLYCONIC PROJECTION
MILES 0   250   500   750
KILOMETERS 0   250   500   750

POPULATION OF CITIES AND TOWNS
■ OVER 2,000,000
▣ 1,000,000 - 1,999,999
● 500,000 - 999,999
◉ 100,000 - 499,999
● 50,000 - 99,999
○ UNDER 50,000

© Copyright by HAMMOND INCORPORATED, Maplewood, N.J. CC-2101-A A
© HAMMOND INC. CD-2108-A
SAME SCALE AS MAIN MAP

Antarctica

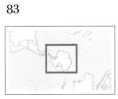

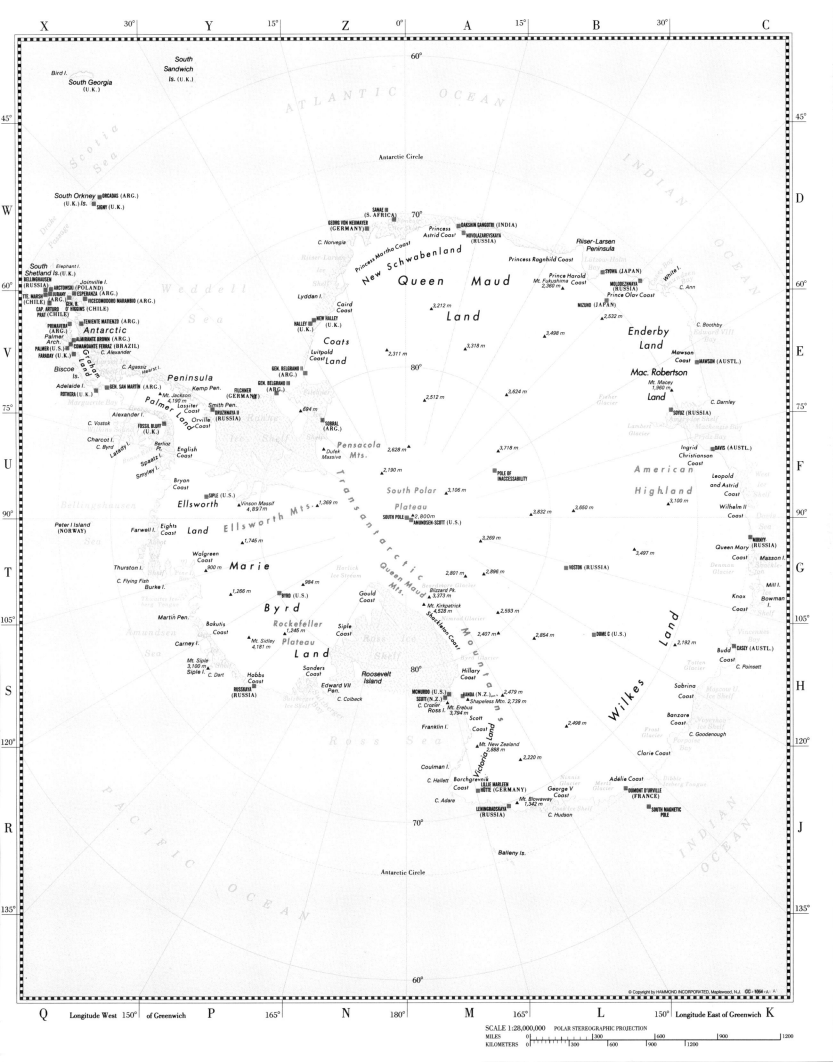

SCALE 1:28,000,000   POLAR STEREOGRAPHIC PROJECTION

© Copyright by HAMMOND INCORPORATED, Maplewood, N.J.   GC-1064·A·A'

North America

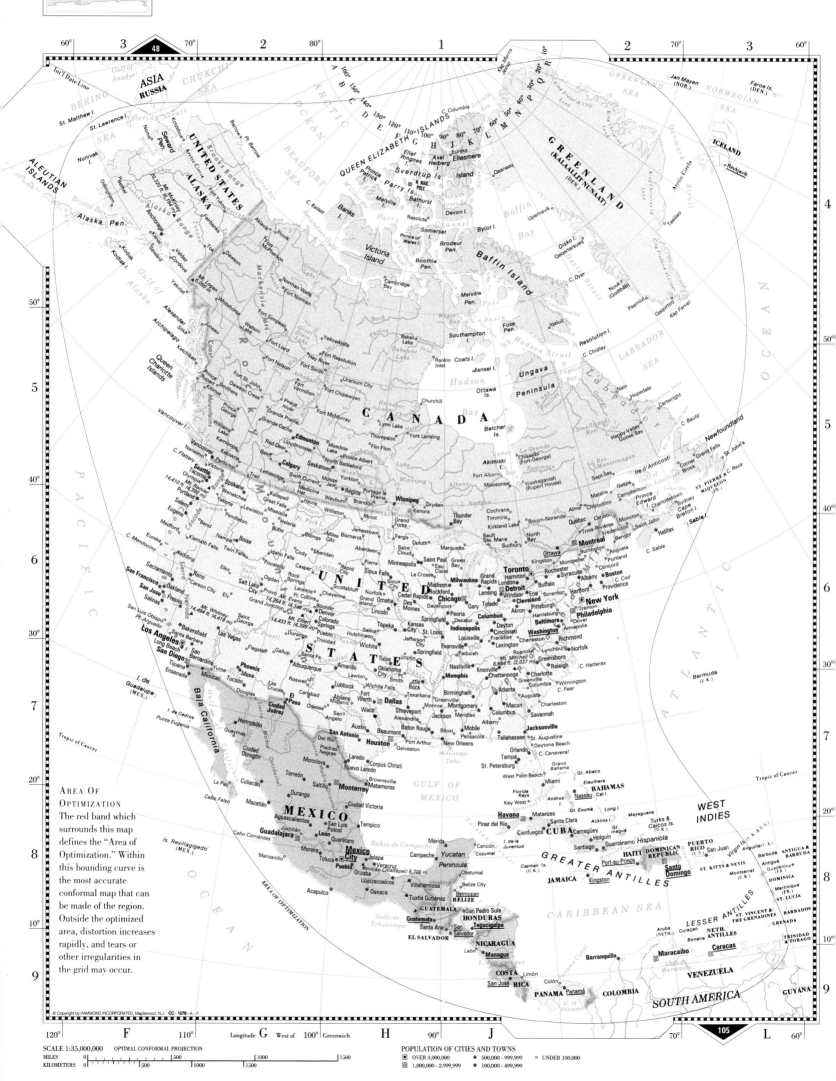

AREA OF
OPTIMIZATION
The red band which
surrounds this map
defines the "Area of
Optimization." Within
this bounding curve is
the most accurate
conformal map that can
be made of the region.
Outside the optimized
area, distortion increases
rapidly, and tears or
other irregularities in
the grid may occur.

© Copyright by HAMMOND INCORPORATED, Maplewood, N.J.   CC · 1076 · A · A

SCALE 1:35,000,000   OPTIMAL CONFORMAL PROJECTION
MILES 0   500   1000   1500
KILOMETERS 0   500   1000   1500

POPULATION OF CITIES AND TOWNS
◼ OVER 3,000,000   ● 500,000 - 999,999   ○ UNDER 100,000
▣ 1,000,000 - 2,999,999   ● 100,000 - 499,999

Alaska

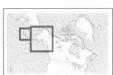

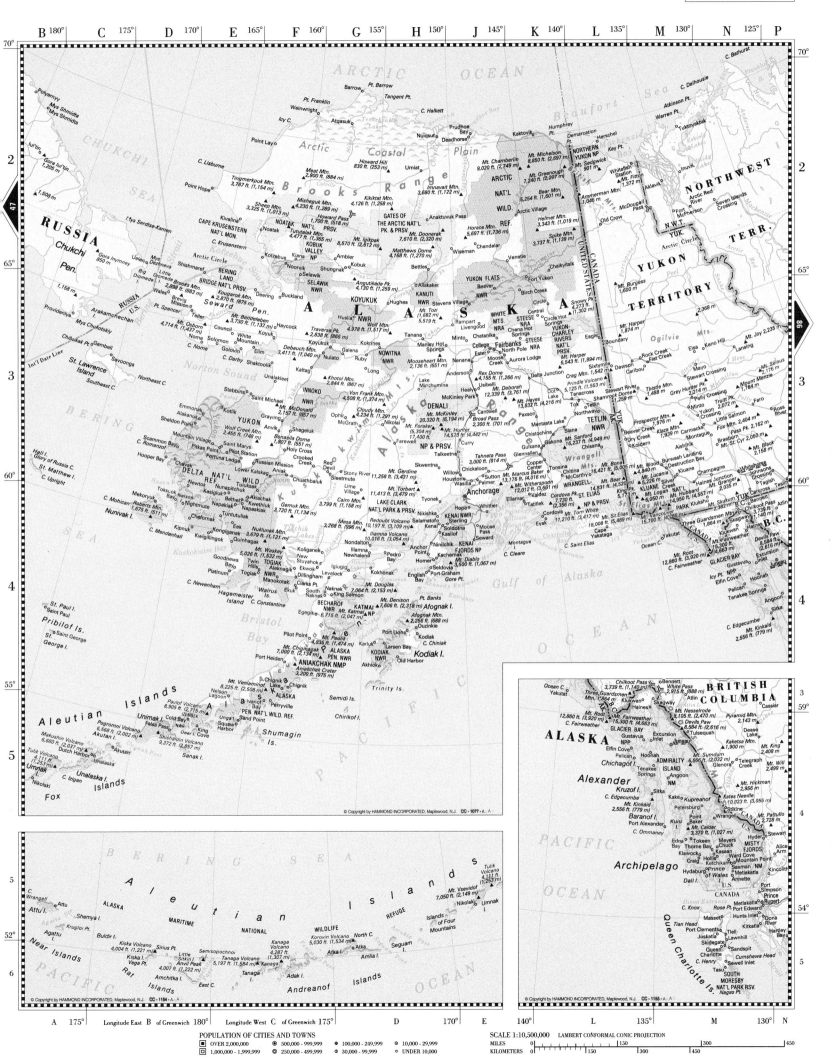

POPULATION OF CITIES AND TOWNS

■ OVER 2,000,000	◉ 500,000 - 999,999	● 100,000 - 249,999	○ 10,000 - 29,999
□ 1,000,000 - 1,999,999	◉ 250,000 - 499,999	● 30,000 - 99,999	○ UNDER 10,000

SCALE 1:10,500,000   LAMBERT CONFORMAL CONIC PROJECTION

MILES   0   150   300   450

KILOMETERS   0   150   300   450

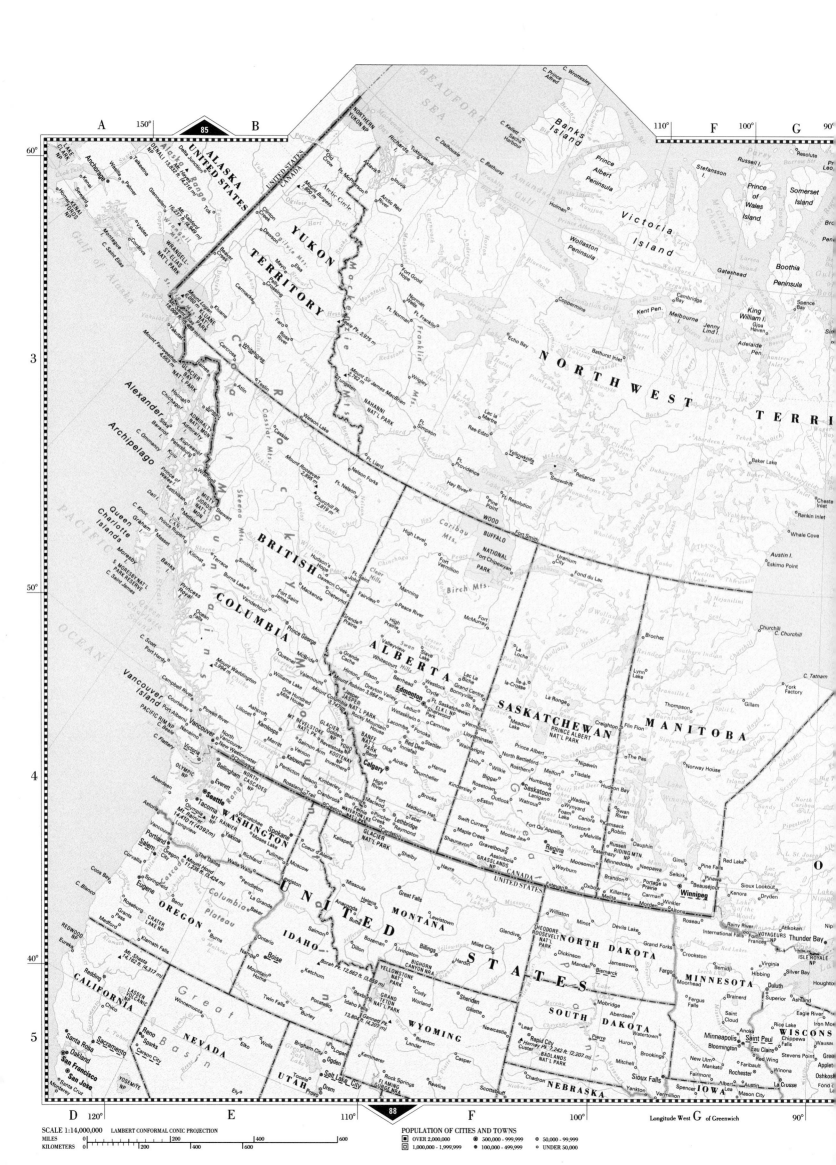

Canada

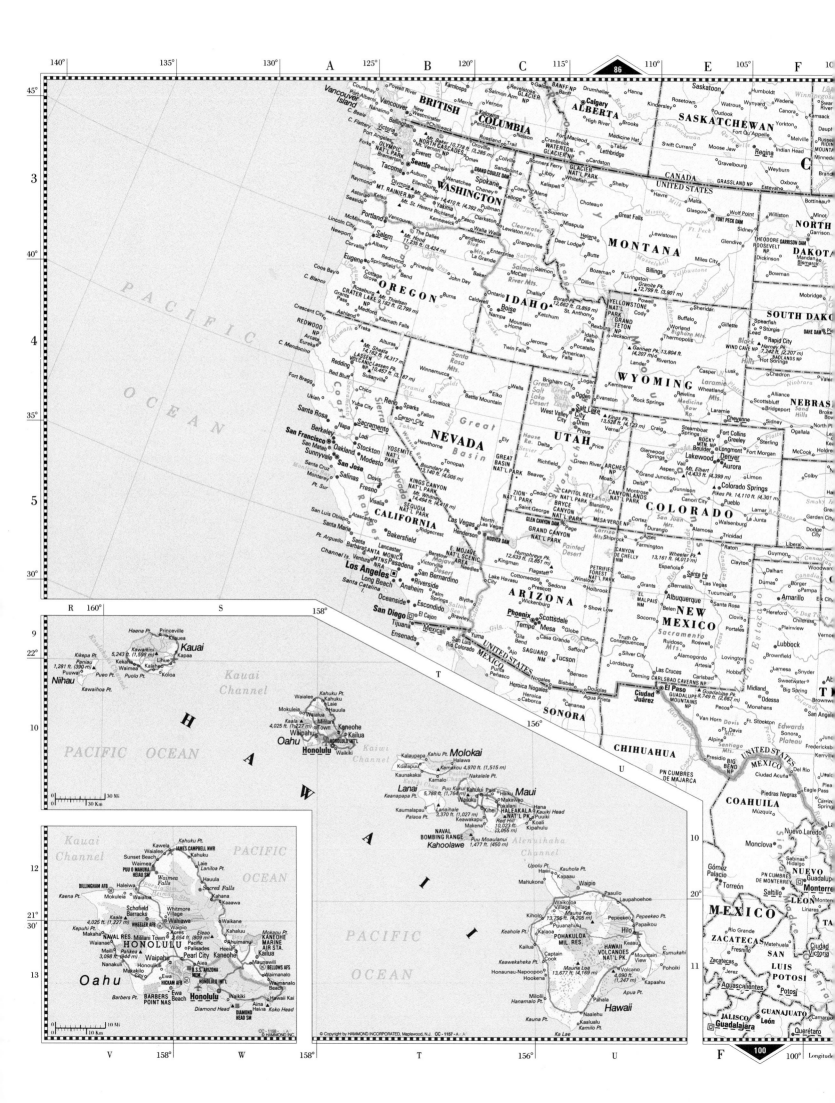

© Copyright by HAMMOND INCORPORATED, Maplewood, N.J. CC - 1157 - A

United States

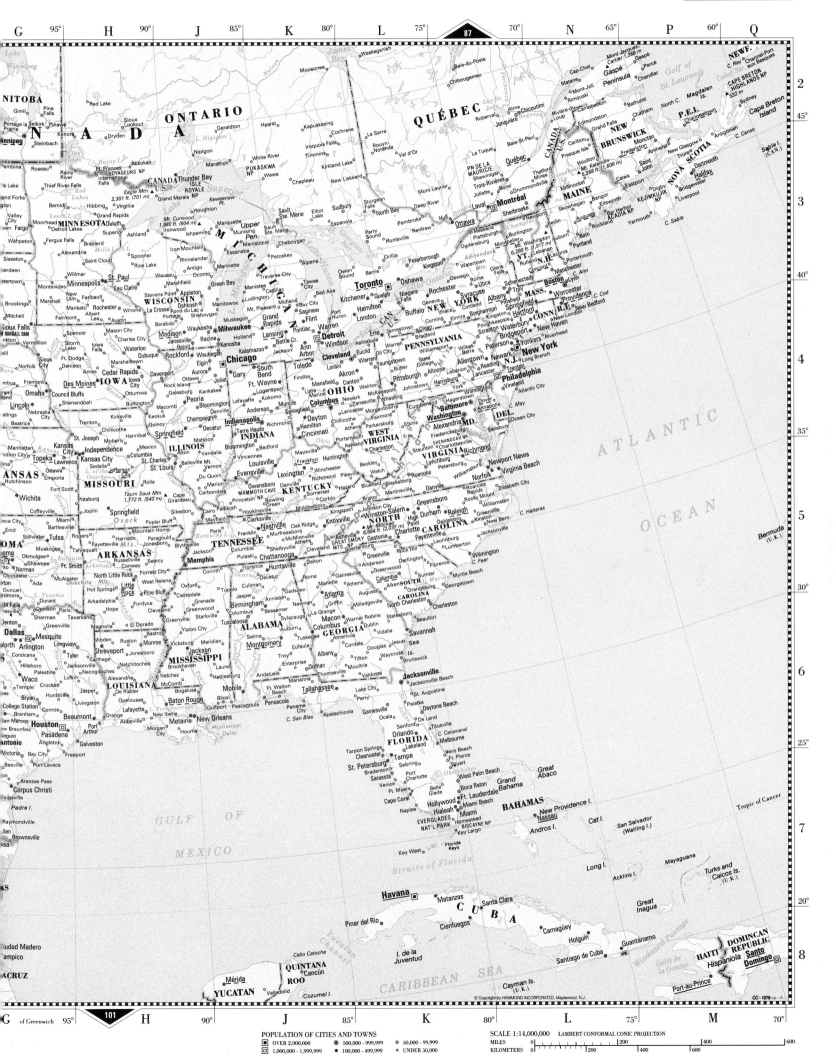

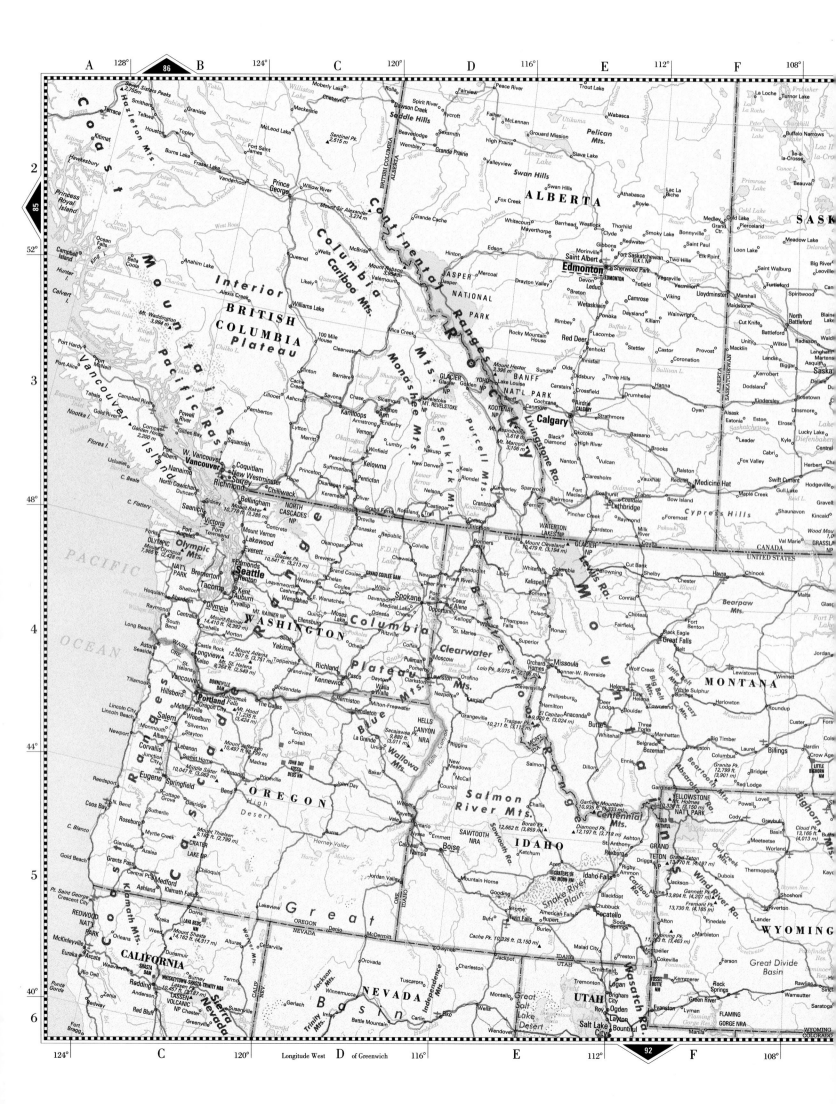

Southwestern Canada, Northwestern United States

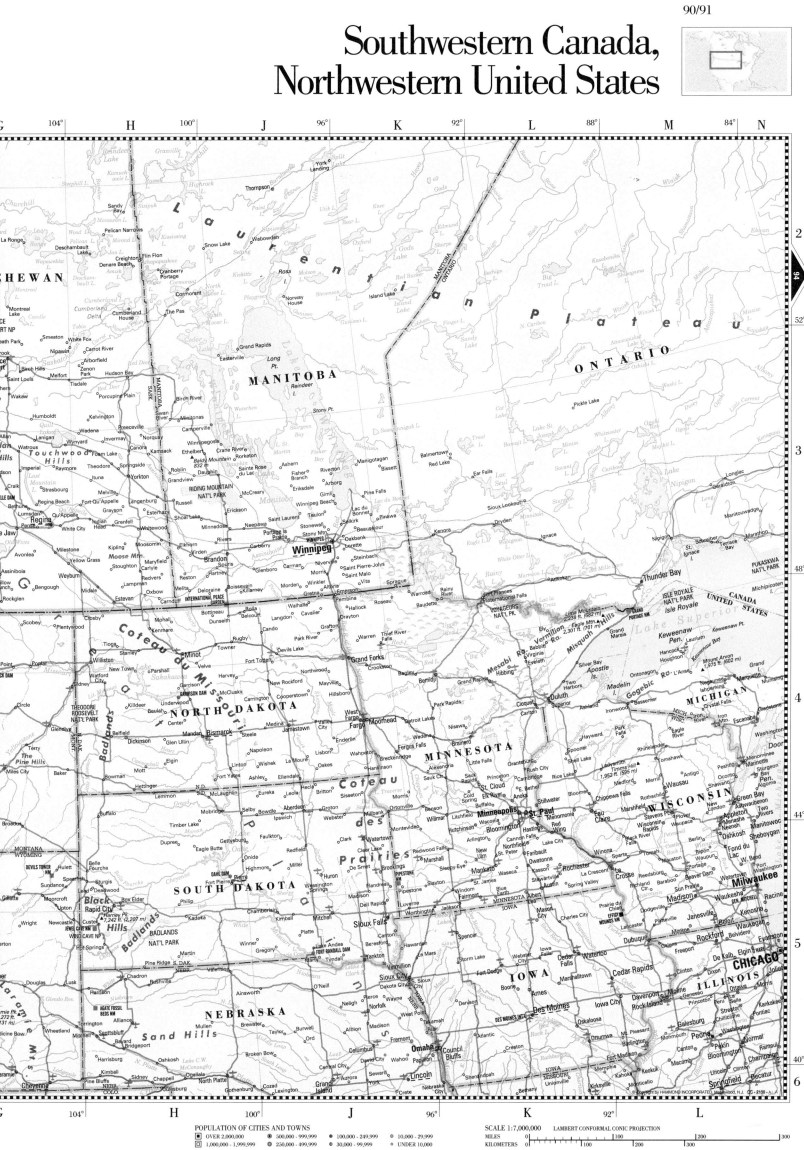

POPULATION OF CITIES AND TOWNS

■ OVER 2,000,000   ● 500,000 - 999,999   ● 100,000 - 249,999   ○ 10,000 - 29,999

□ 1,000,000 - 1,999,999   ● 250,000 - 499,999   ● 30,000 - 99,999   ○ UNDER 10,000

SCALE 1:7,000,000   LAMBERT CONFORMAL CONIC PROJECTION

MILES 0   100   200   300

KILOMETERS 0   100   200   300

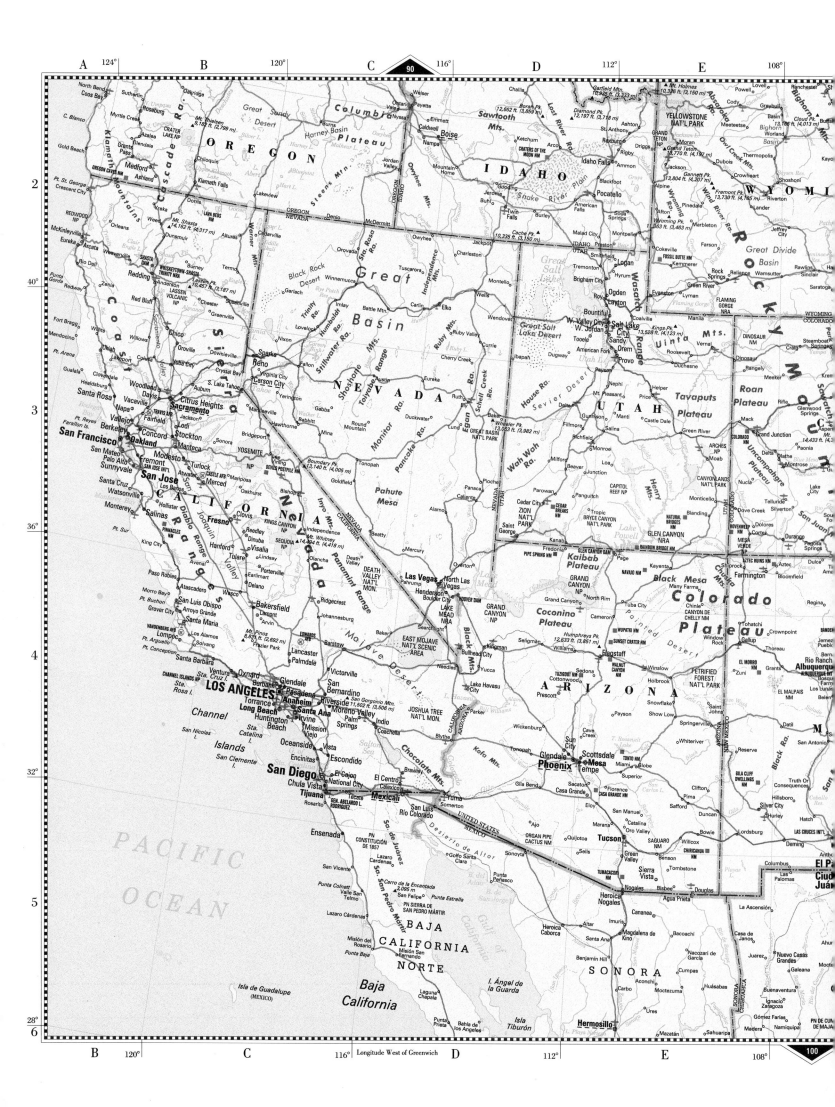

Southwestern United States

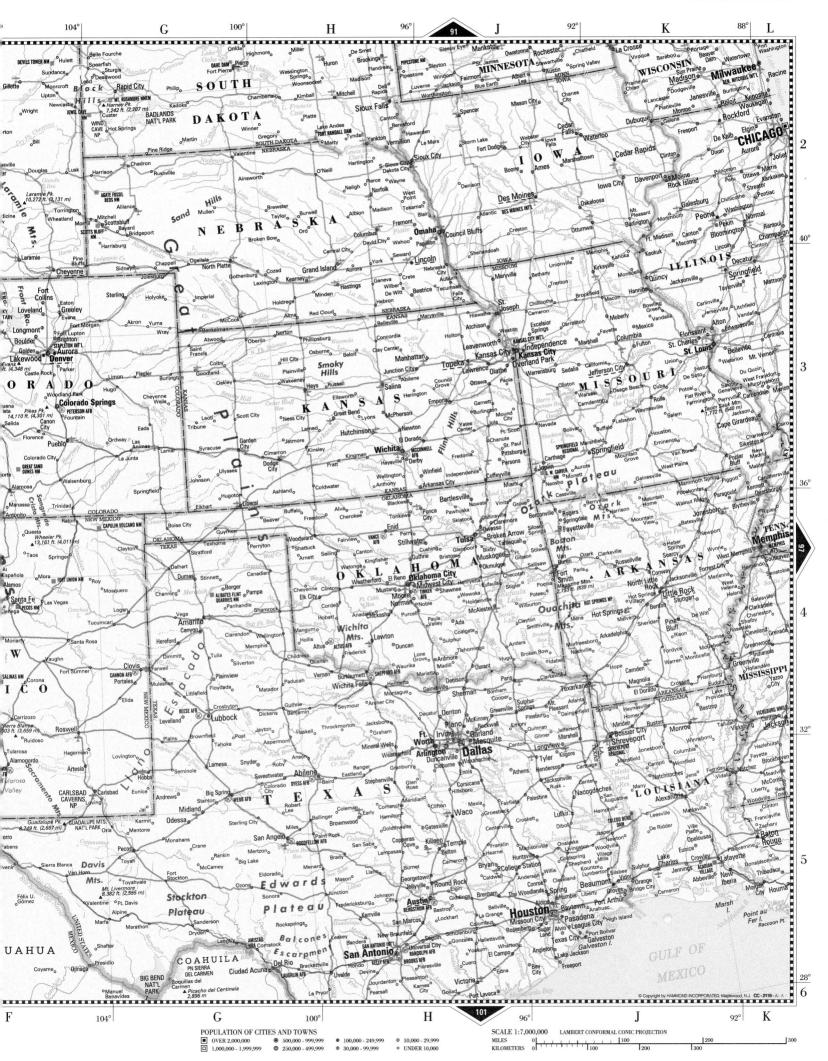

POPULATION OF CITIES AND TOWNS

■ OVER 2,000,000   ⬛ 500,000 - 999,999   ● 100,000 - 249,999   ○ 10,000 - 29,999

⬚ 1,000,000 - 1,999,999   ● 250,000 - 499,999   ● 30,000 - 99,999   ○ UNDER 10,000

SCALE 1:7,000,000   LAMBERT CONFORMAL CONIC PROJECTION

MILES 0 ___ 100 ___ 200 ___ 300

KILOMETERS 0 ___ 100 ___ 200 ___ 300

© Copyright by HAMMOND INCORPORATED, Maplewood, N.J.   CC-2110-A : A

Southeastern Canada,
Northeastern United States

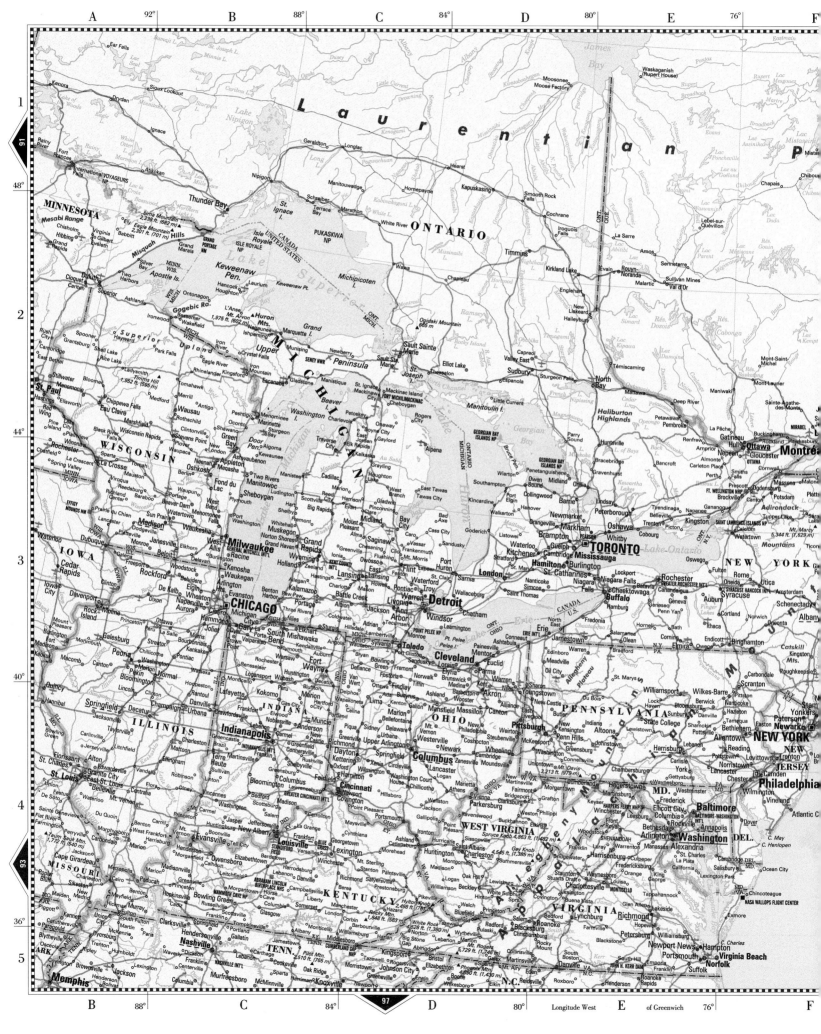

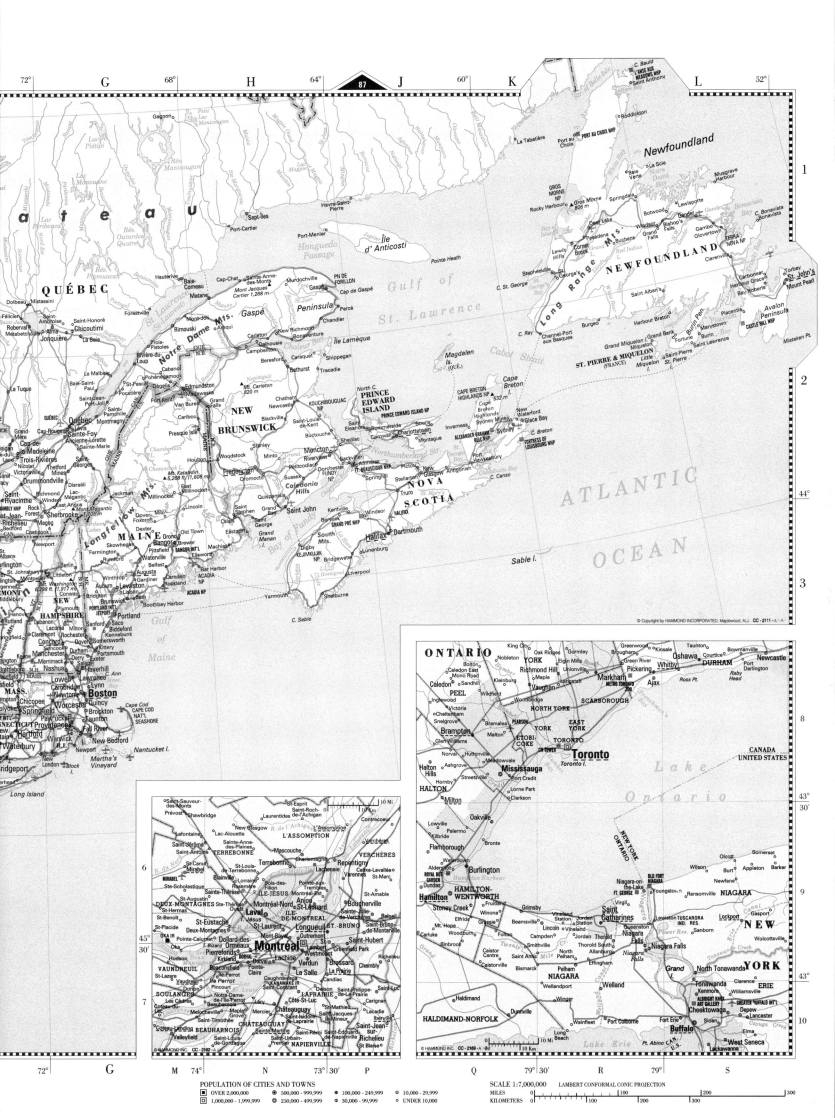

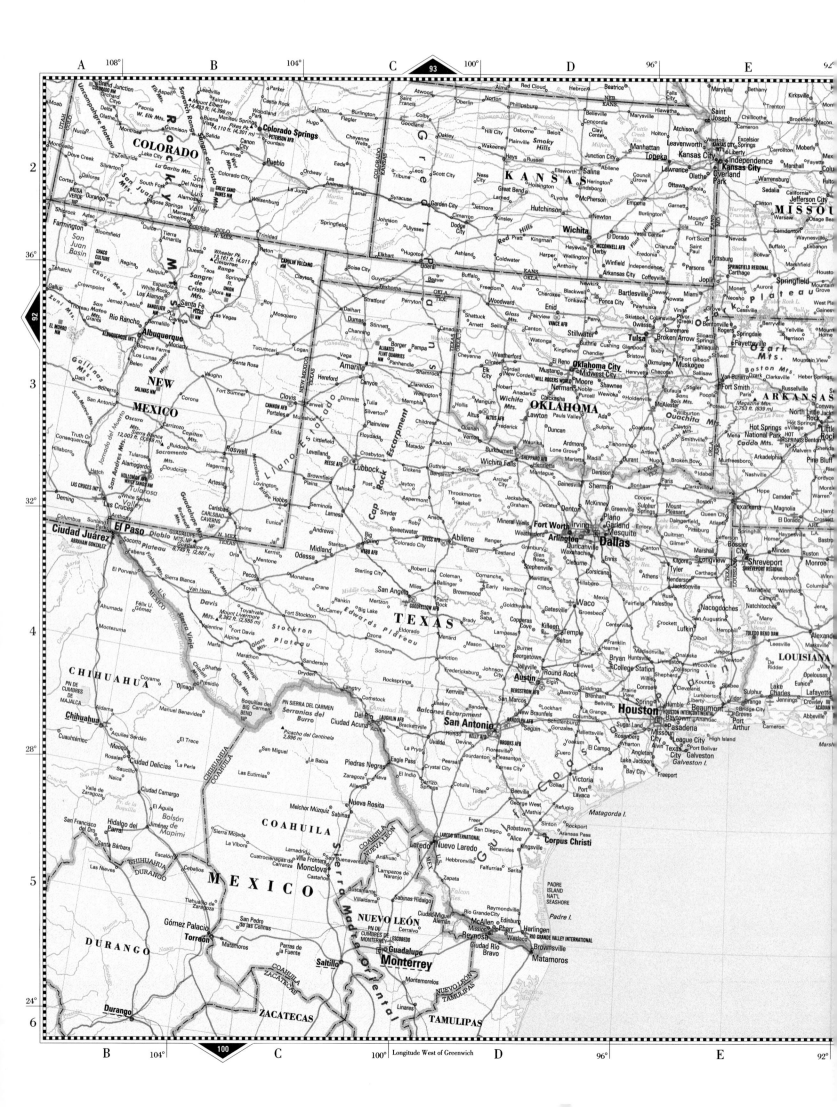

Southeastern United States

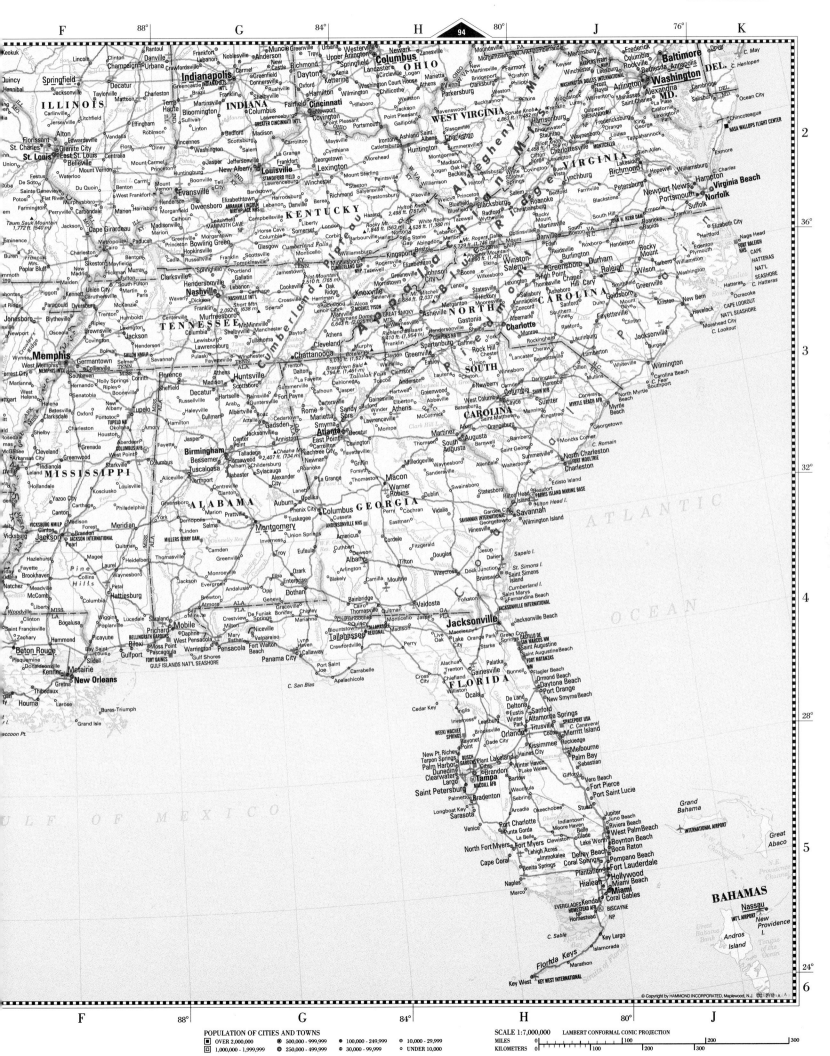

POPULATION OF CITIES AND TOWNS

■ OVER 2,000,000	● 500,000 - 999,999	● 100,000 - 249,999	○ 10,000 - 29,999
□ 1,000,000 - 1,999,999	● 250,000 - 499,999	○ 30,000 - 99,999	○ UNDER 10,000

SCALE 1:7,000,000   LAMBERT CONFORMAL CONIC PROJECTION

MILES 0   100   200   300
KILOMETERS 0   100   200   300

Los Angeles, New York, Philadelphia, Washington

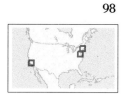

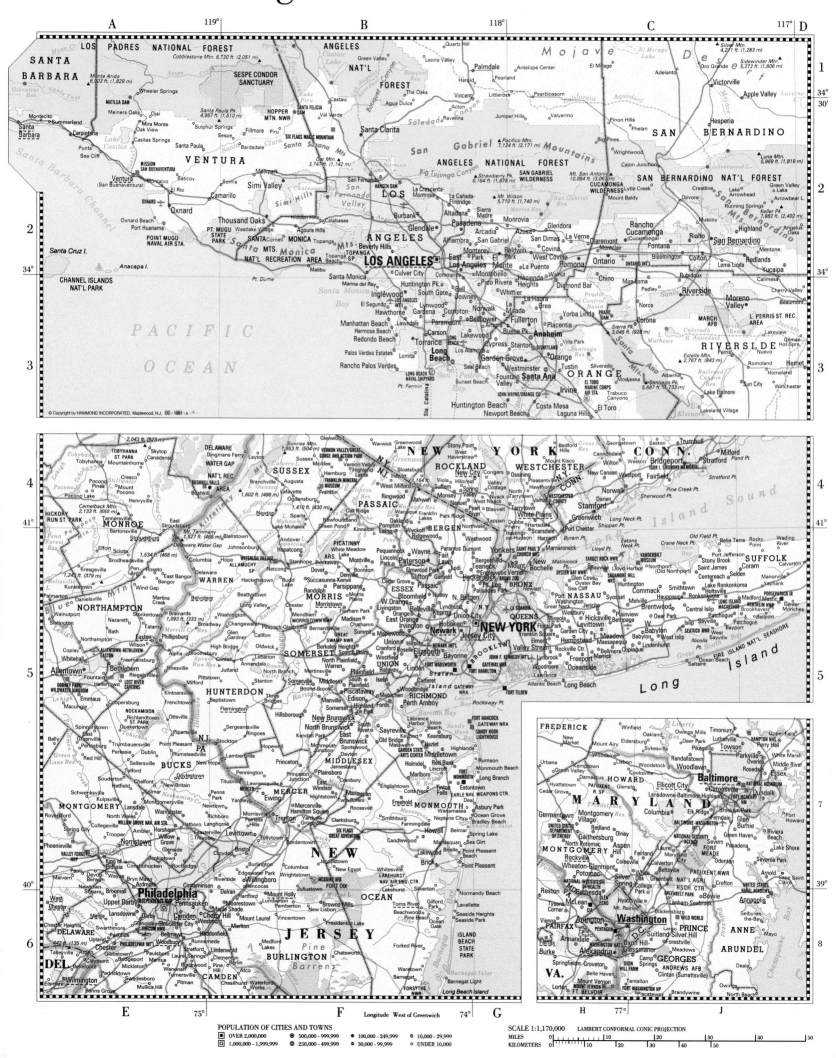

Seattle, San Francisco, Detroit, Chicago

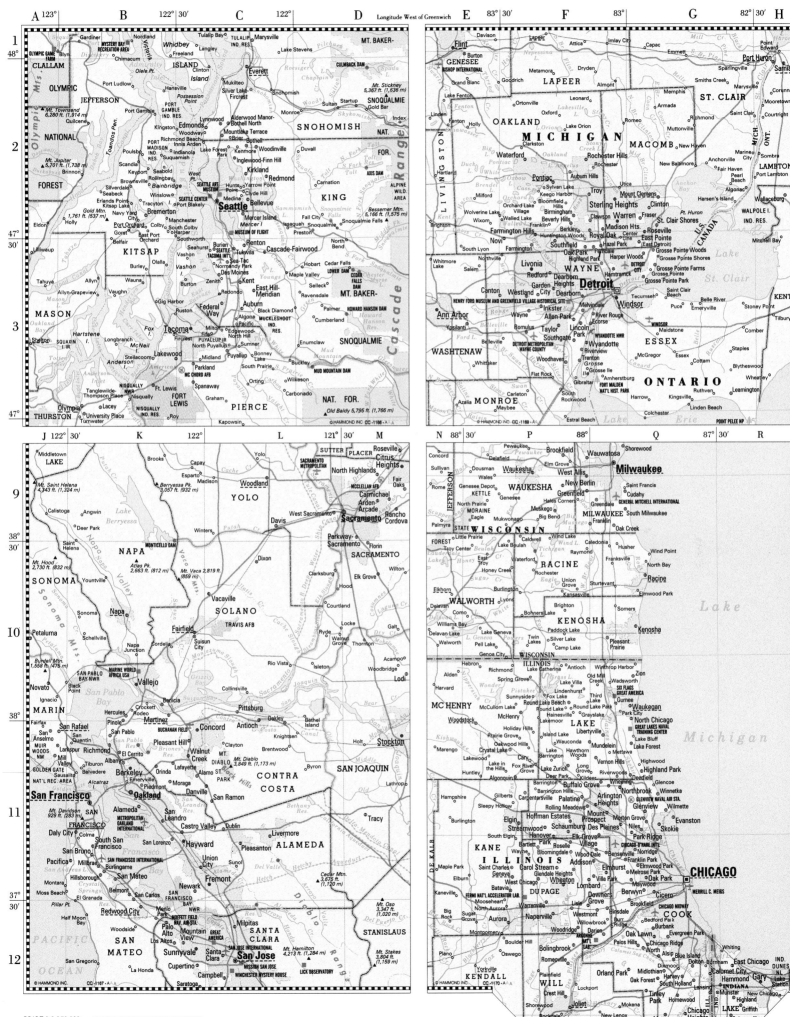

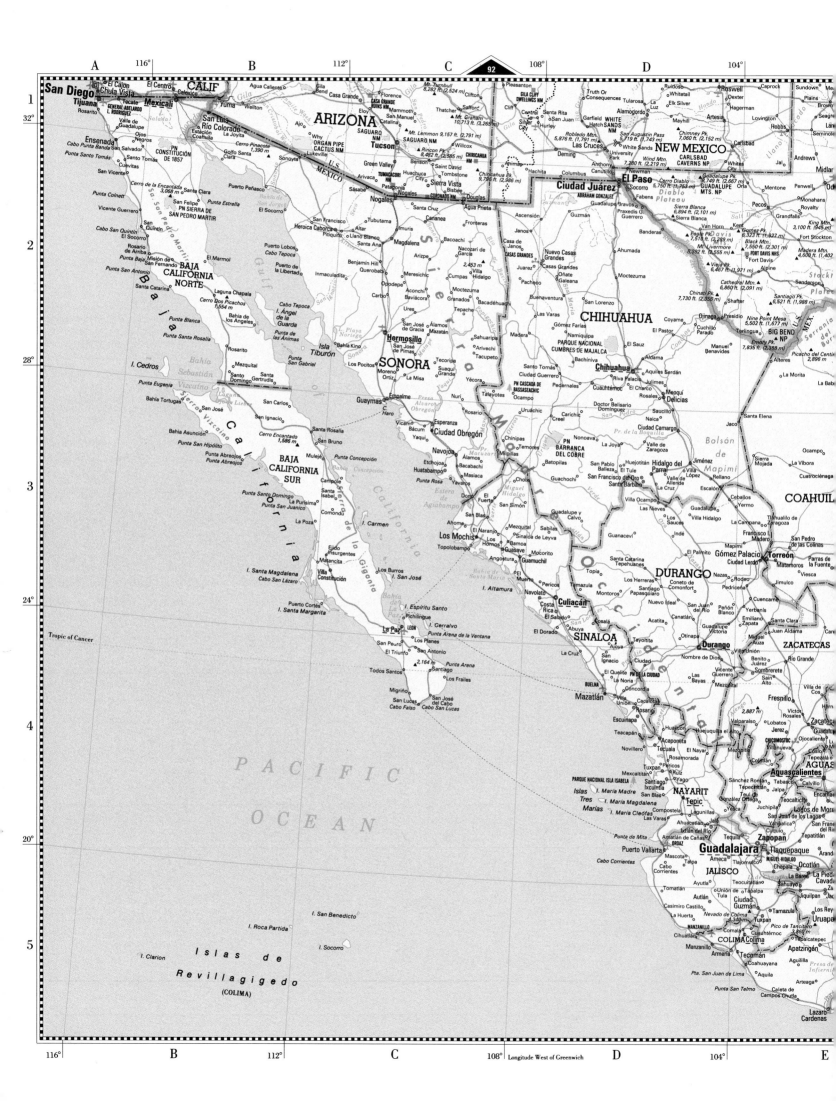

Northern and Central Mexico

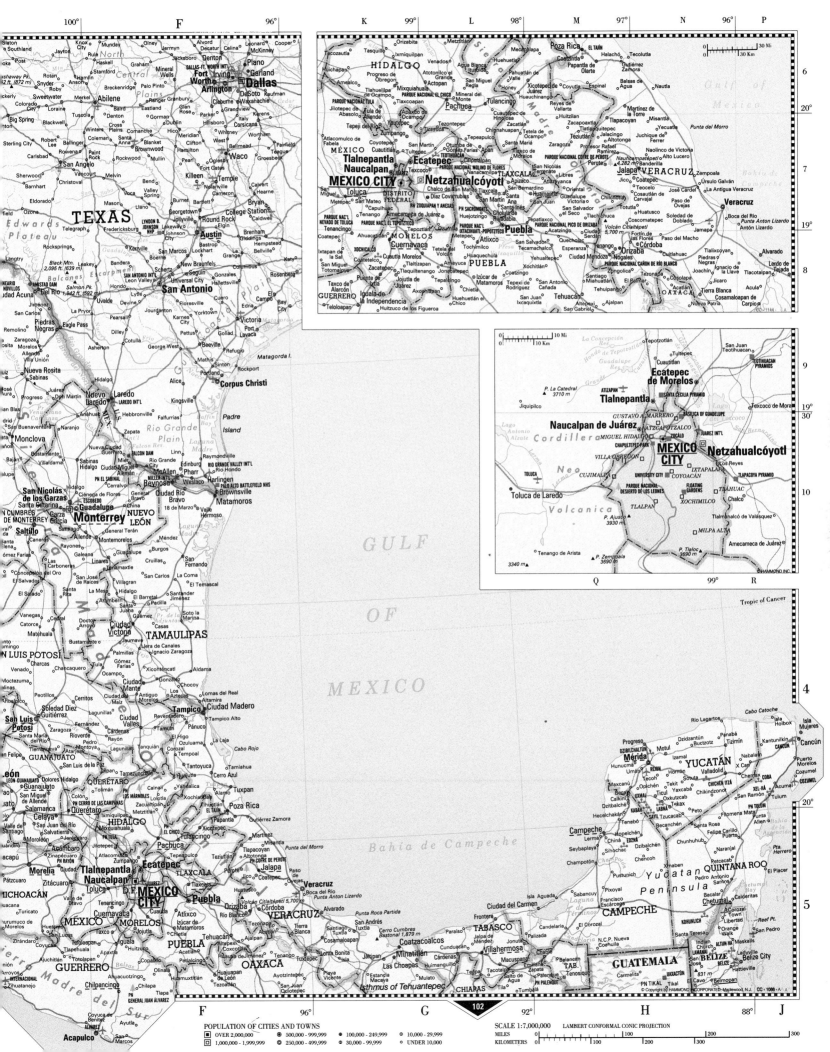

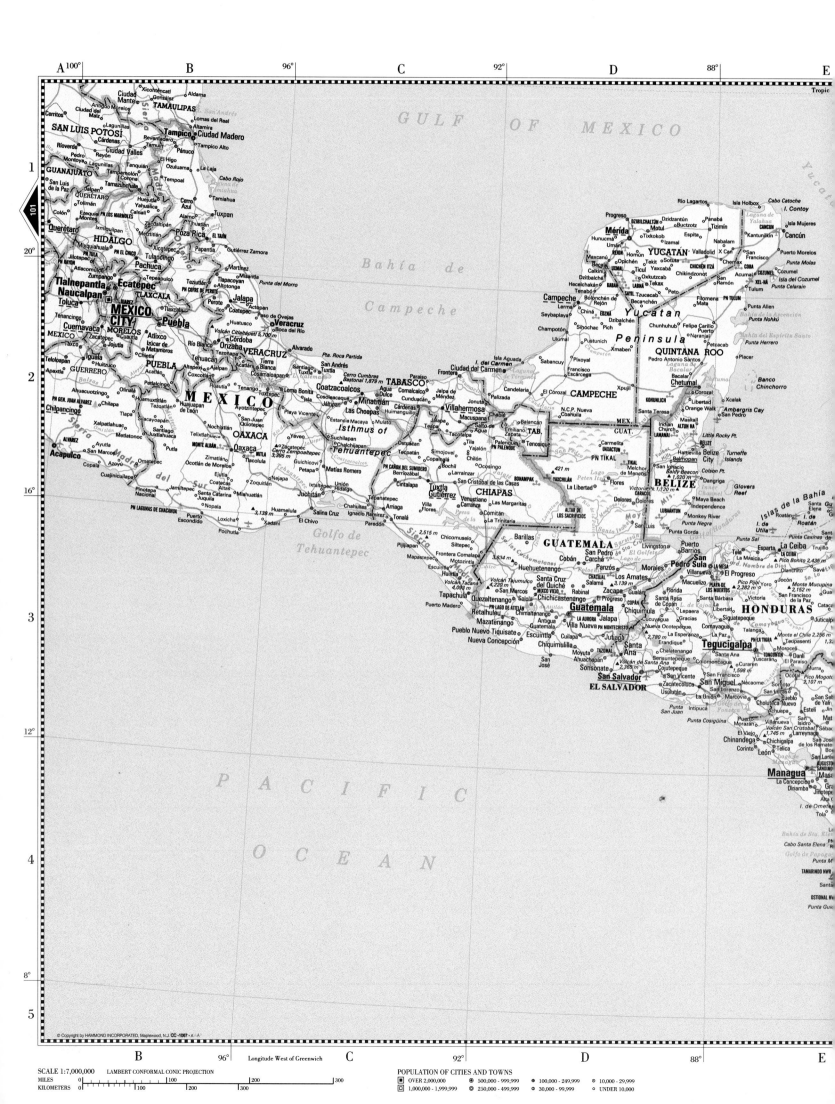

GULF OF MEXICO

Bahía de Campeche

PACIFIC OCEAN

A 100° B 96° C 92° D 88° E

TAMAULIPAS

SAN LUIS POTOSÍ

GUANAJUATO

QUERÉTARO

HIDALGO

Pachuca

Tlalnepantla Ecatepec
Naucalpan
Toluca TLAXCALA
MEXICO CITY Puebla
Cuernavaca MORELOS
MEXICO PUEBLA

Veracruz
VERACRUZ

GUERRERO

Acapulco

OAXACA
Oaxaca
MONTE ALBÁN

Tampico Ciudad Madero

Coatzacoalcos
Minatitlán
TABASCO
Villahermosa

Isthmus of Tehuantepec

CHIAPAS
Tuxtla Gutiérrez

Golfo de Tehuantepec

Ciudad del Carmen

CAMPECHE
Campeche

Mérida
YUCATAN
CHICHEN ITZÁ

Yucatan Peninsula

QUINTANA ROO

Cancún

Chetumal

Tapachula

BELIZE
Belize City

GUATEMALA
Guatemala

Quezaltenango

El Salvador
San Salvador
EL SALVADOR

San Pedro Sula

HONDURAS

Tegucigalpa

Managua

SCALE 1:7,000,000   LAMBERT CONFORMAL CONIC PROJECTION

MILES 0   100   200   300
KILOMETERS 0   100   200   300

POPULATION OF CITIES AND TOWNS

■ OVER 2,000,000   ◉ 500,000 - 999,999   ● 100,000 - 249,999   ○ 10,000 - 29,999
▣ 1,000,000 - 1,999,999   ◉ 250,000 - 499,999   ○ 30,000 - 99,999   · UNDER 10,000

101

Southern Mexico, Central America, Western Caribbean

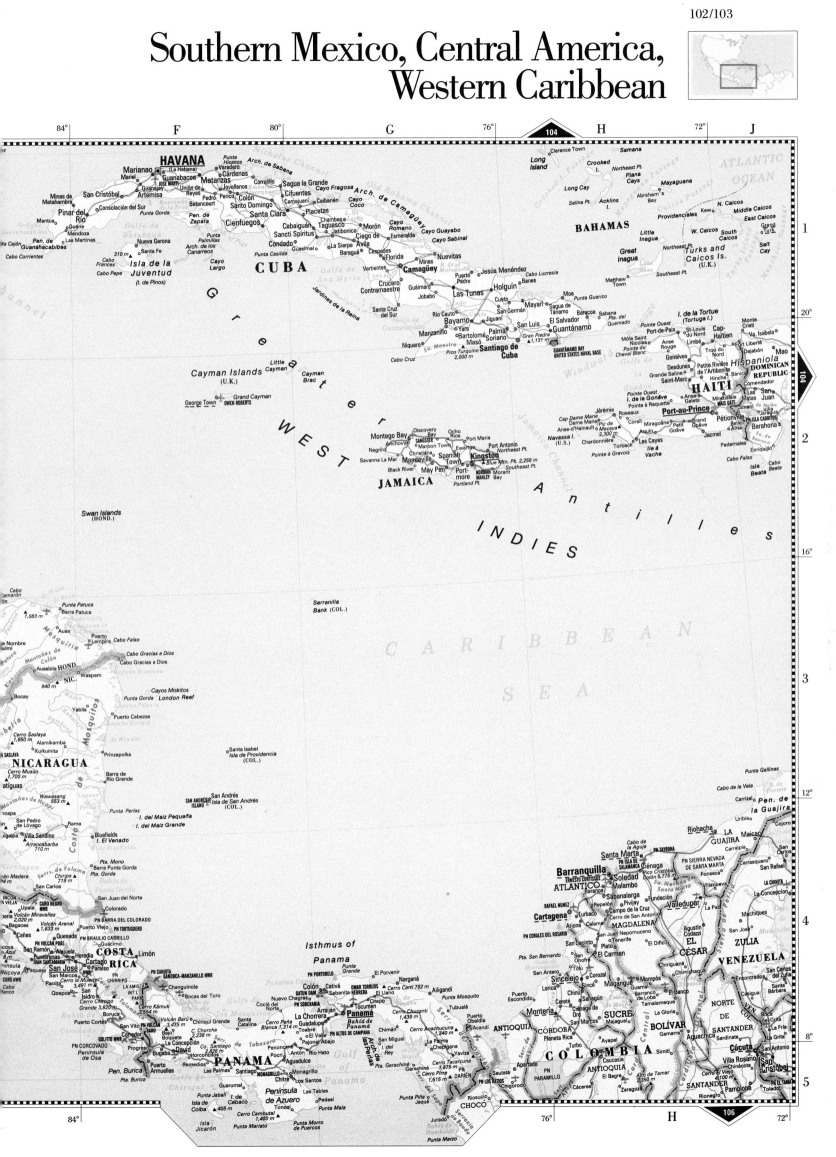

Eastern Caribbean, Bahamas

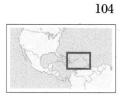

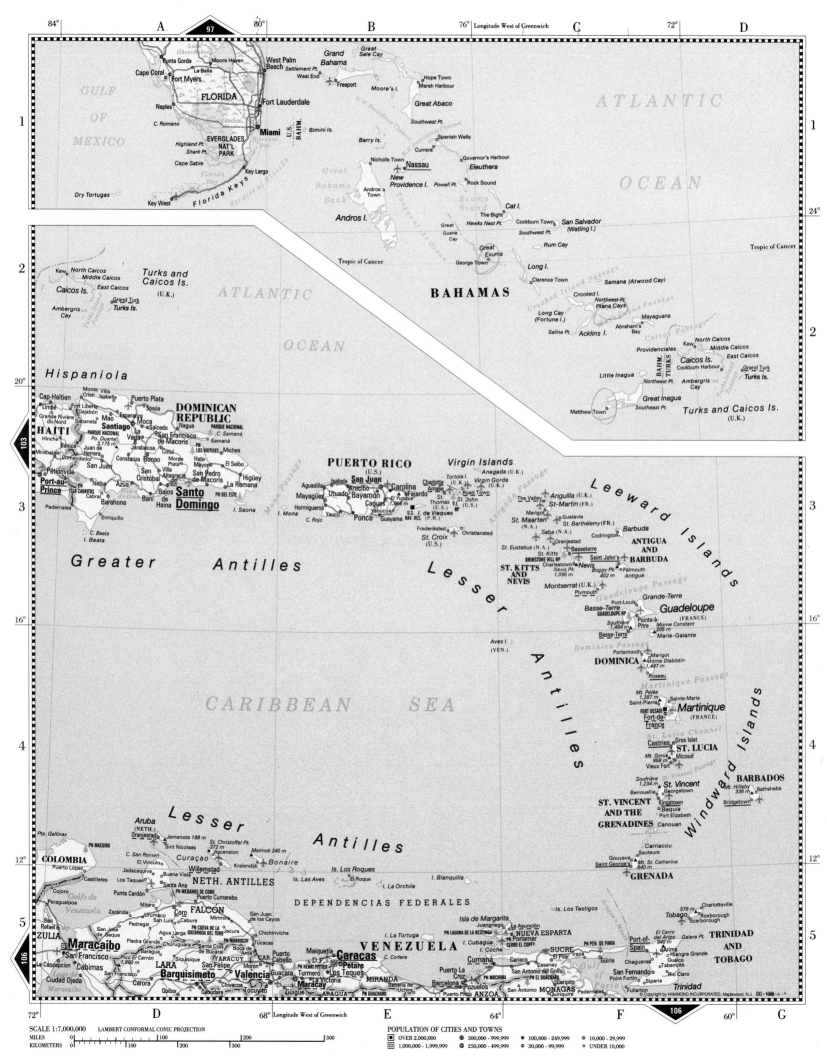

Longitude West of Greenwich

| A | B | C | D |

GULF
OF
MEXICO

Punta Gorda
Cape Coral · Fort Myers
Naples
C. Romano
Highland Pt.
Shark Pt.
Cape Sable
Dry Tortugas
Key West

Moore Haven
La Belle
FLORIDA
EVERGLADES
NAT'L
PARK
Key Largo
Florida Keys

West Palm
Beach · Settlement Pt.
West End
Fort Lauderdale
U.S.
BAHM.
Bimini Is.
Miami

Grand
Bahama
Great
Sale Cay
Freeport
Moore's I.

Hope Town
Marsh Harbour
Great Abaco
Southwest Pt.
Berry Is.
Spanish Wells
Current
Nicholls Town
Governor's Harbour
Nassau
New
Providence I. Powell Pt.
Eleuthera
Rock Sound
Andros
Town

ATLANTIC

OCEAN

24°

Tropic of Cancer

Great
Guana
Cay
Andros I.
Great
Exuma
George Town
Cat I.
The Bight
Hawks Nest Pt.
Cockburn Town
Southwest Pt.
Rum Cay
Long I.
Clarence Town

San Salvador
(Watling I.)

Samana (Atwood Cay)

BAHAMAS

Crooked I.
Northeast Pt.
Plana Cays
Long Cay
(Fortune I.)
Salina Pt.
Acklins I.
Abraham's
Bay
Mayaguana

Tropic of Cancer

2

Kew
North Caicos
Middle Caicos
East Caicos
Caicos Is.
Ambergris
Cay
Turks and
Caicos Is.
(U.K.)
Grand Turk
Turks Is.

ATLANTIC

OCEAN

Providenciales
Caicos Is.
Cockburn Harbour
Little Inagua
Northeast Pt.
Matthew Town
Great Inagua
Southeast Pt.
L.
Rosa
Kew
North Caicos
Middle Caicos
East Caicos
BAHM.
TURKS
Caicos Is.
Ambergris
Cay
Grand Turk
Turks Is.
Turks and Caicos Is.
(U.K.)

2

20°

Hispaniola

Cap-Haïtien
Limbé
Monte
Cristi
Villa
Isabella
Puerto Plata
Sosúa

Fort Liberté
Grande Rivière
du Nord
Dajabón
Sabaneta
Mao
Moca
Salcedo
Esperanza
PARQUE NACIONAL
Santiago
La
Vega
San Francisco
de Macoris
C. Samaná
Samaná
PN
LOS HAITISES
Miches

HAITI
Hinche
Bánica
Comendador
Mirebalais
Port-au-
Prince
ISLA CABRITOS
Pétionville
Pedernales

Juan de
Herrera
Constanza
San Juan
Neiba
Cabral
C. Beata
I. Beata

Jarabacoa
Po. Duarte
3,175 m
Bonao
Monte
Plata
Bani
Barahona
Enriquillo

PARQUE NACIONAL
Cotui
Villa
Altagracia
San
Cristóbal
Bajos
de
Haina
Bahía
de Ocóa

Hato
Mayoro
El Seibo
DOMINICAN
REPUBLIC
Nagua

San Pedro
de Macoris
Santo
Domingo
I. Saona

Higüey
La Romana
PN DEL ESTE

Greater **Antilles**

Mona
Passage
I. Mona
C. Rojo

PUERTO RICO
(U.S.)
Aguadilla
Isabela
San Juan
Mayagüez
Utuado
Arecibo
Bayamón
Carolina
Hormigueros
Yauco
Caguas
Fajardo
Yabucoa
Ponce
Guayama
I. de Vieques
(P.R.)
El Yunque
1,065 m
NAV. RES.

Virgin Islands
Anegada (U.K.)
Tortola I.
(U.K.)
Virgin Gorda
(U.K.)
Charlotte
Amalie
Road Town
St.
Thomas
St. John
(U.S.)
The Valley **Anguilla (U.K.)**
Marigot **St-Martin (FR.)**
St. Maarten
(N.A.)
Gustavia
St. Barthélemy (FR.)
Saba (N.A.)
Oranjestad
St. Eustatius (N.A.)
St. Kitts
ST. KITTS
AND
NEVIS
Basseterre
Charlestown
Nevis Pk.
1,096 m
Montserrat (U.K.)
Plymouth
BRIMSTONE HILL NP
Nevis
Saint John's
Boggy Pk.
402 m
Falmouth
Antigua
ANTIGUA
AND
BARBUDA
Codrington
Barbuda

Leeward **Islands**

3

St. Croix
(U.S.)
Frederiksted
Christiansted

Lesser **Antilles**

16°

CARIBBEAN **SEA**

Aves I.
(VEN.)

Guadeloupe Passage
Port-Louis
Grande-Terre
Basse-Terre
GUADELOUPE NP
Soufrière
1,484 m
Basse-Terre
Pointe-à-
Pitre
Morne Constant
205 m
Marie-Galante
Guadeloupe
(FRANCE)

Dominica Passage
Portsmouth
Morne Diablotin
1,447 m
Roseau
Marigot
DOMINICA

Martinique Passage
Mt. Pelée
1,397 m
Saint-Pierre
FORT DESAIX
Fort-de-
France
Sainte-Marie
Martinique
(FRANCE)

16°

4

St. Lucia Channel
Castries
Mt. Gimie
958 m
Vieux Fort
Gros Islet
ST. LUCIA
Micoud

St. Vincent Passage
Soufrière
1,234 m
Barrouallie
ST. VINCENT
AND THE
GRENADINES
St. Vincent
Georgetown
Kingstown
Bequia
Port Elizabeth
Canouan

Mt. Hillaby
336 m
BARBADOS
Bathsheba
Bridgetown

Windward **Islands**

4

Carriacou
Sauteurs
Gouyave
Saint George's
GRENADA
Mt. St. Catherine
840 m

12°

Lesser
Pta. Gallinas
PN MACURA
COLOMBIA
Puerto López

Aruba
(NETH.)
Jamanota 188 m
Oranjestad
C. San Roman
El Vinculo
Curaçao
Jadacaquiva
Buena Vista
Los Taques
Santa Ana
Punta Cardón
Mitare
Zazárida
PN MEDANOS DE CORO
Puerto Cumarebo

St. Christoffel Pk.
372 m
Ascension
Sint Nicolaas
Willemstad
NETH. ANTILLES
Kralendijk
Malmok 240 m
Bonaire

Antilles

Is. Los Roques
Is. Las Aves
El Roque
I. La Orchila
I. Blanquilla

DEPENDENCIAS **FEDERALES**

Is. Los Testigos

Tobago
Charlotteville
Roxborough
Scarborough
576 m
TRINIDAD
AND
TOBAGO

12°

5

San
Rafael
ZULIA
La Concepción
Ciudad Ojeda
Maracaibo
San Francisco
Cabimas
Lago de
Maracaibo
Pico El Cerrón
1,990 m
La
San José
de Seque

El Vínculo
Cojoro
Paraguaipoa
Golfo de
Venezuela
Agua Larga
Piedra Grande
Churuguara
Baragua
Pedregal
Dabajuro
PN CUEVA DE LA
QUEBRADA DEL TORO
Boca de
Aroa
PN MORROCOY
Siquisique
Quíbor
Carora
San Luis
FALCON
Coro
PN HENRI PITTIER
Tucacas
Puerto
Cabello
Barquisimeto
Chivacoa
San
Felipe
Morón
Valencia
Turmero
Maracay
Güigue
Tocuyito
Maiquetía
D.F.
La Victoria
Caracas
Pétare
Los Teques
MIRANDA
Sabana de
Uchire
ARAGUA
PN GUACHARO

VENEZUELA

San Juan
de los Cayos
Chichiriviche
San
Antonio
Barcelona
Pozuelos
Puerto Piritu
ANZOA.
Puerto La
Cruz
Isla de Margarita
Juangriego
NUEVA ESPARTA
La Asunción
Porlamar
I. Coche
I. Cubagua
SUCRE
Cumaná
Cariaco
El Pilar
San Antonio del Golfo
Casanay
PN PEN. DE PARIA
Güiria
El Cerro
del Aripo
940 m
SUCRE
Port-of-
Spain
Arima
Chaguanas
Galera Pt.
TRINIDAD
AND
TOBAGO
San Fernando
Point Fortin
Siparia
Fullarton
Rio Claro
Guayaguayare
Sangre Grande
I. La Tortuga
I. Coche
Gulf
of
Paria
Chaguaramas
Guaico
Trinidad

© Copyright by HAMMOND INCORPORATED, Maplewood, N.J.

5

| D | E | F | G |

72°
68° Longitude West of Greenwich
64°
60°

SCALE 1:7,000,000   LAMBERT CONFORMAL CONIC PROJECTION

MILES   0   100   200   300

KILOMETERS   0   100   200   300

POPULATION OF CITIES AND TOWNS

| ▣ OVER 2,000,000 | ◉ 500,000 - 999,999 | ● 100,000 - 249,999 | • 10,000 - 29,999 |
| ▢ 1,000,000 - 1,999,999 | ◉ 250,000 - 499,999 | • 30,000 - 99,999 | • UNDER 10,000 |

South America

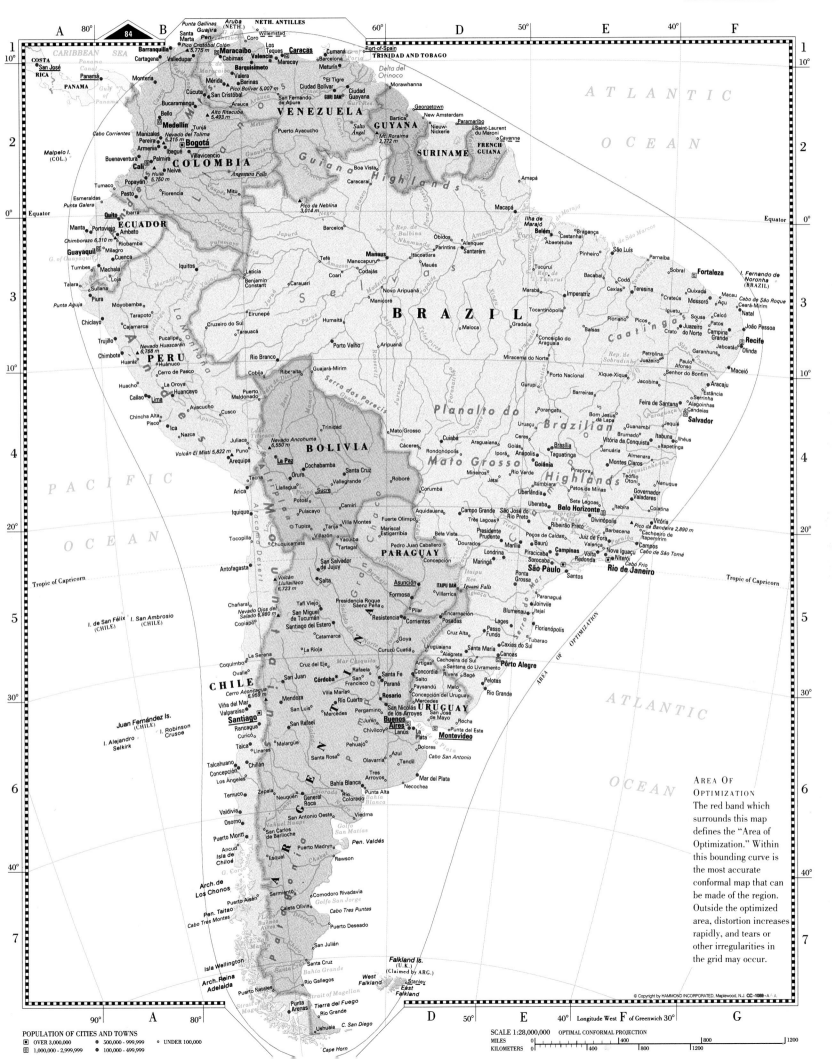

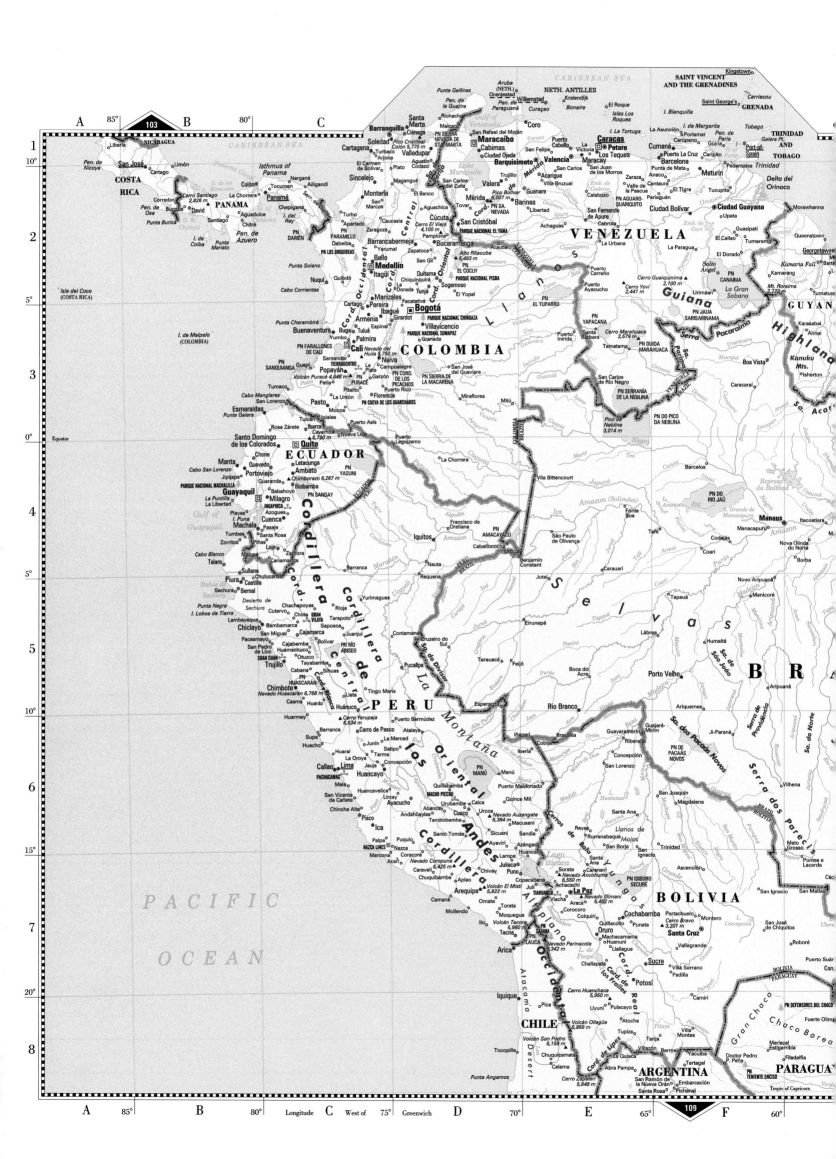

Northern South America

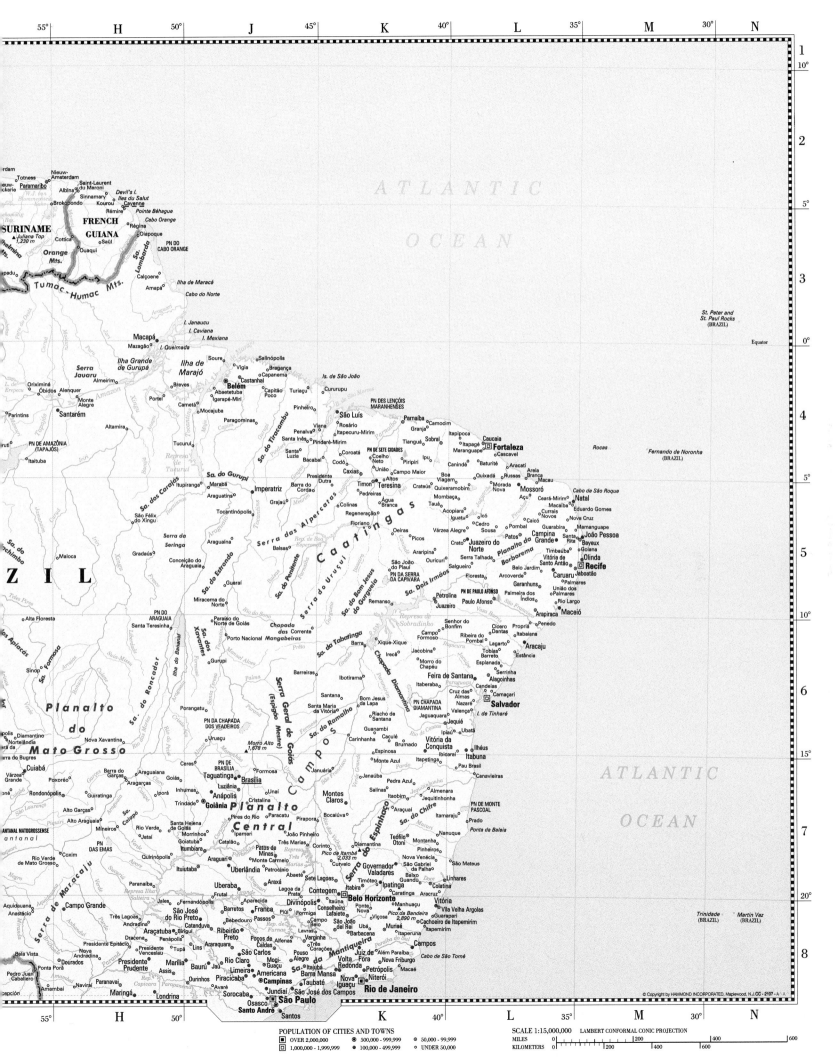

Southeastern Brazil

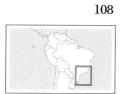

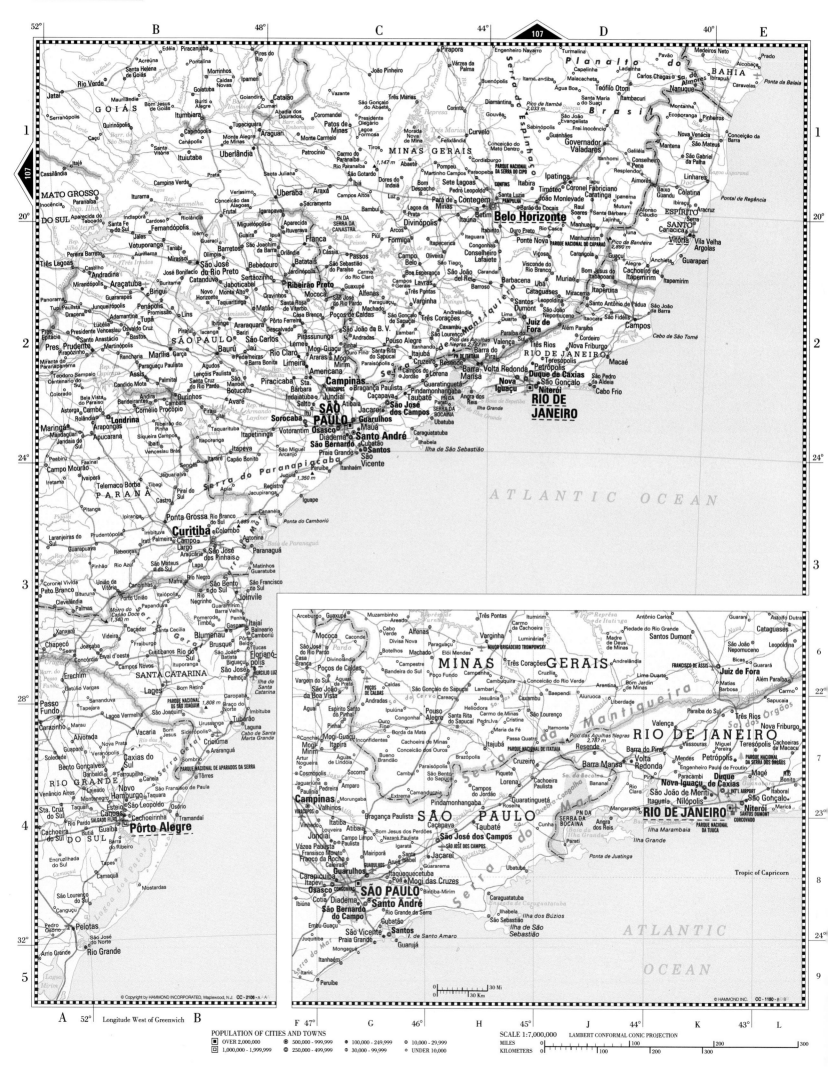

Longitude West of Greenwich

POPULATION OF CITIES AND TOWNS

■ OVER 2,000,000   ● 500,000 - 999,999   ● 100,000 - 249,999   • 10,000 - 29,999
▣ 1,000,000 - 1,999,999   ◉ 250,000 - 499,999   • 30,000 - 99,999   • UNDER 10,000

SCALE 1:7,000,000   LAMBERT CONFORMAL CONIC PROJECTION

MILES   0   100   200   300
KILOMETERS   0   100   200   300

Southern South America

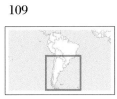

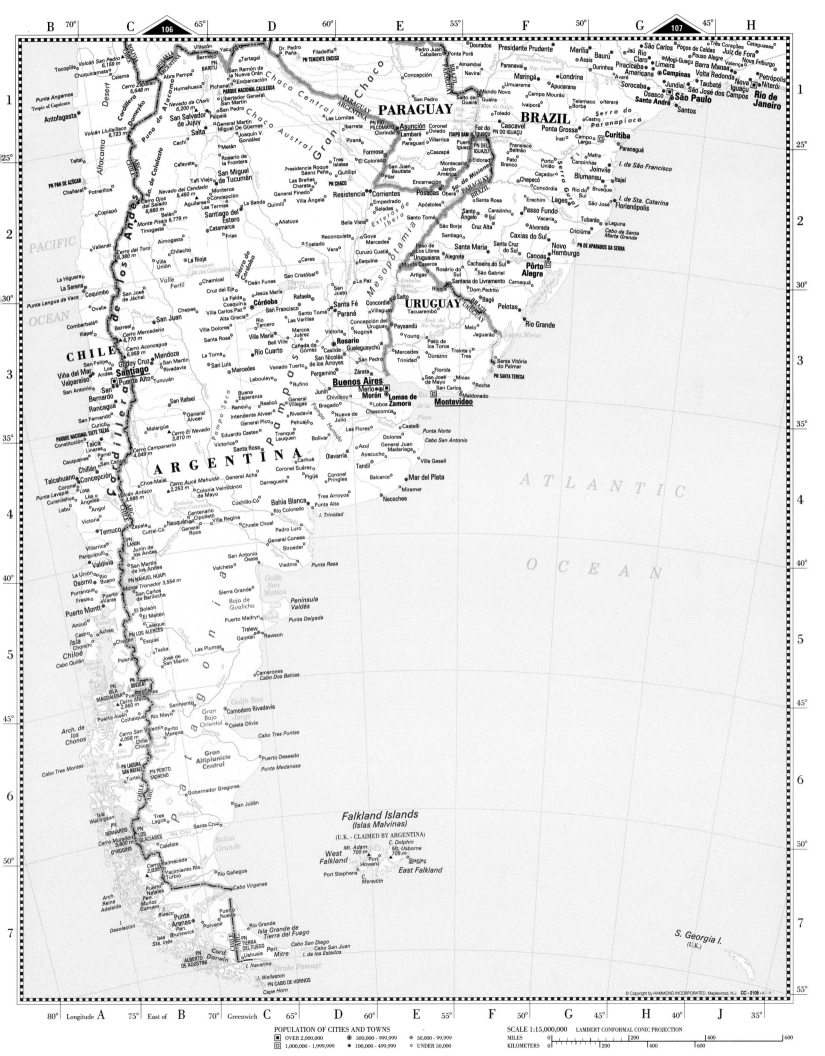

Index of the World

This index lists places and geographic features found in the atlas. Every name is followed by the country or area to which it belongs. Except for cities, towns, countries and cultural areas, all entries include a reference to feature type, such as province, river, island, peak, and so on. The page number and alpha-numeric code appear in blue to the left of each listing. The page number directs you to the largest scale map on which the name can be found. The code refers to the grid squares formed by the horizontal and vertical lines of latitude and longitude on each map. Following the letters from left to right, and the numbers from top to bottom, helps you to locate quickly the square containing the place or feature. Inset maps have their own alpha-numeric codes. Names that are accompanied by a point symbol are indexed to the symbol's location on the map. Other names are indexed to the initial letter of the name. The primary abbreviations used in this index are listed below.

Index Abbreviations

A.F.B.	Air Force Base	**Fed.**	Federal, Federated	**Nat'l Pk**	National Park	**São T. & Pr.**	São Tomé &
Afghan.	Afghanistan	**Fin.**	Finland	**N. Br.**	New Brunswick		Príncipe
Ala.	Alabama	**Fla.**	Florida	**N.C.**	North Carolina	**Sask.**	Saskatchewan
Alg.	Algeria	**for.**	forest	**N. Dak.**	North Dakota	**S.C.**	South Carolina
Alta.	Alberta	**Fr.**	France, French	**Nebr.**	Nebraska	**Scot.**	Scotland
Ant. & Barb.	Antigua & Barbuda	**Fr. Pol.**	French Polynesia	**Neth.**	Netherlands	**S. Dak.**	South Dakota
Antarc.	Antarctica	**Ft.**	Fort	**Neth. Ant.**	Netherlands Antilles	**Sen.**	Senegal
arch.	archipelago			**Nev.**	Nevada	**Sing.**	Singapore
Arg.	Argentina	**Ga.**	Georgia	**Newf.**	Newfoundland	**S. Korea**	South Korea
Ariz.	Arizona	**Ger.**	Germany	**N.H.**	New Hampshire	**S. Leone**	Sierra Leone
Ark.	Arkansas	**Greenl.**	Greenland	**Nic.**	Nicaragua	**Sol. Is.**	Solomon Islands
Austr.	Australia	**Gt.**	Great	**N. Ire.**	Northern Ireland	**Sp.**	Spain, Spanish
aut.	autonomous	**Guad.**	Guadeloupe	**N.J.**	New Jersey	**St.**	Saint, Sainte
		Guat.	Guatemala	**N. Korea**	North Korea	**str.**	strait
Bah.	Bahamas	**Guy.**	Guyana	**N. Mex.**	New Mexico	**St. Vinc.**	
Bang.	Bangladesh			**Nor.**	Norway	**& Grens.**	Saint Vincent &
Belg.	Belgium	**har., harb.**	harbor	**N.S.**	Nova Scotia		the Grenadines
Bol.	Bolivia	**Hon.**	Honduras	**N.W.T.**	Northwest	**Switz.**	Switzerland
Bosn.	Bosnia &	**Hun.**	Hungary		Territories		
	Herzegovina			**N.Y.**	New York	**Tanz.**	Tanzania
Bots.	Botswana	**Ill.**	Illinois	**N.Z.**	New Zealand	**Tenn.**	Tennessee
Braz.	Brazil	**Ind.**	Indiana			**Terr.**	Territory
Br., Brit.	British	**Indon.**	Indonesia	**Okla.**	Oklahoma	**Thai.**	Thailand
Br. Col.	British Columbia	**Int'l**	International	**Ont.**	Ontario	**Trin. & Tob.**	Trinidad & Tobago
Bulg.	Bulgaria	**Ire.**	Ireland	**Oreg.**	Oregon	**Tun.**	Tunisia
Burk. Faso	Burkina Faso	**isl., isls.**	isle, island,				
			islands	**Pa.**	Pennsylvania	**U. A. E.**	United Arab
Calif.	California	**Isr.**	Israel	**Pak.**	Pakistan		Emirates
Camb.	Cambodia	**isth.**	isthmus	**Pan.**	Panama	**U. K.**	United Kingdom
Can.	Canada			**Papua N.G.**	Papua New Guinea	**Ukr.**	Ukraine
cap.	capital	**Jam.**	Jamaica	**Par.**	Paraguay	**Urug.**	Uruguay
Cent. Afr.				**P.E.I.**	Prince Edward	**U. S.**	United States
Rep.	Central African	**Kans.**	Kansas		Island		
	Republic	**Ky.**	Kentucky	**pen.**	peninsula	**Va.**	Virginia
chan.	channel			**Phil.**	Philippines	**Ven. Venez.**	Venezuela
Chan. Is.	Channel Islands	**La.**	Louisiana	**pk.**	park	**V.I. (Br.)**	Virgin Islands
Col.	Colombia	**Leb.**	Lebanon	**plat.**	plateau		(British)
Colo.	Colorado	**Lux.**	Luxembourg	**Pol.**	Poland	**V.I. (U.S.)**	Virgin Islands (U.S.)
Conn.	Connecticut			**Port.**	Portugal,	**Viet.**	Vietnam
C. Rica	Costa Rica	**Madag.**	Madagascar		Portuguese	**vol.**	volcano
Czech Rep.	Czech Republic	**Man.**	Manitoba	**P. Rico**	Puerto Rico	**Vt.**	Vermont
		Mass.	Massachusetts	**prom.**	promontory		
DC	District of Columbia	**Maur.**	Mauritania	**prov.**	province, provincial	**W.**	West, Western
Del.	Delaware	**Md.**	Maryland	**pt., pte.**	point, pointe	**Wash.**	Washington
Dem.	Democratic	**Mex.**	Mexico			**W. Indies**	West Indies
Den.	Denmark	**Mich.**	Michigan	**Que.**	Québec	**Wis.**	Wisconsin
depr.	depression	**Minn.**	Minnesota			**W. Samoa**	Western Samoa
des.	desert	**Miss.**	Mississippi	**reg.**	region	**W. Va.**	West Virginia
dist.	district	**Mo.**	Missouri	**Rep.**	Republic	**Wyo.**	Wyoming
Dom. Rep.	Dominican Republic	**Mong.**	Mongolia	**res.**	reservoir		
		Mont.	Montana	**R.I.**	Rhode Island	**Yugo.**	Yugoslavia
E.	East, Eastern	**Mor.**	Morocco	**riv.**	river		
Ecua.	Ecuador	**Moz.**	Mozambique	**Rom.**	Romania	**Zim.**	Zimbabwe
El Sal.	El Salvador	**mt.**	mount				
Eng.	England	**mtn., mts.**	mountain, mountains	**S.**	South, Southern		
Equat. Guin.	Equatorial Guinea			**sa.**	serra, sierra		
est.	estuary	**N,. No.**	North, Northern	**S. Africa**	South Africa		
Eth.	Ethiopia	**N. Amer.**	North America	**S. Amer.**	South America		

111

Aach – Blue Nile

A

31/F2 **Aachen**, Ger.
36/E2 **Aare** (riv.), Switz.
79/G5 **Aba**, Nigeria
51/G4 **Abadan**, Iran
46/K4 **Abakan**, Russia
79/F5 **Abeokuta**, Nigeria
21/D2 **Aberdeen**, Scot.
91/J4 **Aberdeen**, S. Dak.
90/B4 **Aberdeen**, Wash.
78/D5 **Abidjan**, Côte d'Ivoire
93/H3 **Abilene**, Kans.
93/H4 **Abilene**, Texas
94/D1 **Abitibi** (riv.), Ont.
94/C4 **Abraham Lincoln Birthplace Nat'l Hist. Site**, Ky.
38/C1 **Abruzzi** (reg.), Italy
53/F4 **Abu Dhabi** (cap.), U.A.E.
79/G4 **Abuja** (cap.), Nigeria
95/G2 **Acadia Nat'l Pk.**, Maine
101/E5 **Acapulco**, Mex.
79/E5 **Accra** (cap.), Ghana
46/K4 **Achinsk**, Russia
109/C3 **Aconcagua** (mt.), Arg.
93/H4 **Ada**, Okla.
69/M7 **Adamstown** (cap.), Pitcairn
49/D1 **Adana**, Turkey
52/D3 **Ad Dahnā** (des.), Saudi Arabia
52/F3 **Ad Dammān**, Saudi Arabia
77/N6 **Addis Ababa** (cap.), Eth.
99/Q16 **Addison**, Ill.
73/A2 **Adelaide**, Austr.
77/Q5 **Aden** (gulf), Afr., Asia
52/D6 **Aden**, Yemen
33/J4 **Adige** (riv.), Italy
94/F2 **Adirondack** (mts.), N.Y.
68/D5 **Admiralty** (isls.), Papua N.G.
94/C3 **Adrian**, Mich.
18/E4 **Adriatic** (sea), Europe
39/J3 **Aegean** (sea)
53/H2 **Afghanistan**
74/* **Africa**
76/D1 **Agadir**, Morocco
68/D3 **Agana** (cap.), Guam
93/G2 **Agate Fossil Beds Nat'l Mon.**, Nebr.
57/H7 **Ageo**, Japan
62/C2 **Agra**, India
100/E4 **Aguascalientes**, Mex.
76/F3 **Ahaggar** (mts.), Alg.
62/B3 **Ahmadabad**, India
51/G4 **Ahvaz**, Iran
88/W13 **Aiea**, Hawaii
97/H3 **Aiken**, S.C.
32/F5 **Aix-en-Provence**, France
38/A2 **Ajaccio**, France
62/B2 **Ajmer**, India
56/D3 **Akashi**, Japan
55/M4 **Akita**, Japan
49/D3 **Akko**, Isr.
62/C3 **Akola**, India
94/D3 **Akron**, Ohio
45/L2 **Aktyubinsk**, Kazakhstan
97/G4 **Alabama** (riv.), Ala.
97/G3 **Alabama** (state), U.S.
99/K11 **Alameda**, Calif.
93/F4 **Alamogordo**, N. Mex.
93/F3 **Alamosa**, Colo.
20/G3 **Aland** (isls.), Fin.
85/J4 **Alaska** (gulf), Alaska
85/F4 **Alaska** (pen.), Alaska
85/H3 **Alaska** (range), Alaska
85/* **Alaska** (state), U.S.
34/E3 **Albacete**, Spain
39/F2 **Albania**
97/G4 **Albany**, Ga.
94/F3 **Albany** (cap.), N.Y.
90/C4 **Albany**, Oreg.
87/H3 **Albany** (riv.), Ont.
51/F4 **Al Başrah**, Iraq
77/N7 **Albert** (lake), Africa
91/K5 **Albert Lea**, Minn.
86/E3 **Alberta** (prov.), Can.
20/D4 **Alborg**, Den.
92/F4 **Albuquerque**, N. Mex.
32/B2 **Alderney** (isl.), Chan. Is.
88/T10 **Alenuihaha** (chan.), Hawaii
49/E1 **Aleppo**, Syria
85/E5 **Aleutian** (isls.), Alaska
85/L4 **Alexander** (arch.), Alaska
49/A4 **Alexandria**, Egypt
96/E4 **Alexandria**, La.
94/E4 **Alexandria**, Va.
49/B4 **Al Fayyum**, Egypt
53/G3 **Al Fujayrah**, U.A.E.
76/F2 **Algeria**
75/S15 **Algiers** (cap.), Alg.
98/B2 **Alhambra**, Calif.
52/D6 **Al Ḩudaydah**, Yemen
52/E3 **Al Hufūf**, Saudi Arabia
35/E3 **Alicante**, Spain
62/C2 **Aligarh**, India
49/B4 **Al Jīzah**, Egypt
76/H1 **Al Khums**, Libya
51/F4 **Al Kuwait** (cap.), Kuwait
62/D2 **Allahabad**, India
94/D4 **Allegheny** (mts.), U.S.
99/F7 **Allen Park**, Mich.
94/F3 **Allentown**, Pa.
64/F4 **Allepey**, India
94/D3 **Alliance**, Ohio
46/H5 **Alma-Ata**, Kazakhstan
50/B4 **Al Mahallah al Kubrá**, Egypt
49/B4 **Al Mansūra**, Egypt
34/D4 **Almeria**, Spain
52/B4 **Al Minyā**, Egypt
33/G4 **Alps** (mts.), Europe
36/D2 **Alsace** (reg.), Fr.
98/B2 **Altadena**, Calif.
46/J5 **Altai** (mts.), Asia
94/B4 **Alton**, Ill.
94/E3 **Altoona**, Pa.
54/C4 **Altun** (mts.), China
93/H4 **Altus**, Okla.
57/L10 **Amagasaki**, Japan
93/G4 **Amarillo**, Texas
107/H4 **Amazon** (riv.), S. Amer.
67/G4 **Ambon**, Indon.
92/E2 **American Fork**, Utah
69/J6 **American Samoa**
97/G3 **Americus**, Ga.
93/J2 **Ames**, Iowa
95/H2 **Amherst**, N.S.
30/B4 **Amiens**, France
93/G5 **Amistad Nat'l Rec. Area**, Texas
49/D4 **Amman** (cap.), Jordan
61/H3 **Amoy** (Xiamen), China
62/C3 **Amravati**, India
64/C2 **Amritsar**, India
28/B4 **Amsterdam** (cap.), Neth.
94/F3 **Amsterdam**, N.Y.
48/F5 **Amudar'ya** (riv.), Asia
83/S **Amundsen** (sea), Antarc.
86/D1 **Amundsen** (gulf), N.W.T.
55/M1 **Amur** (riv.), Asia
90/E4 **Anaconda**, Mont.
47/T3 **Anadyr'**, Russia
47/R3 **Anadyr** (gulf), Russia
98/C3 **Anaheim**, Calif.
50/B2 **Anatolia** (reg.), Turkey
85/J3 **Anchorage**, Alaska
33/K5 **Ancona**, Italy
34/C4 **Andalusia** (reg.), Spain
63/F5 **Andaman** (sea), Asia
63/F5 **Andaman** (isls.), India
94/C3 **Anderson**, Ind.
97/H3 **Anderson**, S.C.
105/B3 **Andes** (mts.), S. Amer.
46/H5 **Andizhan**, Uzbekistan
35/F1 **Andorra**
35/F1 **Andorra la Vella** (cap.), Andorra
98/K8 **Andrews A.F.B.**, Md.
104/B1 **Andros** (isl.), Bah.
54/E1 **Angara** (riv.), Russia
54/E1 **Angarsk**, Russia
106/F2 **Angel** (falls), Ven.
32/C3 **Angers**, France
65/C3 **Angkor** (ruins), Camb.
82/C3 **Angola**
104/F3 **Anguilla** (isl.)
50/C2 **Ankara** (cap.), Turkey
75/V17 **Annaba**, Alg.
50/D4 **An Nafūd** (des.), Saudi Arabia
51/F4 **An Najaf**, Iraq
63/J4 **Annamitique** (mts.), Laos, Viet.
98/J8 **Annandale**, Va.
94/E4 **Annapolis** (cap.), Md.
62/D2 **Annapurna** (mt.), Nepal
99/E7 **Ann Arbor**, Mich.
95/G3 **Ann** (cape), Mass.
97/G3 **Anniston**, Ala.
D5/D5 **Anqing**, China
58/B2 **Anshan**, China
49/E1 **Antakya** (Antioch), Turkey
50/B2 **Antalya**, Turkey
81/H7 **Antananarivo** (cap.), Madag.
83/* **Antarctica**
83/V **Antarctic** (pen.), Antarc.
33/G5 **Antibes**, France
95/J1 **Anticosti** (isl.), Que.
104/F3 **Antigua and Barbuda**
49/E1 **Antioch** (Antayka), Turkey
99/L10 **Antioch**, Calif.
109/B1 **Antofagasta**, Chile
81/J6 **Antsiranana** (Diégo-Suarez), Madag.
30/D1 **Antwerp**, Belg.
59/C3 **Anyang**, China
55/N3 **Aomori**, Japan
26/C2 **Apeldoorn**, Neth.
38/C1 **Apennines** (mts.), Italy
69/S9 **Apia** (cap.), W. Samoa
89/K4 **Appalachian** (mts.), U.S.
94/B2 **Appleton**, Wis.
50/C4 **Aqaba** (gulf), Asia
46/H4 **Aqmola** (cap.), Kazakhstan
52/D4 **Arabian** (pen.), Asia
53/H5 **Arabian** (sea), Asia
52/B3 **Arabian** (des.), Egypt
107/L6 **Aracaju**, Braz.
40/E2 **Arad**, Rom.
68/C5 **Arafura** (sea)
35/E2 **Aragón** (reg.), Spain
107/J5 **Araguaia** (riv.), Braz.
51/G3 **Arāk**, Iran
46/G5 **Aral** (sea), Asia
21/H7 **Aran** (isls.), Ire.
51/F2 **Ararat** (mt.), Turkey
98/B2 **Arcadia**, Calif.
42/J2 **Archangel**, Russia
92/E3 **Arches Nat'l Pk.**, Utah
16/A1 **Arctic** (ocean)
51/G2 **Ardabil**, Iran
31/E4 **Ardennes** (for.), Belg.
93/H4 **Ardmore**, Okla.
104/E3 **Arecibo**, P. Rico
106/D7 **Arequipa**, Peru
30/B6 **Argenteuil**, France
109/C4 **Argentina**
99/Q16 **Argonne Nat'l Lab.**, Ill.
39/H4 **Argos**, Greece
20/D4 **Arhus**, Den.
106/D7 **Arica**, Chile
92/D4 **Arizona** (state), U.S.
93/J4 **Arkadelphia**, Ark.
97/E3 **Arkansas** (riv.), U.S.
97/E3 **Arkansas** (state), U.S.
32/F5 **Arles**, France
96/D3 **Arlington**, Texas
94/E4 **Arlington**, Va.
99/Q15 **Arlington Heights**, Ill.
22/B3 **Armagh**, N. Ire.
45/G3 **Armavir**, Russia
45/H4 **Armenia**
28/C5 **Arnhem**, Neth.
70/E2 **Arnhem Land** (reg.), Austr.
33/J5 **Arno** (riv.), Italy
21/C3 **Arran** (isl.), Scot.
104/D4 **Aruba** (isl.)
55/N3 **Asahikawa**, Japan
62/E3 **Asansol**, India
98/G5 **Asbury Park**, N.J.
16/J6 **Ascension** (isl.), St. Helena
78/E5 **Ashanti** (reg.), Ghana
97/H3 **Asheville**, N.C.
51/J2 **Ashkhabad** (cap.), Turkmenistan
97/H2 **Ashland**, Ky.
90/C5 **Ashland**, Oreg.
70/C2 **Ashmore and Cartier Is.** (terr.), Austr.
53/G3 **Ash Shāriqah**, U.A.E.
94/D3 **Ashtabula**, Ohio
48/* **Asia**
52/C5 **Asmera** (cap.), Eritrea
92/F3 **Aspen**, Colo.
98/J7 **Aspen Hill**, Md.
52/E3 **As Salmīyah**, Kuwait
63/F2 **Assam** (state), India
90/C4 **Astoria**, Oreg.
45/J3 **Astrakhan'**, Russia
34/B1 **Asturias** (reg.), Spain
109/E2 **Asunción** (cap.), Par.
52/B4 **Aswân**, Egypt
52/B3 **Asyût**, Egypt
106/E7 **Atacama** (des.), Chile
93/J3 **Atchison**, Kans.
86/F3 **Athabasca** (lake), Can.
97/H3 **Athens**, Ga.
39/H4 **Athens** (cap.), Greece
94/D4 **Athens**, Ohio
39/J2 **Athos** (mt.), Greece
85/C5 **Atka** (isl.), Alaska
97/G3 **Atlanta** (cap.), Ga.
16/G3 **Atlantic** (ocean)
94/F4 **Atlantic City**, N.J.
76/E1 **Atlas** (mts.), Africa
57/H7 **Atsugi**, Japan
52/D4 **Aţ Ţa'if**, Saudi Arabia
85/A5 **Attu** (isl.), Alaska
97/G3 **Auburn**, Ala.
95/G2 **Auburn**, Maine
94/E3 **Auburn**, N.Y.
99/C3 **Auburn**, Wash.
71/R10 **Auckland**, N.Z.
37/G1 **Augsburg**, Ger.
97/H3 **Augusta**, Ga.
95/G2 **Augusta** (cap.), Maine
62/C4 **Aurangabad**, India
93/F3 **Aurora**, Colo.
99/P16 **Aurora**, Ill.
27/K3 **Auschwitz** (Oświęcim), Poland
96/D4 **Austin** (cap.), Texas
70/* **Australia**
73/C3 **Australian Alps** (mts.), Austr.
73/D3 **Australian Cap. Terr.**, Austr.
33/L3 **Austria**
95/L2 **Avalon** (pen.), Newf.
32/F5 **Avignon**, France
25/E2 **Avon** (riv.), Eng.
70/E5 **Ayers Rock** (mt.), Austr.
45/H4 **Azerbaijan**
35/R12 **Azores** (isls.), Port.
44/E3 **Azov** (sea), Europe
92/E3 **Aztec Ruins Nat'l Mon.**, N. Mex.
98/C2 **Azusa**, Calif.
49/B4 **Az Zagāzig**, Egypt

B

77/P5 **Bab el Mandeb** (str.)
41/H2 **Bacău**, Rom.
67/F1 **Bacolod**, Phil.
35/L7 **Badalona**, Spain
26/E4 **Baden-Baden**, Ger.
91/H5 **Badlands Nat'l Pk.**, S. Dak.
87/K1 **Baffin** (bay), N. Amer.
87/H1 **Baffin** (isl.), N.W.T.
52/D2 **Baghdad** (cap.), Iraq
104/B2 **Bahamas**
53/K3 **Bahawalpur**, Pak.
109/D4 **Bahia Blanca**, Arg.
52/F4 **Bahrain**
55/J2 **Baicheng**, China
68/G4 **Bairiki** (cap.), Kiribati
100/B2 **Baja California** (pen.), Mex.
92/C4 **Bakersfield**, Calif.
51/F3 **Bakhtarān**, Iran
45/J4 **Baku** (cap.), Azerbaijan
45/H1 **Balakovo**, Russia
98/C2 **Baldwin Park**, Calif.
35/F3 **Balearic** (isls.), Spain
66/D5 **Bali** (isl.), Indon.
67/E4 **Balikpapan**, Indon.
41/F4 **Balkan** (mts.), Bulg.
46/H5 **Balkhash** (lake), Kazakhstan
18/E3 **Baltic** (sea), Europe
94/E4 **Baltimore**, Md.
53/H3 **Baluchistan** (reg.), Pak.
78/D3 **Bamako** (cap.), Mali
68/F5 **Banaba** (isl.), Kiribati
66/D3 **Bandar Seri Begawan** (cap.), Brunei
67/G5 **Banda** (sea), Indon.
92/F4 **Bandelier Nat'l Mon.**, N. Mex.
66/C5 **Bandung**, Indon.
90/E2 **Banff Nat'l Pk.**, Alta.
62/C5 **Bangalore**, India
65/C3 **Bangkok** (cap.), Thai.
62/E3 **Bangladesh**
95/G2 **Bangor**, Maine
77/J7 **Bangui** (cap.), Cent. Afr. Rep.
40/C3 **Banja Luka**, Bosn.
66/D4 **Banjarmasin**, Indon.
78/A3 **Banjul** (cap.), Gambia
86/D1 **Banks** (isl.), N.W.T.
59/C3 **Baoding**, China
54/F5 **Baoji**, China
59/B2 **Baotou**, China
44/C1 **Baranovichi**, Belarus
104/G4 **Barbados**
94/D3 **Barberton**, Ohio
35/G2 **Barcelona**, Spain
106/F1 **Barcelona**, Ven.
62/C2 **Bareilly**, India
46/D2 **Barents** (sea), Europe
95/G2 **Bar Harbor**, Maine
38/E2 **Bari**, Italy
97/G2 **Barkley** (lake), Ky., Tenn.
46/J4 **Barnaul**, Russia
62/B3 **Baroda**, India
106/E1 **Barquisimeto**, Ven.
106/D1 **Barranquilla**, Col.
94/E2 **Barrie**, Ont.
85/G1 **Barrow** (pt.), Alaska
92/C4 **Barstow**, Calif.
93/H3 **Bartlesville**, Okla.
73/C3 **Bass** (str.), Austr.
36/D2 **Basel**, Switz.
60/B5 **Bassein**, Burma
104/F3 **Basse-Terre** (cap.), Guad.
104/F3 **Basseterre** (cap.), St. Kitts & Nevis
96/F3 **Bastrop**, La.
76/H8 **Batéké** (plat.), Congo
24/D4 **Bath**, Eng.
95/H2 **Bathurst**, N. Br.
87/R7 **Bathurst** (isl.), N.W.T.
75/V18 **Batna**, Alg.
97/F4 **Baton Rouge** (cap.), La.
94/C3 **Battle Creek**, Mich.
45/G4 **Batumi**, Georgia
49/F7 **Bat Yam**, Isr.
26/F4 **Bavaria** (state), Ger.
37/G3 **Bavarian Alps** (mts.), Austria, Ger.
104/E3 **Bayamón**, P. Rico
54/D5 **Bayan Har** (mts.), China
94/D3 **Bay City**, Mich.
32/C2 **Bayeux**, France
47/L4 **Baykal** (lake), Russia
46/G5 **Baykonyr**, Kazakhstan
98/F5 **Bayonne**, N.J.
26/F4 **Bayreuth**, Ger.
96/E4 **Baytown**, Texas
92/E2 **Bear** (lake), U.S.
90/F3 **Bearpaw** (mts.), Mont.
93/H2 **Beatrice**, Nebr.
86/C1 **Beaufort** (sea), N. Amer.
97/H3 **Beaufort**, S.C.
96/E4 **Beaumont**, Texas
94/D4 **Beckley**, W. Va.
49/D4 **Beersheba**, Isr.
61/F4 **Beihai**, China
59/D3 **Beijing** (Peking) (cap.), China
59/E2 **Beipiao**, China
49/D3 **Beirut** (cap.), Leb.
76/G1 **Bejaïa**, Alg.
46/C4 **Belarus**
107/J4 **Belém**, Braz.
95/G2 **Belfast**, Maine
22/C2 **Belfast** (cap.), N. Ire.
62/B4 **Belgaum**, India
26/C3 **Belgium**
44/F2 **Belgorod**, Russia
40/E3 **Belgrade** (cap.), Yugo.
102/D2 **Belize**
102/D2 **Belize City**, Belize
62/C4 **Bellary**, India
94/B4 **Belleville**, Ill.
98/F5 **Belleville**, N.J.
94/E2 **Belleville**, Ont.
99/C2 **Bellevue**, Wash.
98/B3 **Bellflower**, Calif.
90/C3 **Bellingham**, Wash.
83/U **Bellingshausen** (sea), Antarc.
102/D2 **Belmopan** (cap.), Belize
108/D2 **Belo Horizonte**, Braz.
94/B3 **Beloit**, Wis.
98/K7 **Beltsville**, Md.
41/H2 **Bel'tsy**, Moldova
91/K4 **Bemidji**, Minn.
62/D2 **Benares** (Varanasi), India
90/C4 **Bend**, Oreg.
62/E4 **Bengal** (bay), Asia
59/D4 **Bengbu**, China
77/K1 **Benghazi**, Libya
82/B3 **Benguela**, Angola
79/F4 **Benin**
76/G6 **Benin City**, Nigeria
95/F3 **Bennington**, Vt.
93/J4 **Benton**, Ark.
94/C3 **Benton Harbor**, Mich.
76/G6 **Benue** (riv.), Nigeria
58/B2 **Benxi**, China
56/B4 **Beppu**, Japan
33/K3 **Berchtesgaden**, Ger.
94/C4 **Berea**, Ky.
43/N4 **Berezniki**, Russia
33/H4 **Bergamo**, Italy
20/C3 **Bergen**, Nor.
47/T4 **Bering** (sea)
85/E3 **Bering** (str.)
99/K11 **Berkeley**, Calif.
27/G2 **Berlin** (cap.), Ger.
95/G2 **Berlin**, N.H.
84/L6 **Bermuda**
36/D4 **Bern** (cap.), Switz.
36/D5 **Bernese Alps** (range), Switz.
99/Q16 **Berwyn**, Ill.
36/C3 **Besançon**, France
97/G3 **Bessemer**, Ala.
98/J8 **Bethesda**, Md.
94/F3 **Bethlehem**, Pa.
49/D4 **Bethlehem**, West Bank
98/B2 **Beverly Hills**, Calif.
62/E2 **Bhagalpur**, India
62/B3 **Bhavnagar**, India
62/C3 **Bhopal**, India
62/E2 **Bhutan**
27/M2 **Bialystok**, Pol.
32/C5 **Biarritz**, France
95/G3 **Biddeford**, Maine
29/F4 **Bielefeld**, Ger.
27/K4 **Bielsko-Biala**, Poland
63/J5 **Bien Hoa**, Viet.
96/C4 **Big Bend Nat'l Pk.**, Texas
90/F4 **Bighorn** (mts.), Wyo.
90/G4 **Bighorn** (riv.), U.S.
96/C3 **Big Spring**, Texas
62/B2 **Bikaner**, India
68/F3 **Bikini** (atoll), Marshall Is.
34/D1 **Bilbao**, Spain
90/F4 **Billings**, Mont.
97/F4 **Biloxi**, Miss.
104/B1 **Biminis, The** (isls.), Bah.
94/F3 **Binghamton**, N.Y.
86/E3 **Birch** (mts.), Alb.
23/E5 **Birkenhead**, Eng.
97/G3 **Birmingham**, Ala.
25/E2 **Birmingham**, Eng.
99/F6 **Birmingham**, Mich.
92/E5 **Bisbee**, Ariz.
32/B4 **Biscay** (bay), Europe
97/H5 **Biscayne Nat'l Pk.**, Fla.
46/H5 **Bishkek** (cap.), Kyrgyzstan
80/D4 **Bisho**, S. Africa
91/H4 **Bismarck** (cap.), N. Dak.
68/D5 **Bismarck** (arch.), Papua N.G.
78/B4 **Bissau** (cap.), Guinea-Bissau
90/E4 **Bitterroot** (range), U.S.
46/J4 **Biysk**, Russia
75/W17 **Bizerte**, Tun.
44/D4 **Black** (sea)
90/E5 **Blackfoot**, Idaho
36/D2 **Black** (for.), Ger.
91/H5 **Black Hills** (mts.), U.S.
23/E4 **Blackpool**, Eng.
97/H2 **Blacksburg**, Va.
98/K8 **Bladensburg**, Md.
55/K1 **Blagoveshchensk**, Russia
36/C6 **Blanc** (mt.), Europe
82/G4 **Blantyre**, Malawi
75/S15 **Blida**, Alg.
95/G3 **Block** (isl.), R.I.
80/D3 **Bloemfontein**, S. Africa
98/F5 **Bloomfield**, N.J.
94/B3 **Bloomington**, Ill.
94/C4 **Bloomington**, Ind.
91/K4 **Bloomington**, Minn.
90/D4 **Blue** (mts.), Oreg.
97/H2 **Bluefield**, W. Va.
77/M5 **Blue Nile** (riv.), Africa

Jundi – Madras

Rainb – Somer

Venice – Zwolle